What About Us?

The PLC at Work® Process for Grades PreK–2 Teams

DIANE KERR
TRACEY A. HULEN

JACQUELINE HELLER
BRIAN K. BUTLER

Foreword by Douglas Reeves

Solution Tree | Press

a division of
Solution Tree

555 North Morton Street
Bloomington, IN 47404
800.733.6786 (toll free) / 812.336.7700
FAX: 812.336.7790
email: info@SolutionTree.com

SolutionTree.com

Visit **go.SolutionTree.com/PLCbooks** to download the free reproducibles in this book.

Printed in the United States of America

Library of Congress Cataloging-in-Publication Data

Names: Kerr, Diane, 1960- author. | Hulen, Tracey A., author. | Heller,
    Jacqueline, author. | Butler, Brian K., author.
Title: What about us? : the PLC process for grades PreK-2 teams / Diane
    Kerr, Tracey A. Hulen, Jacqueline Heller, and Brian K. Butler.
Description: Bloomington, IN : Solution Tree Press, [2020] | Includes
    bibliographical references and index.
Identifiers: LCCN 2020014330 (print) | LCCN 2020014331 (ebook) | ISBN
    9781949539691 (paperback) | ISBN 9781949539707 (ebook)
Subjects: LCSH: Early childhood teachers--In-service training. |
    Professional learning communities.
Classification: LCC LB1775.6 .K47 2020 (print) | LCC LB1775.6 (ebook) |
    DDC 372.21--dc23
LC record available at https://lccn.loc.gov/2020014330
LC ebook record available at https://lccn.loc.gov/2020014331

Solution Tree
Jeffrey C. Jones, CEO
Edmund M. Ackerman, President

Solution Tree Press
President and Publisher: Douglas M. Rife
Associate Publisher: Sarah Payne-Mills
Art Director: Rian Anderson
Managing Production Editor: Kendra Slayton
Senior Production Editor: Todd Brakke
Content Development Specialist: Amy Rubenstein
Copy Editor: Evie Madsen
Proofreader: Kate St. Ives
Cover Designer: Rian Anderson
Editorial Assistants: Sarah Ludwig and Elijah Oates

Dedication

· · · · · · · · · · · · · · · · · · · ·

This book has been a labor of love and a calling that we began over three years ago with a mentor and dear friend who sat with us on a fall day in Charlottesville, Virginia. That woman was Rebecca DuFour. Although we lost Becky all too soon, her legacy as the kind, giving, generous, and gracious megastar of the PLC at Work movement lives on. Becky, with Richard DuFour and Robert Eaker, created a wave felt around the world. We hope this book contributes to the continued vision they, along with Solution Tree, established to transform education worldwide, ensuring learning for all! Becky, the following pages are for you and for every educator who wants to ensure that our youngest learners have the life that they deserve, one full of limitless possibilities.

Acknowledgments

· ·

It's hard to put into words how blessed and fortunate I am; this same educator who, as a young boy, had a lot of self-doubt about his academic abilities and who struggled to learn to read fluently. A young boy who, during his primary school years, had the term *retention* mentioned to his parents by a well-meaning teacher; but his parents basically said, "No, we've got this. He won't be retained." It's equally hard to put into words how my paternal grandparents, with only a third- and fifth-grade education, made a choice in the 1940s during the height of segregation and Jim Crow laws to encourage my father to go to college. They subsequently lost their right to sharecrop and live on their land because of their decision to give him a chance at breaking a multigeneration cycle of poverty. To both sets of grandparents—my mother's parents and my father's parents—I am honored to be living their wildest dreams. I also dedicate this book to my parents, Paul and Doris Butler Sr., who taught me that being kind, working hard, pursuing an education, and not giving up was a recipe for success. Even though I experienced early academic struggles, the talk in our house was where and when my siblings and I were going to college, not if. To my parents, I owe everything. I am only sorry that my dad, who was a reading teacher and principal and passed away in January of 2020, did not live to read this book.

I also owe so much to my wonderful wife, Kathleen, and my two daughters, Alison and Emily, who keep me grounded and are a constant source of encouragement. There are too many teachers, coaches, colleagues, mentors, and friends to mention without slighting how important they were to my journey, but they know who they are, and I am so thankful for your gift of kindness toward me.

Jacquie Heller, Tracey Hulen, and Diane Kerr have been colleagues of mine for over a decade, and during that time, I realized that they were the most amazing, caring, and decent educators whom I would have loved for my own children to have as teachers. I pinch myself every day to get to call them my coauthors.

—Brian Butler

To my parents, who believed I could do things I had not yet envisioned, my husband, Tom, who offers support and encouragement beyond measure, and my children, Tessa and Griffith, who are simply magical and make me want to dig deeper. Thank you for the love that fuels me to do this work.

To the indescribable crew of educators, colleagues, and friends who opened Mason Crest Elementary, and to those that came after the founding members who helped us grow into the model PLC that shaped this book. It was a once-in-a-lifetime professional and personal experience, and I forever carry you with me.

To every single person at Solution Tree who has paved the way for this work to happen in schools and graciously supported us in telling the story of that work in this book. Thank you for the thousand ways you accomplish things behind the scenes that allow more students to learn at high levels.

To the frontline educators working with our youngest learners, who know the importance of building a solid foundation for learning and the power of early intervention and who are so vested in their students' success that, after a day of pouring their heart and soul into meeting the ever-increasing needs of their students, still find the energy to pick up this book and try to find a way to do it better tomorrow. You are my heroes.

—Jacquie Heller

In a PLC, it is never an *I*; it is always *we*. We could not have written this book without the influence of the countless educators we have had the privilege to work alongside throughout our careers. So much of my personal growth in early childhood education came from my work at Mason Crest Elementary while learning and collaborating with outstanding and dedicated professionals.

To my longtime colleague and friend, Jennifer Deinhart, you have been my mathematics partner for most of my career, someone who always inspires and challenges me and who has taught me to believe in myself and all those around me.

To my parents and family, especially my husband and dedicated partner, Anthony, who has wholeheartedly supported me through my educational journey. And to my three wonderful sons, T.J., Nathan, and Kyle, who help me to see things through their young eyes and continue to fuel my passion for social-emotional learning.

Finally, to my three coauthors and amazingly talented colleagues: Jacquie, Diane, and Brian. You each have dedicated your hearts and souls to this profession and have inspired students, parents, and educators around the world. I am forever indebted to you for showing me and so many others the benefits of hard work and true collaboration.

—Tracey Hulen

I awkwardly stumbled into the field of education one day at the encouragement of an amazing educator and friend, Sue Goldstein. Since then, I've dedicated my work to students with diverse backgrounds, and I became a teacher of the English language, working with English learners from all over the world. From those first days, I knew that team collaboration was the only way for students and adults to learn at high levels. I thank every single educator with whom I have crossed paths and collaborated. You have influenced me and shaped me as a learner, teacher, and leader. I could never name you all, but you know who you are. Thank you!

I appreciate the support that Solution Tree provides its authors, and I thank them for the opportunity to write a book they published. Not only do they expect high-quality products, but they support us in the process. Their encouragement and guidance along the way ensures that the result is of the highest standards. Also, their thoughtful approach to our work is rooted in a vision that all educators can support: transforming education worldwide to ensure learning for all. This has been my mantra for a very long time—learning for *all*.

To my coauthors, Brian, Jacquie, and Tracey, it was life changing for me to work with you at Mason Crest Elementary (along with the rest of our amazing staff), and this book has only lifted you higher in my esteem and deeper into my heart. Thank you for being you and being courageous enough to want to partner in this endeavor. I continue to learn from you, and for that, I am forever grateful.

I would never have written this book if it wasn't for the support of my entire family. My parents, who gave everything for me to grow up healthy and happy; my wonderful daughters and their husbands, Kirstin and Seamus and Allie and Matt, who are always my cheerleaders; and my granddaughter, Rory, the center of my world. Most importantly, I thank my life partner, best friend, and biggest fan—my husband, Gib. He tells me I can when I think I can't, and he goes to the earth's end to support me in my dreams. He has been very patient with me during these few years, and I'm the luckiest; thank you.

—DIANE KERR

Solution Tree Press would like to thank the following reviewers:

Tricia Brickner
Principal
Jefferson Elementary School
Goshen, Indiana

Rosella Evaro
Instructional Coach
Spring Hill Elementary School
Pflugerville, Texas

Katie Brittain
Principal
Rose Haggar Elementary School
Dallas, Texas

Natalie Fish
Kindergarten Teacher
Welchester Elementary School
Golden, Colorado

Leigh Anne Neal
Assistant Superintendent and Principal
Shawnee Mission Early Childhood
  Education Center
Overland Park, Kansas

Rachel Perez
Kindergarten Teacher
Spring Hill Elementary School
Pflugerville, Texas

Curt Schwartz
Principal
Jefferson Elementary School
Goshen, Indiana

Amy Stoker
Interventionist and RTI Coordinator
Harvest Elementary School
Harvest, Alabama

Dawn Vang
Assistant Principal
McDeeds Creek Elementary School
Southern Pines, North Carolina

Table of Contents

By Douglas Reeves

1   Creating a Foundation for Learning

2   Building a Curriculum

3   Determining Essential Standards and Curriculum Mapping

What Do We Want Our Students to Learn?

4   Unwrapping Standards and Setting Goals

5   Designing Assessments

6   Discussing Data and Monitoring Progress

About the Authors

Diane Kerr is an educational consultant and former assistant principal at Mason Crest Elementary School in Fairfax County Public Schools (FCPS), Virginia. She supports schools on their journey to become high-functioning professional learning communities (PLCs) and especially enjoys working with schools with diverse student populations. During her tenure as a coprincipal at Mason Crest, the school earned the distinction of becoming the very first recipient of the coveted DuFour Award, which recognizes top-performing PLCs around the world.

Before joining the Mason Crest team in 2012, Diane was one of two English for speakers of other languages coordinators for the FCPS, which has more than 180,000 students. She supervised and led multiple teams that provided services to schools, parents, and students and was a sought-after resource about other central office programs. Working in Connecticut, Bahrain, and Virginia, Diane's career focuses on collaboratively supporting students with diverse needs and specifically on teaching English to speakers of other languages of all ages.

Throughout her career in education, Diane has provided professional development in many venues, including presenting to large groups of school leaders, school board members, teachers, and teacher teams. She has taught university-level classes on differentiation and meeting the needs of diverse learners. She was a part of a team who helped contributing author Brian K. Butler write chapter 3, "Collaborating in the Core," of *It's About Time: Planning Interventions and Extensions in Elementary School.* Diane presented at the 2018 and 2019 Solution Tree Soluciones Institutes and select PLC at Work Institutes in 2018 and 2019. She also presented at the first-ever Culture Keepers Institute in 2018.

Diane earned an education specialist degree and a preK–12 administration and supervision endorsement from the University of Virginia, and she holds a master's degree in teaching with an endorsement in teaching English to speakers of other languages from Sacred Heart University in Fairfield, Connecticut. She holds a bachelor of science degree in economics from the College of Charleston.

Diane and her husband Gib have two adult daughters, Kirstin and Allie, two son-in-laws, Seamus and Matt, and a granddaughter, Rory.

To learn more about Diane's work, follow @diane_KerrWerx on Twitter

Tracey Hulen, an education consultant and elementary and middle school mathematics specialist, has been part of the leadership team at two model professional learning communities (PLCs) in Fairfax County, Virginia. She specializes in mathematics and social-emotional learning and has a wide range of experience collaborating about data-driven instruction. She served as a mathematics specialist at Mason Crest Elementary School in Annandale, Virginia, the first model PLC to receive Solution Tree's annual DuFour Award in 2016. While serving in this role, Tracey worked with preK–6 teams of teachers and was instrumental in helping build and support the school's innovative mathematics program. Under her leadership, Mason Crest consistently achieved outstanding results in mathematics on the Standards of Learning for Virginia Public Schools. Her work also included supporting early childhood teams with integrating social-emotional learning with academic learning.

In addition to her work at Mason Crest, Tracey worked with the mathematics team in the FCPS Instructional Services Department for four years, which serves 140 elementary schools. During that time, she supported the development of FCPS's rigorous mathematics curriculum, assessments, and instructional programs. Tracey's work included creating and facilitating FCPS's mathematics professional development for administrators, instructional coaches, and elementary teachers. In addition, she provided more individualized support to schools in planning, creating assessments, discussing data, determining lesson study, differentiating instruction, and utilizing best practices in mathematics.

In 2006, Tracey was a Title I mathematics coach who passionately led other mathematics specialists and resources teachers in Fairfax County's Title I schools. Tracey previously served as a member of the National Council of Teachers of Mathematics Educational Materials Committee, advising board members on matters related to the council's publications, as well as proposing, reviewing, and approving manuscripts for publication. She has been published in *AllThingsPLC Magazine* and *The Journal of Mathematics and Science: Collaborative Explorations* from the Virginia Mathematics and Science Coalition.

Tracey earned a bachelor of science in education from Pennsylvania State University and a master's in education (mathematics specialist) from the University of Virginia.

To learn more about Tracey's work, follow @traceyhulen on Twitter.

Jacqueline Heller focuses on building capacity and collective efficacy with teachers to ensure all students learn at high levels. As a literacy teacher and coach at Mason Crest Elementary School in Annandale, Virginia, she helped the school become the first model professional learning community (PLC) to receive the DuFour Award.

She has extensive experience collaborating about data-driven instruction, spending most of her twenty-five-year career working with and learning from diverse language learners and students living in poverty in Title I schools. Jacqueline has been published in the *Journal of Literacy Research*. She has presented at the state and international levels and served on the leadership teams of two model PLCs in Fairfax County, Virginia.

Jacqueline received a bachelor of science from the University of Virginia and a master of education from George Mason University where she is pursuing a PhD in education with an emphasis in literacy and change management.

To learn more about Jacqueline's work, follow @JacquieHeller on Twitter.

Brian K. Butler is an education consultant who has worked with thousands of schools throughout the United States, Australia, and Canada presenting on the PLC at Work and RTI at Work models. Brian is a retired principal who last served at Mason Crest Elementary School in Annandale, Virginia in 2017. Under Brian's leadership, Mason Crest received Solution Tree's first annual DuFour Award in 2016. The honor, named for PLCs at Work process architect Richard DuFour, credits high-performing PLCs that demonstrate exceptional levels of student achievement. The recipient of the DuFour Award is the highest award that a PLC at Work school can achieve. In 2016, Mason Crest was the model of all model schools from around the world and received $25,000 as part of the award.

Brian has also been a principal and an assistant principal for other schools in Fairfax County Public Schools (FCPS). While principal of Mount Eagle Elementary (2006–2011), it was also recognized as a model PLC at Work school. During his tenure, Brian was named a finalist for FCPS Principal of the Year for demonstrating superior leadership qualities and creating an exceptional educational environment. As assistant principal of Lemon Road Elementary, Brian, with Principal Carolyn Miller, helped lead staff to high levels of collaboration—an approach he shares with parent groups, teachers, school staff, and administrators to encourage teamwork among stakeholders. Lemon Road was also a model PLC at Work school.

A former professional basketball player in the European League, Brian holds a bachelor's degree in speech communications from George Washington University. He also has a teacher's certification in physical education and a master's degree in school counseling from George Mason University. He earned an administrative endorsement from the University of Virginia.

Brian and his wife Kathleen have two adult daughters Alison and Emily.

To learn more about Brian's work, follow @bkbutler_brian on Twitter.

To book Diane Kerr, Tracey A. Hulen, Jacqueline Heller, or Brian K. Butler for professional development, contact pd@SolutionTree.com.

Foreword

· · · · · · · · · · · · · · · · · ·

By Douglas Reeves

In more than two decades of observing over a thousand collaborative teams committed to the professional learning community (PLC) model, I had never heard the word *play* uttered in the context of a PLC; that is, until reading the pages of this wonderful book. With compelling evidence and richly described case studies, *What About Us?* takes the reader on a journey through the challenges and successes of teachers, students, and leaders in the primary grades. As you pursue the successful implementation of an early childhood team in a school that functions as a PLC, you will explore not only the essentials of learning, assessment, intervention, and extensions of learning but also the sheer joy that play and deep attention to the social and emotional needs of students provide to educators who are courageous enough to take on these challenges.

In this book, readers will transcend the perilous ground of what Rick DuFour and I called *PLC Lite* (DuFour & Reeves, 2016) and create vibrant and engaging communities of professionals who fearlessly challenge themselves and one another. While some readers may already be familiar with the PLC process, my experience suggests that all educators, particularly those who are part of an early childhood team, will benefit from the practical application of that process that the following pages provide. Effective PLCs do far more than look at data or ask questions regarding learning, assessment, intervention, and extension. This book provides specific tasks and elaborates on the deep inquiry in which professionals must engage to be worthy of the name *professional learning community*.

Careful readers will want to study this book and not merely breeze through it. Your study will be rewarded with insights into seven key ideas.

1. **Context:** Context includes the mission, vision, and fundamental values of the school and every classroom within it.

2. **Culture:** Culture is the sum of the actions, practices, and traditions that, while not inscribed in policy and procedure, represent the values and habits that influence students and faculty.

3. **Curriculum:** As this book's authors explain, curriculum is far more than a set of state, provincial, or national standards. It gives clarity to students and teachers about learning that is most important, and it illustrates how all essential learning fits together.

4. **Competence:** Competence represents the practices that professionals hone and improve throughout their careers. Its importance reminds us that we never arrive in this profession but are always learning from research, from our colleagues, and from our students.

5. **Collaboration:** Collaboration is at the very heart of PLCs, as teachers and school leaders not only share their most effective practices but fearlessly learn from their mistakes.

6. **Conscious teaching:** Conscious teaching requires that educators abandon the notion that, because they probably know more mathematics than a five-year-old, they can teach like automatons. The demands of conscious teaching require that educators consider far more than the right answer to the sum of two digits. It demands they care deeply about the answer to questions for which there is no absolutely correct response, such as, "How are you feeling?" and "What is making you happy, sad, or anxious right now?"

7. **Continuous learning:** Continuous learning requires a degree of humility that is not easy in an environment full of expert educators, but it is essential. While readers may take great satisfaction in the affirmations this book provides regarding what they already know, they will learn and grow best when they allow themselves to be challenged by the books they read, their colleagues, and their students.

Enjoy the journey ahead. Share it with your colleagues. Study it in detail. Correspond with the authors. You will find the benefits you reap from this text far exceed your investment of time and intellectual energy.

Douglas Reeves is the author of more than forty books, including *Achieving Equity and Excellence*.

Introduction

· ·

When a student first walks through a school's front doors, an entire world of opportunity lays ahead for every educator in the building. These first steps are the beginning of a formal learning journey educators control, and they have the responsibility to ensure high levels of learning for students—*all* students. How do educators purposefully guide that journey? They do it together using the Professional Learning Communities at Work (PLC) process (DuFour, DuFour, Eaker, Many, & Mattos, 2016).

This book focuses on the early years of learning and how the PLC process supports early childhood programs. It aligns with our own experiences and learning through our work at Mason Crest Elementary School in Fairfax County Public Schools (FCPS) and with that of colleagues from across the United States. Mason Crest, located in Annandale, Virginia, is a diverse, Title I preK–5 elementary school. It humbly holds the honor of being the very first DuFour Award recipient in 2016 as a top model PLC school in the world. Schools with this distinction must meet these criteria:

- Demonstrate a commitment to PLC concepts.
- Implement those concepts for at least three years.
- Present clear evidence of improved student learning. (AllThingsPLC, n.d.)

This award in no way suggests Mason Crest ended its learning journey with this achievement. Instead, it suggests our years of effort, experiences, and laser-like focus on the PLC process have benefited student and adult learning; this includes the learning of the youngest students, those in preschool. The Mason Crest preschool team includes the Family and Early Childhood Education Program and Head Start, a full-day program that primarily serves income-eligible students. There are also self-contained special education classrooms that provide targeted services to students with Individual Education Programs. One additional classroom for the Early Childhood Inclusion Program features co-teaching from an early childhood program teacher and a special education teacher. Mason Crest has between eighty and one hundred students in each grade level starting in preschool. Its teachers always assume learning is continuous and there should be a direct connection between preschool and the rest of the school.

This tightly connected relationship between grades preK–5 educators provides students with a network of support for their many needs as they grow, learn, and prepare for the future. This is the bedrock of the PLC process—to prepare all students for successful adult lives.

As you begin this book, this background knowledge is important as we lay out the case for including early childhood education teams in the PLC process and then establish how the teams can effectively implement processes and a culture to not only improve learning in preK–2 but also establish the foundation for students' learning throughout their educational careers. The rest of this introduction provides the following information about the content you will find in this book.

- Essential terminology

- The importance of understanding students' social-emotional needs

- The role of play in early childhood education

- Key understandings about the physical and cultural aspects of the learning environment

- A primer on collective inquiry and job-embedded professional development

- An explanation of what you can expect from each chapter

Essential Terminology

Throughout this book, we use the terms *early childhood*, *preschool*, and *primary grades*. According to the National Association of Education of Young Children (NAEYC; 2009), the term *early childhood* refers to birth through age 8. For this book, we apply that definition but break it down into categories (see figure I.1). While we encourage educators working with students younger than age four to read this book and apply PLC big ideas and concepts to their practices, the examples in this book target grades preK–2.

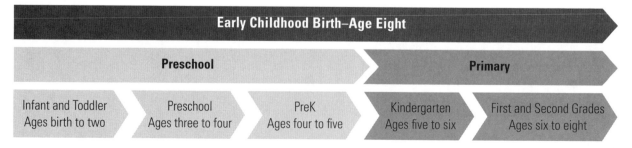

Figure I.1: Early childhood classifications.

Preschool and kindergarten programs vary greatly; they can be private, public, half day, or full day. Districts sometimes house these programs in an elementary school and sometimes offer independent programs and locations. When we refer to *primary grades*, we include students in kindergarten through second grade. While many eight-year-old students begin the school year as third graders, this grade serves as a transitional year from *early primary grades* (K–2) to *upper primary grades* (4–6) and is often the start of standardized testing for students. Just as we hope educators of preK–2 students will apply the PLC concepts, we also believe those working with students in upper primary grades can gain insights and ideas to improve their practices.

Regardless of grade level or organization, it is teams that drive this work. In *Learning by Doing*, PLC architects Richard DuFour, Rebecca DuFour, Robert Eaker, Thomas W. Many, and Mike Mattos (2016) define a team as "a group of people working together *interdependently* to achieve a *common goal* for which members are *mutually accountable*" (p. 42). The ultimate question teams must collectively answer is, "Do team members have a shared responsibility for responding to the four critical questions in ways that enhance students' learning?" (DuFour et al., 2016, p. 60). We address the concept of the four critical questions of a PLC in chapter 1 (page 13). What is important about this statement is what it says about the work of teams. There are a number of team structures that support meaningful collaboration, including the following:

- **Same-course or grade-level teams** are those in which, for example, all the geometry teachers or all the second-grade teachers in a school form a collaborative team.

- **Vertical teams** link teachers with those who teach content above or below their students.

- **Electronic teams** use technology to create powerful partnerships with colleagues across the district, state, or world.

- **Interdisciplinary teams** found in middle schools and small high schools can be an effective structure if members work interdependently to achieve an overarching curricular goal that will result in higher levels of student learning.

- **Logical links** put teachers together in teams that are pursuing outcomes linked to their areas of expertise. (DuFour et al., 2016, p. 64)

DuFour et al. (2016) say the most powerful structure that supports student learning is one in which a team of educators teaches the same course or grade level; however, the ultimate message to any person engaged in the PLC at Work process is that *everyone* in the school should be a part of a team. Even if a teacher is the only one teaching that grade level or course, there are team structures that allow them to collaborate. Sometimes that may require creative solutions and structures, like electronic teams and logical-links teams, but in all cases, collaboration is essential.

Incorporating Social, Emotional, and Academic Learning

A critical consideration for schools is to maintain an intentional focus on incorporating both academic and social-emotional needs of each student into the school's instructional plan. The social-emotional development of the youngest learners is critical, and educators should not push it aside. In our travels, we have heard about and witnessed teachers complain about how their district leadership pushes a focus on academic skills while saying nothing about and brushing aside social and emotional skills. This was a constant theme from teachers who attended Brian's breakout session, "What About Us?" at the PLC at Work Institute (Butler, 2019).

Researchers Joseph A. Durlak, Roger P. Weissberg, Allison B. Dymnicki, Rebecca D. Taylor, and Kriston B. Schellinger (2011) support social-emotional learning (SEL) for all students and show how it can improve academic performance. Their work is based on findings from a meta-analysis of over two hundred school-based SEL programs that involved over two hundred-thousand students showing that academic achievement increased by 11 percentile points when teachers embedded SEL in their instruction. Additionally, as we work with teachers across the country, teachers consistently share their experience-based convictions that students cannot learn academic skills without instruction and reinforcement of social-emotional skills. When Brian created his PLC at Work Institute presentation (Butler, 2019), he asked a kindergarten teacher at Mason Crest why teaching SEL is so important. She succinctly said, "The development of social skills is most important because we can teach the academic skills more directly if students have developed social competencies" (Louise Robertson, personal communication, May, 2017). Coauthors Damon E. Jones, Mark Greenberg, and Max Crowley (2015) further find the following SEL skills make a lifelong impact on children.

- Handling frustration
- Taking turns
- Coping with being told, "No."
- Being kind to others

Many states have established a set of SEL standards and many address these concepts and skills for preschool learners as well. The NAEYC's (2009) position on SEL states, "All the domains of development and learning—physical, social and emotional, and cognitive—are important, and they are closely interrelated. Children's development and learning in one domain influence and are influenced by what takes place in other domains" (p. 11). The most skillful early childhood programs incorporate all domains throughout the day. Throughout this book, we provide examples of how teams include social-emotional skills in their planning, teaching, and assessment practices to ensure they are teaching with the developmental needs of the whole child in mind.

Learning Through Play and Intentional Teaching Practices

A school administrator shared with Brian in a breakout session (Butler, 2019), that her kindergarten teachers no longer regarded the kindergarten classroom as the fun place and time they experienced when they were children. Her teachers lamented that kindergarten had come to encompass the demands of what used to be for first grade and that drill-and-kill pencil-and-paper tasks had become the order of the day.

We push back on the idea that these early years of learning are no longer fun or filled with play. It can be exactly the opposite—both engaging and academic. Play serves its own purpose, building executive-functioning skills, cognitive flexibility, and working memory through social interaction and giving students opportunities for healthy challenge (Suh, 2019). We suggest integrating academic learning with play. Tools of the Mind program developers Deborah J. Leong and Elena Bodrova (2012) contend, "Research provides more and more evidence of the positive effects that well-developed play has on various areas of child development, such as children's social skills, emerging mathematical ability, mastery of early literacy concepts, and self-regulation" (p. 28).

Instead of the youngest learners sitting in their chairs working quietly, we believe walking into a classroom of young learners should reveal a flurry of activity, as students participate in meaningful play *and* engage in learning opportunities that the teacher directs and students initiate. When we walk into these classrooms, we see students talking with one another, pretending, taking turns, and interacting with materials that support their SEL, as well as develop their academic skills of numeracy and literacy. We see teachers moving around the classroom, guiding the play through purposeful talk that happens authentically in the moment, as well as proactively using planned and intentional prompts and questions that shape how students play, learn, and interact with one another. These teachers carefully design and plan classroom activities. In fact, Kimberly Brenneman (2014) of the Rutgers University National Institute for Early Education Research shares:

> Using an engaging and interactive *planned* lesson to show and explain how a tool or material is used need not mean that play and self-guided exploration have been stifled. Instead these teaching strategies could mark the beginning of higher quality play and increased learning, guided by children, but inspired by their teacher. (p. 1)

As students progress through the early childhood years, this focus on play morphs into classrooms of inquiry and engaging problem-solving activities where learning is fun and prepares students for learning in subsequent grades. Crafting these sorts of classroom experiences also requires teams to focus on both the physical and cultural aspects of the learning environment.

The Learning Environment in Early Childhood

A foundational building block of a well-managed classroom includes a set of rules, routines, and procedures. In many contemporary classrooms, teachers and students collaborate to establish these rules, routines, and procedures, setting up clear expectations and accountability for everyone. The implications of this collaboration reflect in both the physical and cultural environment, of which each play an active role in students' learning. Let's examine each of these environments.

The Physical Environment

If educators want learners to be creative and critical thinkers, and active collaborators and communicators, then the physical environment must be conducive for those types of interactions. Setting up the physical space to include a whole-group area—plus a variety of areas where teachers can facilitate learning with small groups of students and learning spaces where students can explore and engage in play—is an important step for all early educators. Lucy Calkins (n.d.) of the Teacher's College Reading and Writing Project writes that because one size does not fit all, teachers must set up an environment that allows for flexibility and a range of activities. In her workshop model, she emphasizes the following points (Calkins, n.d.):

- help teachers address each child's individual learning;
- explicitly teach strategies students will use not only the day they are taught, but whenever they need them;
- help students work with engagement so that teachers are able to coach individuals and lead small groups;
- support small-group work and conferring, with multiple opportunities for personalizing instruction;
- tap into the power of a learning community as a way to bring all learners along;
- build choice and assessment-based learning into the very design of the curriculum.

The routines and structures of reading and writing workshop are kept simple and predictable so that the teacher can focus on the complex work of teaching in a responsive manner to accelerate achievement for all learners. (Calkins, n.d., p. 6)

Teachers must also carefully consider the variety of materials they put out for play and learning to intentionally include those that support the specific content as well as those that allow students to stretch their boundaries in physical, cognitive, language, and SEL skills. As teachers get to know their students, the environment should be flexible and adapt to the needs of individual learners as well as the development of the whole group as students grow and progress.

The Cultural Environment

When teachers have a well-created physical space and procedures, they can focus on creating a culturally responsive classroom that encourages and promotes student inquiry and developing an academic mindset. In *Culturally Responsive Teaching and the Brain*, former teacher and author Zaretta Hammond (2017) provides a framework for culturally responsive teaching, which involves four key components: (1) awareness, (2) learning partnerships, (3) information processing, and (4) a community of learners and learning environment. Each of these are critical when striving for fairness and giving all students what they need when they need it to ensure they are learning at grade level or better. In this book, we focus on the community of learners and the learning environment. Hammond (2017) stresses the importance of the following components of a culturally responsive classroom.

- Create an environment that is intellectually and socially safe for learning.

- Make space for student voice and agency (so students can become leaders of their own learning).

- Build classroom culture and learning around communal (sociocultural) talks and task structures.

- Use classroom rituals and routines to support a culture of learning.

- Use principles of restorative justice to manage conflicts and redirect negative behavior.

A culturally responsive classroom leads students toward taking control of their learning through goal setting, creating a plan to reach those goals, and monitoring that plan. Students will ultimately become independent learners who are not afraid of taking risks with a growing sense of self-efficacy. Early childhood classrooms focused on this type of learning environment provide students with not only the academic learning they require but also the social-emotional skills they need to be successful in life. NAEYC (n.d.) reports that in high-quality preschool programs, teachers do the following.

- Provide opportunities for students to develop positive relationships between peers and with themselves.

- Provide materials and activities that interest and challenge students.

- Balance group activities and instruction with activities students choose.

- Provide enough time for students to get deeply involved in activities and learning.

- Pay attention to and support students' interests, skills, and knowledge.

- Take notes regularly on what students do and say.

- Collect samples of students' work.

As teams strive to create classroom environments with these features, they set the stage for students' success as they collectively plan for learning, assessing, and meeting all students' needs.

Collective Inquiry and Job-Embedded Professional Development in Early Childhood Education

When implemented with skill and precision, the PLC process supports early childhood teachers and teams' improvement first by treating them as the experts they are. It supports them, second, through a coordinated, collaborative approach of on-the-job learning and professional development. We explore the fundamental elements of a PLC in detail in chapter 1 (page 13). The important takeaway at this point is that abandoning the idea of the isolated classroom teacher in favor of collaborative teams that take collective responsibility for ensuring high levels of learning for *all* students is a superior approach to learning (Buffum, Mattos, & Malone, 2018; DuFour et al., 2016; Many, Maffoni, Sparks, & Thomas, 2018; Marzano, Warrick, Rains, & DuFour, 2018; Williams & Hierck, 2015).

To develop collective responsibility, the entire school organization—that is, all educators, teachers, administration, and support staff—must commit to a schoolwide effort to learn together so that they can move forward as one. There are multiple ways to do this. All staff members must have the opportunity to collectively learn about schoolwide approaches to instruction. Whether the topic is SEL, mathematics, or literacy, *everyone* (including specialist teachers, instructional assistants, and so on) should be included in the learning. This ensures common language, common knowledge, and common expectations regarding all major facets of the school.

The inclusion of the preschool and primary teachers (along with specialists and upper-grades teachers) sends three very clear messages to the entire school: (1) all staff members are integral to the school, (2) all staff members benefit from the expertise throughout the school, and (3) each specialty area has a multitude of strategies that benefit other areas. Early childhood teams' strategies can benefit other grade levels and specialty areas; the same is true of the upper-grades teams and specialty-area teachers. Additionally, all staff members are seen as leaders who can lead schoolwide professional development. We agree with DuFour et al. (2016) that leadership is not an individual endeavor but should be widely dispersed.

This whole-staff learning sets the tone and seamlessly leads to deepening the work of teams through the various collaborative teacher team–meeting structures. Here are the team-meeting structures, which we discuss in detail later in this book.

- Planning meetings
- Having data discussions
- Holding progress-monitoring meetings

During these meetings, team members continue to learn from one another as they try new approaches, share data, and evaluate the impact of any initiatives on student learning. This is job-embedded professional development. In *Learning by Doing*, DuFour et al. (2016) stress that teachers cannot opt-out of the work of teams as it is their professional responsibility:

> Educators in a PLC at Work work together collaboratively in constant, deep collective inquiry into the questions, "What is it our students must learn?" and "How will we know when they have learned it?" The dialogue generated from these questions results in the academic focus, collective commitments, and productive professional relationships that enhance learning for teachers and students alike. (p. 149)

A fourth type of team meeting is available as needed—the *team-observation-reflection meeting* in which teams observe other grade-level teams to learn from and with their vertical colleagues. As an example, a preschool team may want to learn new ways to differentiate and integrate academic skills into center activities (some educators may refer to centers as *stations*, *small-group time*, or *rotations*) and decide to observe the kindergarten team during a mathematics workshop. Observing, reflecting on their learning, and creating a plan for next steps is another form of collective inquiry and job-embedded professional development.

None of these learning opportunities are possible, especially the different team-meeting purposes (planning, data discussions, and progress monitoring) without a master schedule that provides time for the early childhood team to meet. A foundational component of a school striving to become a PLC is to find uninterrupted time during the contracted day for educators teaching the same grade level to collaborate (DuFour et al., 2016). At Mason Crest, we were able to provide teacher collaboration time by setting aside one hour for language arts and one hour for mathematics every week. However, this may not work at other schools. Principals must be creative with the resources they have to ensure that teams have time to meaningfully collaborate. To learn more about how different model PLC schools makes this happen, visit the AllThingsPLC website (www.allthingsplc.com). Creating a schedule that allows time for teams to meet is a first step in creating a collaborative culture.

About This Book

The goal of this book is to provide early childhood teams with not only the research base for the work of a PLC but also the tools for collaborating about the teams' work. Chapter 1 provides a baseline for how the PLC process supports the work of early childhood teams. Chapters 2–7 walk teams through the PLC process in the context of early childhood education. Chapter 2 starts with how teams can examine the curriculum to determine what they want students to learn (what they must know and be able to do). Each subsequent chapter builds on the chapter before it, moving logically through the PLC process. So, chapter 3 covers how teams identify the essential standards within the curriculum and set up a curriculum outline to plan instruction. Chapter 4 addresses how teams unwrap standards, develop learning progressions, and set student goals so they can determine how they will know if students have learned. Chapter 5 focuses on assessments and how early childhood teams can use them to collect data about students' learning. Chapter 6 helps teams understand the data they collect and what the information is communicating about students' learning. Finally, chapter 7 provides insight into planning lessons that help teams apply the collected data to further support students who are struggling or extend learning for those who've achieved proficiency.

If you are already familiar with PLC concepts and processes, you will likely recognize the four critical questions of a PLC (DuFour et al., 2016). Figure I.2 clarifies the role of these questions and how they apply to key learning tasks teams. If you're unfamiliar with the four critical questions of a PLC or any of the concepts you see in figure I.2, don't worry. You will learn much more about them in chapter 1 and throughout this book.

Each chapter also includes tools and resources for teacher teams to immediately use in their work. Although certain tools have examples from a specific grade level, they are applicable to all, and we have provided blank versions of them online (visit www.SolutionTree.com/PLCbooks). However, they may need further adaptation for your specific grade level. Also, a series of vignettes with examples and scenarios will help you visualize the work of teams. Look for the vignettes after each chapter introduction to set the stage for the new topic. In each chapter, there are also Tips boxes that include a series of tips specifically for administrators, coaches, and teachers to engage with and reflect on. At the end of each chapter, there are guiding questions for all educators to consider as they continue their learning journey together.

As you read this book through the lens of an early childhood educator, be willing to accept that your journey does not have an end point. This is a journey about continuous improvement and a willingness to work collaboratively with your colleagues to make that happen. We also want you and your team members to affirm and celebrate the things both students and educators are doing in the name of *learning for all*. In essence, we suggest you read this book all the way through with new and proud eyes. The contemporary educational system needs significant cultural shifts if early childhood educators are to realize the daunting but achievable task of having all students learn at high levels. It takes courage to challenge the status quo and to ensure these shifts occur, and we believe the power of PLC-supported collaboration can ensure every early childhood teacher can achieve success.

Critical question one: What do we want our students to learn?
• Task one: Evaluate your current early childhood curriculum.
• Task two: Identify standards of learning for social, emotional, physical, language, and cognitive development, and choose a set of essential (priority) standards.
• Task three: Develop a curriculum outline and map out major formative assessments for the year.
Critical question two: How will we know if each student has learned it?
• Task four: Unwrap essential standards and develop common understanding about the learning targets.
• Task five: Create learning progressions for essential standards and establish student goal-setting procedures.
• Task six: Build and enhance effective unit plans considering the developmental needs of the whole child.
• Task seven: Collectively create developmentally appropriate common formative assessments and determine student proficiency.
Critical question three: How will we respond when some students do not learn it?
Critical question four: How will we extend learning for students who have demonstrated proficiency?
• Task eight: Using a data protocol, analyze common assessment results to identify effective teaching strategies and plan for instruction that supports and extends student learning.
• Task nine: Monitor student progress and develop a system of interventions and extensions to support all learners.
• Task ten: Plan engaging developmentally appropriate early childhood lessons using researched-based effective teaching practices.

Source: Adapted from Kramer & Schuhl, 2017; Nielsen, 2019.

Figure I.2: Early childhood team tasks and the four critical questions of a PLC.

*Visit **go.SolutionTree.com/PLCbooks** for a free reproducible version of this figure.*

Creating a Foundation for Learning

How Can the PLC Process Support Collaborative Teams?

1

In his TED Talk, Simon Sinek (2009) says very few organizations know their why, their purpose, their beliefs, or even why their organization exists. This *why* or *purpose* is the mission pillar of the PLC at Work process, which we explain in detail later in this chapter. For now, know that when a school or district commits to ensuring high levels of learning for both students and adults as its purpose, "every practice, policy, and procedure of the school is assessed on the basis of how it will impact learning. Every aspect of the PLC process flows from this fundamental premise regarding why the school exists" (DuFour & DuFour, 2012, p. 10).

In this chapter, we begin by looking at why schools and districts must include early childhood education in the PLC process. To ensure full understanding of the language common to all PLCs that underpins the rest of the book, we also review the following components of PLC culture each member of the school organization must understand (DuFour et al., 2016).

- **The four pillars:**
  1. Mission
  2. Vision
  3. Values (collective commitments)
  4. Goals

- **The three big ideas:**

    1. A focus on learning
    2. A collaborative culture and collective responsibility
    3. A results orientation

- **The four critical questions:**

    1. What do we want our students to learn?
    2. How will we know if each student has learned it?
    3. How will we respond when some students do not learn it?
    4. How will we extend learning for students who have demonstrated proficiency?

We conclude the chapter with a series of guiding questions for implementing the PLC process to improve instruction for preK–2 learners.

Before we begin our exploration of PLC structures, we start here not with a fictional vignette (as in forthcoming chapters) but with a message from an elementary leadership team that successfully applied the work of a PLC to early childhood education. In less than five years, their organization was named a national model PLC at Work school. We believe this story is indicative of a school that embraces the PLC process because these team members realized that to ensure high levels of learning for students—preschoolers, kindergarteners and first graders—they had to change their culture to one of collective responsibility. Although this school happens to include just preK through first grade, this example is relevant to all early childhood and elementary schools. Whether a school has a large or small comprehensive early childhood and primary program, young learners are the responsibility of each educator in the building.

Vignette:
The Story of Freeport Elementary

By the Leadership Team at Freeport Elementary School

In 2015, things did not look good for Freeport Elementary School (formerly O. A. Fleming Elementary School) in the Brazosport Independent School District in Texas. Back then, it was a preK–4 campus, and the Texas Education Agency (2015a) labeled the school as *Improvement Required*, a status that could have led to a state takeover of the school (Evans, 2018). Our school scored the lowest across all subject areas and all grade levels in the district and in-state testing. Morale was low, and teacher turnover was high. These were dark times for our school and our district, and the superintendent and district cabinet took drastic measures to transform the campus into a preK–1 early childhood campus. A nearby sister school, Velasco Elementary, was restructured to accommodate grades 2–4. The district also brought in new school leadership, while those existing teachers who were passionate about student learning stayed. Our school got to work. The primary focus for every educator became literacy and teaching students to read at grade level because students who can read can do anything!

Since that time, the school has transformed into a high-performing, happy, and productive learning environment. It has grown from 350 students to 520 students, and the staff doubled. We strive to ensure our students are future ready and that all students leave the campus reading on grade level or above. Yet it still has the same student population it always had, including a high percentage of students who are at risk and live in high poverty and a large percentage of English learners. In June of 2019, district staff reported at a school board meeting that Freeport Elementary had become one of the top-performing schools for its grade span in the district. Its kindergarten students had the biggest gain in the district, twenty-four points from the beginning of the year to end of year on their literacy assessment, and its first-grade students scored the highest on the iStation assessment as compared to the other campuses (Clara Sale-Davis, personal communication, April 28, 2020).

In 2020, Freeport was named a national model PLC at Work school. How did we turn things around so drastically, and how did we experience success year after year such that we became a national model PLC school in 2020? By working together as a collaborative team and having shared accountability for students' learning. We are firm believers in the PLC process, and we believe *all* students can learn. These practices have helped us transform our school into a place where great things are happening!

Early Childhood Education and the PLC Process

We define the scope of *early childhood education* as including preschool through second grade. It's important to stress the importance of including preschool educators in particular in the PLC process. It may seem redundant to say it's important to include preK as part of a PLC's commitment to early childhood education, but in our work locally and across the United States, we find that few schools consider doing so; as a result, they do not see preschool learners as part of their collective responsibility. Additionally, the staff at these schools do not see the teachers and teacher teams of preschool students as members of the larger grades K–6 system. This exclusion of early education professionals reflects the professional development opportunities they receive and impacts structural decisions. For example, when preK teachers are not a part of a vertical team of K–2 teachers, these teachers are rarely included in the development of the master schedule or structures that provide for common planning time.

We believe this does not happen purposefully but is the result of the laser-like focus on grade levels required to participate in end-of-year state assessments to meet federal accountability requirements. We've also seen this happen when administrators have a lack of comfort and understanding of preschool education, allowing teachers to do their work in isolation. Some districts separately support preschool programs and have separate curricula and separate professional development opportunities. To be fair, there are times when teachers require separate training opportunities; however, this structure implies there isn't a connection between preschool and the primary grades. In a preK–12 school district, the district actions and behaviors must align for *all* members of the community in embracing and taking collective responsibility for *all* students.

There are a variety of factors that support why schools should include early childhood educators in the PLC process, even though these early years are not tied to the standardized testing for progress and achievement that often begin in third grade. However, there are two factors of particular importance.

1. No one teacher has all the skills, experiences, and strategies to meet the needs of each student in his or her classroom regardless of the number of degrees, years of experience, or the quality of his or her preservice programs.

2. The early childhood years provide a solid foundation for student success in the upper-elementary grades (grades 3–5) and beyond by eliminating gaps in experiences and readiness.

Learners ages three to five enter school with widely varying academic and SEL needs. Although parents do their very best the moment their children enter the world to provide a strong foundation for their children to learn from, early learning experiences vary from family to family. This variation does not exist because any particular parent cares more or less about his or her child's growth than other parents, but because of many mitigating factors. These factors can include varying levels of parent education, access to resources (at-home interaction, physical and mental healthcare, family support, and so on), and the demands of long workdays (Ferguson, Bovaird, & Mueller, 2007). As a result, these new students often head into a more formal learning environment with very different levels of academic readiness and different social-emotional needs.

In our experience, the *only* way to ensure the needs of each student are met is to have the collective responsibility for all students a PLC ensures. This eliminates the expectation and pressure on teachers to know it all and unilaterally provide everything to every student in their charge. Instead, when teachers operate as a preK–12 PLC, the focus on the success of every student becomes the foundation for how the school does business from the very first moment each student is exposed to a formal school experience to the moment he or she graduates. By starting the PLC process during early childhood education, schools form the foundation for future learning. It also opens the door for teachers to consider how they might deploy strategies proven effective in the upper grades to serve the needs of preK–2.

Developing a strong preschool program is a first step. A study from early education researchers Linda Bakken, Nola Brown, and Barry Downing (2017) reports children from economically disadvantaged homes in high-quality early childhood programs receive benefits ranging from improved academic outcomes (outperforming peers on standardized testing in third and fourth grade) to stronger social skills (appropriate behaviors, emotional maturity, and social interactions that result in fewer discipline referrals) and positive attitudes (exemplified by higher school attendance rates). Strong preschool programs provide immediate and long-term results for students and impact society. The U.S. Department of Education (n.d.) states, "High-quality preschool provides the foundation for children's success in school and helps to mitigate educational gaps that exist between children from high- and low-income families before they enter kindergarten."

High-quality preschool is also a wise economic investment. In "The Productivity Argument for Investing in Young Children," leading economists James J. Heckman and Dimitriy V. Masterov (2007) find for every one dollar invested in high-quality preschool, taxpayers save an average of seven dollars in future costs due to reductions in remedial education costs, increased labor productivity, and a reduction in crime. Walk into any kindergarten classroom, and ask the teacher whether preschool has a positive impact on school readiness for learners. You will hear a resounding, "Yes!" Imagine schools or districts with high-quality preschool programs also follow the PLC process to ensure teachers collectively respond when students don't learn or exceed expectations. The impact can only magnify!

While leveling the playing field in preschool is an important first step, continuing that focus as students progress through the primary years is critical. The Annie E. Casey Foundation (2010) report "Early Warning! Why Reading by the End of Third Grade Matters" shares concerning statistics that should make any early childhood educator feel an urgency for changing traditional practices in primary grades. The report finds that low-income fourth graders not reading on grade level are "all too likely to become our nation's lowest-income, least skilled, least-productive, and most costly citizens tomorrow. Simply put, without a dramatic reversal of the status quo, we are cementing educational failure and poverty into the next generation" (Annie E. Casey Foundation, 2010, p. 7). If reading on grade level by the start of third grade is an indicator of future success (in fourth grade and beyond), then it is imperative that schools focus on strategies and programs for preschool and K–2 to ensure students meet or exceed grade-level reading standards by the start of third grade.

Research also supports the importance of collaboration to guide the work of teams and learning for all students at all grade levels. University of Melbourne (Australia) Professor of Education and Director of the Melbourne Education Research Institute John Hattie (2016) identifies collective teacher efficacy at the top of the list of factors that influence student achievement. Based on a synthesis of more than 1,500 meta-analyses, his research shows collective teacher efficacy is greater than three times more powerful and predictive of student achievement than socioeconomic status. In this context, *collective efficacy* refers to "a group's shared belief in its conjoint capability to organize and execute the courses of action required to produce given levels of attainment" (Bandura, 1997, p. 477).

At his website (https://visible-learning.org), Hattie (n.d.) provides information on 252 influences on student learning based on nearly 1,200 meta-analyses. Each influence has an effect size that indicates its positive or negative impact on student achievement. Any influence above zero has some positive impact on student achievement; however, the factors most worthy of educators' focus are those above the 0.40 hinge point. This hinge point (.40) is the expected growth teachers are likely to see from a student just by him or her being alive and in the average teachers' classroom for a year. Collective teacher efficacy has an effect size of 1.57, which is statistically significant and merits educator's attention (Hattie, 2016). Therefore, when teacher teams come together to plan, assess, and respond to each student's learning, and to evaluate their own practices and ultimate impact on student learning, all students will learn at high levels and be appropriately challenged. Together, teachers learn from their mistakes and successes and translate their learning into teaching practices that have a high impact on student achievement.

Imagine that a collective focus on each student begins in preschool and continues through the primary grades (K–2). By this point, teacher teams will have addressed any variance in student readiness during these early years; as a result, all students will be poised for high levels of learning as they finish elementary school and enter secondary school (grades 6–12). It is clear that creating a solid foundation is critical for preK–2 students to have an opportunity to be successful in subsequent school years and later as adults; the same holds true for a school or district beginning or continuing its journey as a PLC.

With an understanding of the importance of a PLC culture to early childhood education in place, it's important to have a shared understanding of the foundational PLC concepts.

The Four Pillars

The early childhood years of school (preK–2) can create a solid foundation for each student to have a successful adult life. Students who have a solid foundation in early literacy, numeracy, *and* behavior will have multiple opportunities to build on and extend these skills throughout their school years. On the other hand, students who do not have a solid foundation in these areas will stand on shaky ground and continually need support to close learning gaps.

Rebecca DuFour, educator and coauthor of *Learning by Doing* (DuFour et al., 2016), shares an analogy from her brother, "Russ the builder," in emphasizing the importance of laying a solid foundation (personal communication, April 8, 2018). Russ is a veteran housing contractor in southwest Virginia and raves about the beautiful houses he builds. When building a house, Russ does not start with the roof or second floor. He starts planning and then builds a solid foundation to support the rest of the structure. He understands that if he builds the foundation with inattention to detail and sloppiness, it won't be solid or sturdy, and everything built on top of it—no matter how well it's built—will eventually have problems. A structure without a solid foundation will eventually show cracks and gaps in the floors and walls, among many other potential problems. As a homeowner, you may not see the foundation, but it is the most important step to building the house of your dreams.

Much in the same way that building a solid foundation is critically important to a physical structure, so is creating a solid foundation for a PLC school to build on. DuFour et al. (2016) identify four pillars for the foundation of a PLC.

1. Mission

2. Vision

3. Values (collective commitments)

4. Goals

Because this book is for early childhood collaborative teams in schools that already function as PLCs, we will not go into great detail about the four pillars (our assumption being that staff members have already collaborated to create them). The point we would like to emphasize is building a solid foundation is the first step for any school that wishes to become a high-functioning PLC. *Teams cannot overlook this step!* The following sections provide a brief overview of the four pillars, along with examples from our experiences at Mason Crest Elementary School.

Mission: Why Do We Exist?

The *mission* of every school is its statement of purpose. Having clear agreement on the purpose of the school is fundamental to a learning-focused organization. Incessant debate among the staff on the school's purpose will make it virtually impossible for all students to learn at high levels. When schools don't have clear agreement on what high levels of learning means, it's left to the discretion of each teacher to define, which leads to an educational lottery. Each student's education then depends on the teacher to which the school assigns him or her. However, when there is a clear mission that all staff members live up to, it no longer matters which teacher a student has. If he or she experiences difficulty, the staff will guarantee collectively that the student receives the additional time and support he or she needs to learn at high levels.

> **Example Mission Statement**
>
> "The purpose of Mason Crest is to ensure high levels of learning for all—students and adults" (Mason Crest Elementary School, n.d.).

Vision: What Must Our School Become to Accomplish Our Mission?

If asked to write a story painting a picture of the future of learning for your school's students in five years, would the educators in your school write the same headline and have almost identical key points? A school's *vision* tasks a school with defining a compelling visual about its future, what it must become to accomplish its mission. This is the second pillar PLCs must address to collaboratively create a solid foundation (DuFour et al., 2016). Having a clear, coherent vision as an organization moves your school one step closer to ensuring learning for all.

> **Example Vision Statement**
>
> "[When we collectively fulfill that purpose], our students will have the knowledge, skills and dispositions essential to pursuing their goals and dreams throughout their lives" (Mason Crest Elementary School, n.d.).

Values (Collective Commitments): How Must We Behave to Achieve Our Vision?

Having a mission and vision as the first two pillars is a must for any PLC, but they mean nothing if stakeholders don't start *doing*. The third pillar, *values*, or as we prefer to call them, *collective commitments*, asks the question, "How must we behave to achieve our vision?"

In developing collective commitments, "educators shift from offering philosophical musings on mission or their shared hopes for the school of the future to making commitments to act in certain ways—starting today" (DuFour et al., 2016, p. 41). In our work around the world, we find most schools have mission and vision statements that (understandably) all sound very similar, but very few schools have collective commitments. The phrase *all talk and no action* comes to mind when it comes to staff not cocreating and adhering to schoolwide collective commitments. *The Will to Lead, the Skill to Teach*, by consultants and authors Anthony Muhammad and Sharroky Hollie (2012), emphasizes this point perfectly, stating:

> There is a direct link between the belief system of a staff and its behaviors and actions. A staff that aligns its intentions around

student achievement develops a commitment to the essential behaviors that have been proven to boost student performance. (p. 10)

Collective commitments put into words the actions schools must take to move from visualizing what they want to become to committing to specific actions that start the journey of actually doing the work.

Example Staff Collective Commitments

"In order to honor and advance our shared purpose, vision, and goals, we pledge to honor the following collective commitments. We will:

- Identify and teach the agreed-upon essential outcomes, adhere to the curriculum pacing established by the team and help our students discover what they can do with that knowledge.

- Create both common formative and summative assessments and administer them according to the team's agreed-upon timeline.

- Use the results from our common assessments to improve our individual and collective practice and to meet the enrichment and intervention needs of our students.

- Contribute to an effective system of intervention and enrichment.

- Be positive contributing members of our team as we work interdependently to achieve shared goals and demonstrate mutual accountability.

- Engage in open frequent two-way communication among all stakeholders, provide families with ongoing information about their children, and offer specific ideas and materials to help families become full partners in the ongoing education of their children.

- Embrace shared responsibilities and help others grow in their leadership responsibilities.

- Contribute to a culture of celebration by acknowledging the efforts and achievements of our students and colleagues as we continually strive for even greater success.

- Agree to a common language about behavioral expectations, model that behavior, and consistently reinforce our expectations.

- Consider all points of view and come to our work each day as the best versions of ourselves."
(Mason Crest Elementary School, n.d.)

Example Administration Collective Commitments

"In order to create the school we have described in our shared vision, we make the following commitments. We pledge that we will:

- Promote and protect our shared mission, vision, collective commitments, and goals and keep them at the forefront of all decisions and actions. In doing so we will confront staff whose actions are incongruent with our shared purpose and priorities and will attempt to buffer the staff from competing initiatives so they can devote their full energies to the professional learning community process.

- Build shared knowledge around the term "collaborative team" and the various structures they can take.

- Support the collaborative teams by providing them with sufficient time to meet, clear direction regarding the work to be done, ongoing feedback, and the training and resources necessary to help them succeed at what they are being asked to do.

- Provide all teams the Program of Studies, pacing guides, and resources and ensure the specialists working with those teams facilitate dialogue to promote a deep understanding of essential standards-learning outcomes.

- Build shared knowledge around team-developed common formative assessments and provide training that will enable them to easily and effectively disaggregate data to:

    ○ better meet the intervention and extension needs of individual students,

    ○ inform and improve practice of individual members of the team, and

    ○ improve the teams' collective ability to achieve its SMART goals.

- Provide examples of systems of intervention, extension and enrichment and work with staff to create an effective system for Mason Crest.

- Help staff understand the definition of and their role as a team member.

- Model open communication by sharing important information in a timely manner.

- Create opportunities for leadership throughout the staff based on individual expertise and interest.

- Model, encourage, and plan for celebration as a part of our culture and approach initial efforts that do not achieve the intended results as opportunities to begin again more intelligently rather than as failures." (Mason Crest Elementary School, 2016)

Goals: How Will We Mark Our Progress?

A school or district that functions as a PLC does not judge its work based on teacher activities (*Did I teach it? How good did the lesson look?*), but on tangible student results (*Did they learn it?*). The *goals* pillar addresses this outcome by asking, "How will we mark our progress?"

Noted educator, author, and speaker Kenneth C. Williams (2010) often says a team or school without goals is not a team but a group of highly skilled individuals who have good intentions but lack the mutual accountability and collective desire necessary to accomplish anything as one unit. Since the hallmark of the PLC journey is knowing whether you are making progress or not, the only way to do so is by setting a goal. With goals in place, school teams can monitor progress toward the goal and reassess and reflect at short stopping points along the way. The teams then continue the journey with the knowledge of what did or did not work. Additionally, an awareness of progress toward goals facilitates celebrations as teams and the school accomplish short- and long-term wins. These celebrations are the fuel that helps educators continue this never-ending journey.

Another analogy Rebecca DuFour (2015a) offers is to have educators think of a stool that has four legs and then picture that same stool with one leg missing, then another leg: "Would a stool missing one or more of its legs be wobbly?" she asks. Of course it would. No educator would want to put a student, let alone him- or herself, on that stool. Now, think of a PLC school resting on the four pillars. What would happen if one or more of these pillars is missing? Rebecca DuFour (2015a) asserts the foundation will constantly remind staff to assess any practice, program, policy, and procedure by asking the question, "Does this help more students learn at high levels or prevent students from learning at high levels?" When the answer is the former, teachers must keep doing it and get better at it. If the answer is the latter, teachers must abandon it. For an in-depth examination of the shared foundation of the PLC pillars, we recommend *Learning by Doing* (DuFour et al., 2016).

Example Goals Statement

The following hypothetical goals (derived from our current work) each list a schoolwide goal and each grade level's aligned goal.

- By the end of the 2020–2021 academic year, the number of students in preK–2 scoring proficient in reading will increase from 70 percent to 75 percent as demonstrated by the end-of-year reading assessment. Individual grade levels will increase as follows.

    ○ *Preschool*—75 percent to 80 percent

    ○ *Kindergarten*—64 percent to 69 percent

    ○ *First grade*—81 percent to 86 percent

    ○ *Second grade*—65 percent to 70 percent

continued ➜

- By the end of the 2020–2021 academic year, the number of students in preK–2 scoring proficient in mathematics will increase from 72 percent to 78 percent as demonstrated by the end-of-year mathematics assessment. Individual grade levels will increase as follows.
  - *Preschool*—71 percent to 77 percent
  - *Kindergarten*—54 percent to 60 percent
  - *First grade*—94 percent to 99 percent
  - *Second grade*—73 percent to 78 percent

The Three Big Ideas

Schools and districts that function as PLCs have an unwavering focus on three big ideas (DuFour et al., 2016).

1. A focus on learning

2. A collaborative culture and collective responsibility

3. A results orientation

These three ideas apply to all teams, all grade levels, and all content areas. How teams do the work may look different, but the focus on these three big ideas remains clear and constant regardless of the content or age of the students. The following sections explore each of these big ideas.

A Focus on Learning

If you were to ask teachers, "Do schools focus on learning?" you may get very surprised or incredulous responses like, "Of course we focus on learning" or "It's my job to teach and the student's job to learn." If equity in schools truly concerns educators, then they must be ready to make some fundamental shifts away from the way traditional schools do business to the way schools that function as PLCs do business. This shift requires being able to make the promise to every parent that "it does not matter which teacher his or her child is assigned to, as every student receives the additional time and support needed to learn at high levels" (Buffum et al., 2018, p. 26). Table 1.1 documents some of these shifts.

Engaging teams in identifying the most important knowledge, skills, and dispositions students must learn in each unit, course, or subject is critical to this first big idea. As Rebecca DuFour (2015a) notes, "This idea, a focus on learning, is the biggest of the big."

Table 1.1: Cultural Shifts for Creating a Focus on Learning

Traditional School	PLC School
From a focus on teaching . . .	to a focus on learning
From an emphasis on what is taught . . .	to a fixation on what students learned
From coverage of content . . .	to demonstration of proficiency
From providing individual teachers with curriculum documents such as state standards and curriculum guides . . .	to engaging collaborative teams in building shared knowledge regarding essential curriculum

Source: DuFour et al., 2016, p. 258.

A Collaborative Culture and Collective Responsibility

The second big idea of a PLC, a collaborative culture and collective responsibility, compels schools to abandon the idea of the isolated classroom teacher in favor of collaborative teams of teachers who take collective responsibility for the learning of all students. This is non-negotiable if schools are to ensure adherence to a focus on learning (the first big idea). The reason schools exist is to ensure learning for all. We know of no study that finds working in isolation is more effective for student achievement than working collaboratively on the right work (the four critical questions of a PLC) and taking responsibility as a team for every student's success. Table 1.2 lists some of the fundamental shifts necessary to realize a collaborative culture.

Table 1.2: Cultural Shifts for Creating a Collaborative Culture

Traditional School	PLC School
From isolation . . .	to collaboration
From each teacher clarifying what students must learn . . .	to collaborative teams building shared knowledge and understanding about essential learning
From individual teachers attempting to discover ways to improve results . . .	to collaborative teams of teachers helping each other improve
From privatization of practice . . .	to open sharing of practice
From decisions made based on individual preferences . . .	to decisions made collectively by building shared knowledge of best practice
From an assumption that these are "my students, those are your students" . . .	to an assumption that these are "our students"

Source: Adapted from DuFour et al., 2016, p. 259.

We cannot overstate the importance of a collaborative culture. Educator, author, and presenter Luis F. Cruz (2019) shares, "People are less likely to tear down a fence if they helped to build it." Creating the conditions and expectations that *all* stakeholders will be collaborating to build a culture of shared ownership ensures not only adherence to the process but also ownership of the success of each student. "Teacher teams can only function within a PLC when they are operating within a culture that values and promotes collaboration" (Many et al., 2018, p. 30).

A Results Orientation

No matter how well educators embrace the first two big ideas of learning and collaboration, they will ultimately be judged on *results*—or the evidence that more students are learning at higher levels because of what the educators are doing. Using the evidence of results effectively activates what we call two *levers* (or *arms*) *of learning* in this continuous cycle of improvement.

1. **The student lever of learning:** When teams look at the results of team-developed *common formative assessments* (assessments teams collaboratively develop and issue to all of their students), they can immediately see what students learned (the intended essential curriculum) and what students did not learn. The teams' responsibility is to respond immediately, unit by unit, to ensure students have proper interventions (so they won't fall farther behind) and, if they are already proficient, provide appropriate extension on the standard (to prevent student boredom and to continue to challenge students appropriately).

2. **The teacher lever of learning:** Teams embrace the idea of true collective responsibility by creating norms and *SMART goals* (strategic and specific, measurable, attainable, results oriented, and time bound; Conzemius & O'Neill, 2014). Team members see all students as *their* students and become interdependent and mutually accountable. You can access examples of SMART goals on the AllThingsPLC website's Tools & Resources page (www.allthingsplc.info/tools-resources; select the Set SMART Goals box and choose Apply).

Teams' use of common formative assessments (assessments *for* learning; Stiggins, Arter, Chappuis, & Chappuis, 2004; Wiliam, 2011) ensures interdependence and mutual accountability, both at the core of these two levers. The collaborative development, execution, and review of these assessments leads to trusting relationships; individual team members are willing to be transparent and trusting in sharing individual and collective data. Richard DuFour (2016a) calls team-developed common assessments the "lynchpin of the PLC at Work process" because it not only improves student learning but also adult learning.

Let's examine *why* team members willing to share and compare data are sure to learn from and with one another. If teacher A shows outstanding results on a specific learning target or skill from a team-developed common assessment—and teacher B's, C's, and D's results on that particular learning target or skill are much lower than teacher A's—wouldn't it make sense for all four team members to examine what teacher A did to get those results? Maybe teachers B, C, and D could co-teach with teacher A, observe teacher A in the classroom, or use a team meeting to simply have teacher A walk them through the teaching process from beginning to end for that skill? This continuous, unit-by-unit, job-embedded learning and professional development is the heart of the PLC process. It drives both students and teachers to learn at high levels. As PLC experts and presenters Sharon V. Kramer and Sarah Schuhl (2017) state, "In the end, the proof is in the tangible results" (p. 3).

As with the first two big ideas, there are some significant cultural shifts schools and teams must make to make a results orientation a reality. Table 1.3 lists these shifts.

Table 1.3: Cultural Shifts for Creating a Results Orientation

Traditional School	PLC School
From a focus on inputs . . .	to a focus on results
From goals related to completion of projects and activities . . .	to SMART goals demanding evidence of student learning
From assessing impact based on teacher satisfaction ("Did you like it?") . . .	to assessing impact based on evidence of improved student learning
From infrequent summative assessments . . .	to frequent common formative assessments
From individual teacher assessments . . .	to collaborative team-developed assessments
From each teacher determining the criteria to use in assessing student work . . .	to collaborative teams clarifying the criteria and ensuring consistency among team members when assessing student work
From focusing on average scores . . .	to monitoring each student's proficiency in every essential skill

Source: Adapted from DuFour et al., 2016, pp. 258–260.

The Four Critical Questions

The four critical questions of a PLC are the glue that holds the three big ideas together. These questions are the focus of every collaborative team, whether a preschool team, a third-grade team, or a secondary algebra team. The following four questions keep a team's focus on student learning and results (DuFour et al., 2016).

1. **What do we want our students to learn?** Have we identified the essential knowledge, skills, and dispositions each student is to acquire as a result of each unit of instruction in early childhood?

2. **How will we know if each student has learned it?** Are we using ongoing formative assessments in our classrooms? Are we gathering evidence of student learning through one or more team-developed common formative assessments for each unit of instruction?

3. **How will we respond when some students do not learn it?** Can we identify students who need additional time and support by the student, by the standard, and for every unit of instruction in the early childhood grades? Do we use evidence of student learning from

common formative assessments to analyze and improve our individual and collective instructional practice?

4. **How will we extend learning for students who have demonstrated proficiency?** Can we identify students who have reached proficiency on identified learning targets to extend their learning?

To answer these questions effectively, the very first thing collaborative teams must do is learn together, building shared understandings about what these questions mean and clarifying the work they must do to answer them. Learning together can take many forms, such as formal professional development, including classes, courses, and book studies. Less formal professional development is learning through collective inquiry, the cornerstone of a collaborative team's work.

Focusing on the high-impact practice of "teachers, working together, as evaluators of their impact" is the process teacher teams follow as they answer these questions together (Hattie, 2013). Not only are team members learning about and agreeing on a curriculum to guarantee but also creating common assessments to monitor students' learning. The data teams gather from those assessments is what makes this analysis a learning process. Teams learn about student learning and which students need additional time and support or extensions and, pivotal to the inquiry process, teams learn which teaching strategies were most effective—and which were not.

As teachers learn from one another, they improve their practices, which results in more student learning. Chapters 2 through 7 each provide an in-depth exploration of an aspect of teaching and learning related to these critical questions, including examples of the kinds of work teams should engage in to support learning for early childhood students. As your school engages in this work, have all team members reflect on the tips in this section.

Tips for **Administrators**	*Tips for* **Coaches**	*Tips for* **Teachers**
Promote and protect the shared mission, vision, collective commitments, and goals of the PLC, and keep them at the forefront of all decisions and actions.	Model for teams the behaviors and cultural shifts that make up the three big ideas of a PLC. For example, when teams work on shifting from a focus on teaching to a focus on learning, affirm to team members, "Yes, you did teach that standard; now let's look at the evidence of student learning," and guide them through the work.	In your team meetings, routinely refer to and review the third pillar (the school's collective commitments and team norms) and hold one another accountable to both. If needed, develop an accountability protocol that team members can use to address broken team norms.
Be willing to confront staff whose actions are incongruent with the school's shared purpose and priorities.		
Be vigilant in attempting to buffer the staff from competing initiatives so they can devote their full energies to the PLC process.		

Start any decision-making process with staff by learning together to build shared knowledge.

Ensure teams understand the three big ideas are foundational guiding principles, and the more the school aligns with the right work regarding these ideas, the better chance the school has of achieving its mission of learning for all.

Start any decision-making process with teams by learning together to build shared knowledge.

Start any decision-making process with colleagues by learning together to build shared knowledge.

Guiding Questions

Use the following guiding questions to learn together and build shared knowledge.

- How are your early childhood and primary grades included in the school-improvement process at your school? Are they separate entities? Do early childhood teams have opportunities to learn together with their upper-elementary counterparts?

- Does your school have urgency and systems to close student achievement and SEL gaps to support students before they reach upper-elementary grades?

- Does your school have a strong foundation? Does it have a clear mission (purpose), a shared vision for what the school wishes to become, values for how staff will behave to realize the mission and vision (collective commitments), and clearly set goals teams monitor?

- How stable is your foundation? Is there an area you need to collectively build and strengthen? If so, what is your first step?

- How well does your district or school understand the three big ideas of a PLC? How will you develop a plan to build shared understanding so all staff consider, understand, and embrace these ideas?

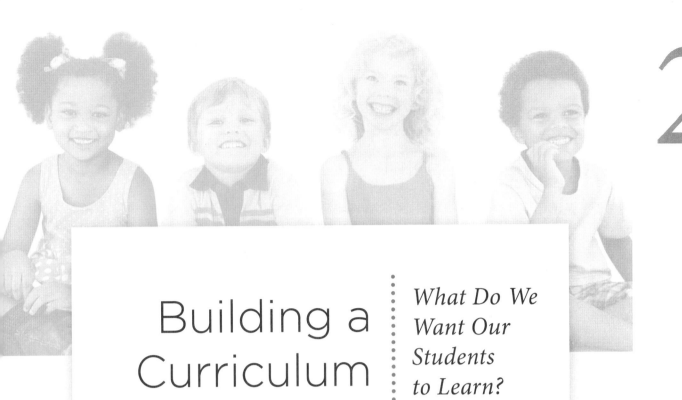

Building a Curriculum

What Do We Want Our Students to Learn?

The work of early childhood teams is not a linear process team members can check off on a sequential list, but rather a multifaceted process with one team task leading into, supporting, and focusing the work of the next layer in a ripple effect that leads to high levels of learning for both students and teachers (see figure 2.1, page 32). As Richard DuFour (2015b), an architect of the PLC at Work process writes:

> The journey will undoubtedly require hard work. But if there is one undeniable reality for every educator every year, it is that we are going to work hard. The real question is this: Will we work hard and succeed or work hard and fail? (p. 252)

The first step toward working hard and succeeding is focusing on answering the first critical question: What do we want our students to learn? (DuFour et al., 2016). The younger the students your team works with, the more difficult this question may seem at first. In this chapter, we'll help you begin to answer this question by thinking about curricula in the context of the first critical question of a PLC and by analyzing what your early childhood curriculum is based on with respect to your team's pedagogy, the state or province learning standards, and the school or district requirements for the curriculum itself. We end the chapter with an examination of how the factors contribute to a guaranteed and viable curriculum that supports the learning of the whole child, including the SEL and academic needs of your students.

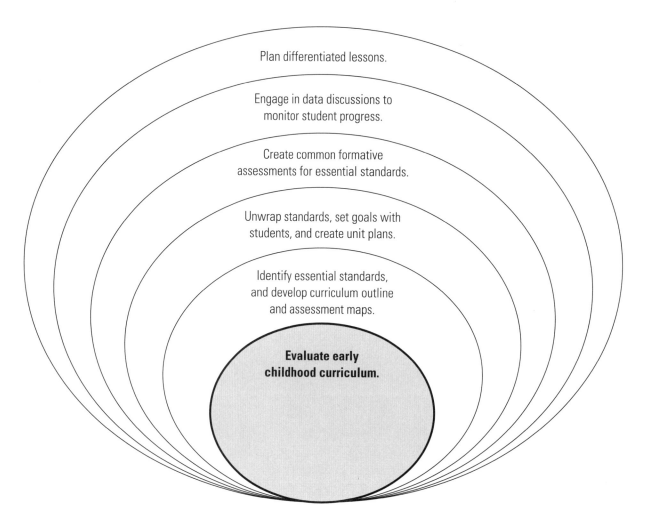

Figure 2.1: The work of early childhood teams in a PLC—Evaluate curriculum.

Vignette:

A Preschool Team Sets the Stage for Learning

This vignette, which we originally published in AllThingsPLC Magazine (Hulen, Heller, Kerr, & Butler, 2019), features a team of preschool teachers engaging in job-embedded professional development through collaborative team planning and lesson study. Team members learned from one another and provided instruction focused on academic skills and concepts in a play-based setting. The team included a mathematics and language arts specialist, classroom teachers, and administrators who all met to learn about questioning strategies that encourage students to discover the main ideas of texts through interactive read-alouds. The reading specialist presented background information to the team, and members prepared to go into the classroom where she would model an interactive read-aloud with students. As part of this lesson study, the team selected a book to use during the read-aloud. Team members specifically chose *Fill a Bucket* by childhood specialists and authors Carol

McCloud and Katherine Martin (2018) because it supports students' learning of essential standards for SEL

After choosing stopping points in the story and crafting questions to help students understand the main meaning of the text, the team observed the reading specialist read the story and engage a classroom of preschool students in discussion. The team members (including the mathematics specialist and an administrator) sat with the students on the carpet and observed evidence of learning while engaging with students during the interactive read-aloud. This was true *learning by doing* for all active participants.

After finishing the interactive read-aloud, the team met to discuss the evidence of student learning they observed and how the team could improve the lesson to target learning. During the discussion, the mathematics specialist posed questions to the team asking how they could use ideas from the book to incorporate essential learning standards focused on counting into daily learning stations. The team generated a list of ideas based on the book's illustrations of buckets filling with hearts and stars when people say kind things or are positive toward others.

- Students count and sort assorted plastic hearts and stars in small buckets.

- Students have opportunities to have free play with the hearts, stars, and buckets the teacher provides.

- Teachers teach specific mathematics counting games using the hearts and stars.

- Teachers provide students with materials during free-play time, with each teacher acting as a facilitator during play and asking specific questions related to the essential mathematics standards.

Of these ideas, the preschool team focused on the last one and what materials they could introduce during free-play time to help students with their mathematics skills. The following example highlights how this exercise played out in the classroom.

A student, Juan, continuously dumps the hearts and stars out of the buckets into different containers at the play-kitchen area.

Teacher: Juan, that looks fun. I think I want to try to dump all these hearts and stars into this small cereal box. Do you think they will fit?

Juan: I think there are too many.

Teacher: Want to try it? Can you help me? Can we work together as a team?

Juan helps the teacher carefully dump the hearts and stars into the small cereal box and as he predicted, they do not all fit.

Teacher: How many stars and hearts do you think didn't make it into the box?

Juan: I don't know.

Teacher: Let's take a guess.

Juan: Eight?

Teacher: How can we check to see if we are close to our guess?

Juan: We can count them.

Teacher: Great idea!

Juan counts from one to eight, but there are more pieces. When he gets to ten, he doesn't know what comes next.

Teacher: What comes after ten? I wonder if we could look in our classroom to see what comes after ten.

Juan points to the pocket calendar and points to eleven but does not know how to say, "eleven." The teacher puts a star or heart into each pocket of the calendar, and they count together. By this time, other students have become interested in what Juan and the teacher are doing.

Teacher: Can anyone help us count these stars and hearts?

With this prompt from the teacher, another student who can count past ten begins to help, and they all determine they have fifteen leftovers after counting to eight. Before the teacher leaves the student group at the learning play station, she says, "I wonder how many just hearts there are?" and then walks away. For the remainder of the free-play time, she observes students from a distance working either in pairs or independently sorting and counting the hearts and stars and putting them into larger and smaller buckets. One student sorted red hearts in one bucket and blue stars in the other bucket, and so on. Two students reenacted examples from the book. A student said something kind to another student and as he did, she filled his bucket with a handful of stars and hearts. The teacher made a note to use these two students' exchange with the class as an example to build on when working on communication and SEL goals.

The next day the teacher's goal is to collect evidence of student learning in mathematics. She decides to see if the students in her class can count a set of five objects, one by one. During students' play, she creates opportunities for them to count the objects they are playing with (perhaps that day's hearts and stars or whatever happens to be capturing students' attention the next day) and records the data on an informal checklist the team created during a weekly planning session.

Curriculum and the First Critical Question of a PLC

At this point, you may be asking yourself the following.

- "What was the main purpose of the preschool team meeting?"

- "How often do teachers meet, and are all their meetings structured the same way?"

- "How were the teachers getting job-embedded professional development on interactive read-alouds?

- How did the teacher choose counting a set of five objects as the mathematics assessment for the next day?

These are all great questions, but the one we most often hear teachers say is, "We have so much to do, so where do we even start?" The answer to this resides in the four critical questions of a PLC. The remaining chapters give you numerous examples that show how you can put all the pieces together when you use your time to collaborate about the right work. We start here with the first critical question.

As educational researchers Thomas A. Angelo and K. Patricia Cross (1993) state, "Learning can and often does take place without the benefit of teaching—and sometimes even in spite of it—but there is no such thing as effective teaching in the absence of learning. Teaching without learning is just talking" (p. 3).

Inherent in the first critical question is the idea of knowing what teams want students to know *and* be able to do. If teams want to ensure teaching leads to learning in early childhood, they must consider *how* learning happens for these young students. While the learning process is often similar across grade levels and content areas, early childhood educators must consider more than just academics while answering the four critical questions by keeping the whole child in mind when determining what they want students to know and be able to do. While this is true at all learning levels, we find it particularly so in early childhood because, as early childhood educators know, young students learn through play. Much of a teacher's work with these students centers on learning-to-learn activities and helping them develop a love of learning, things that may seem difficult to express as *know* and *be able to do*. Some preK–2 classrooms have a defined curriculum that drives the teachers' answer to the first critical question, but even more student-centered curricula still expect all students to learn and grow. So, what does your early childhood team believe is most important for your students to be able to do?

Things like self-advocating, appropriately sharing group attention, and engaging in parallel play don't just happen for some students unless the teacher explicitly teaches these skills. So, if your team is focusing on teaching these skills in preschool, then that is the answer to what you want students to be able to do. This is just as valid a focus for your collaborative work as having students identify numbers up to ten, write the letters in their name, and learn the vocabulary of shapes and colors. Unfortunately, in many schools, the focus on explicitly teaching SEL skills and academic behaviors tends to decrease as students age, when the focus of answering the first critical question shifts more to content areas. However, teaching these SEL skills is a crucial part of the early childhood curriculum, and it is vital for students to have several years to continually develop these important foundational skills from preschool through second grade.

Balancing SEL and academic content is even more challenging in U.S. states and other countries in which we have had the privilege to work, like Canada and Australia, where the curriculum could be a mile wide and seem to include more each year. This type of curriculum also makes it difficult to answer critical question one because *all* students will not be able to know and do everything in the curriculum at the same time. In a PLC, learning must be the *constant* and time the *variable* (DuFour et al., 2016). Teams must sort learning standards into essential *need-to-know* standards and nonessential *nice-to-know* standards. We cover this process and the criteria teams use in detail in chapter 3 (page 47). This process of identifying agreed-on essential standards also gives team members a chance to discuss each standard and ensure there is common understanding about what the standard expects from students.

Only after a team has answered the first critical question can members begin to unpack the standards, develop common pacing for teaching units, clarify the level of rigor they expect, create common formative assessments, create common end-of-unit assessments, and develop lessons that teach what the students will need to know and be able to do to be successful. (These are all topics we cover in subsequent chapters.) This is the work that allows teachers to work hard and succeed rather than work hard and fail.

Components of an Early Childhood Curriculum

An issue we frequently hear early childhood educators debate is the effect of early childhood programs on students' social-emotional development. Some educators fear academic-focused programs will take precedent over social-emotional development as is often the case in the upper-elementary grades. When considering your youngest learners, it makes sense to ask, "Why can't there be a focus on both?"

When educators convey the notion that academics and play are two separate and independent uses of time during the school day, this inadvertently reveals their limited knowledge of early childhood education. Learning in subject-matter domains is *not* separated into academics and play, but rather early childhood students learn academics *through* games and play. For example, high-quality implementation of mathematics curricula in preschools shows the transfer of skills to other domains, including both language and self-regulation (Sarama, Clements, Wolfe, & Spitler, 2012). Other research shows preschool curricula can successfully combine social-emotional, literacy, language, science, and mathematics learning (Sarama, Brenneman, Clements, Duke, & Hemmeter, in press)—all while enhancing, rather than competing with, play-based approaches (Farran, Aydogan, Kang, & Lipsey, 2006). By establishing consensus that early childhood education students learn best when learning through play, teams can focus on the important work of determining how to facilitate high-level learning. Achieving this requires that all stakeholders have a common understanding of the early childhood curriculum, no matter what that curriculum is based on.

The reason we write *no matter what that curriculum is based on* is because education evolves and changes over time as educators seek to engage in continuous research to improve practices. The standards change over time, and each new year teams have a new set of learners. That creates an ongoing need to adapt curricula with the times. Therefore, teams must ensure they are working collectively throughout the year on a daily, weekly, and monthly basis and are using the same guaranteed and viable curriculum to ensure equity for all learners.

As teams focus on the three big ideas of a PLC, they *collaborate* to improve the *learning* of the adults to impact the *results* for students. The learning adult educators engage in while collectively answering the critical questions improves their pedagogy and, ultimately, their practices to ensure every student learns at high levels. We find that as teams work together to answer critical question one, they are likely to use the terms *learning standards* frequently, *curriculum* occasionally, and *pedagogy* rarely. In reality, the work of teams in answering this question involves each of those three things intricately woven together (see figure 2.2, page 38), so the following section clarifies what each means.

Pedagogy

According to the National Research Council (2001b), *pedagogy* is a deliberate process of cultivating development through three basic components:

> (1) curriculum, or the content of what is being taught; (2) methodology, or the way in which teaching is done; and (3) techniques for socializing children in the repertoire of cognitive and affective skills required for successful functioning in society that education is designed to promote. (p. 182)

In simpler terms, *pedagogy* is a teacher's techniques, methods, and approaches to the curriculum. Teachers learn about pedagogy during their preservice training and then must put theory into practice when they begin to work with students in schools. Sound pedagogy is rooted in research and helps teachers understand *how* to best teach a particular concept. Inherently, it is the first tool teachers put in their toolbelts and the one they continue to refine through changes to their instructional practices. However, because pedagogy is more theoretical than the other terms in

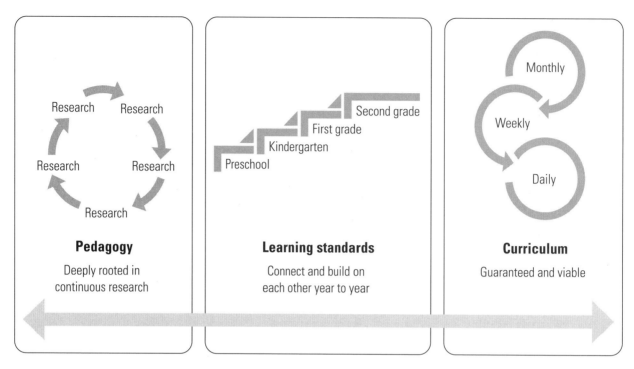

Figure 2.2: Pedagogy, standards, and curriculum connection.

figure 2.2, we find it common for busy teachers to get bogged down in the more practical learning standards or curriculum. That is why it's so important to collaborate as a team and reflect weekly on the teaching and learning that is happening. In doing so, early childhood teachers develop as reflective practitioners with a stronger understanding of the pedagogy that works for them.

Learning Standards

Learning standards (or just *standards*) explicitly describe *what* students learn in each grade level or content area. Standards set specific learning objectives for a particular area of study. Most often, countries, states, or provinces select the standards educators must teach. U.S. states have increasingly begun to include preschool standards in addition to long-standing grades K–12 learning standards. Many preschool learning standards have been developed based on recommendations from the NAEYC, Association for Early Learning Leaders, or National Education Association. *Head Start*, a federally funded early childhood program for low-income families, has its own set of learning outcomes or standards. While public preschool programs usually have predetermined standards and provide curricula to support instruction, private preschools may need to develop their own standards to teach along with the curriculum they use to teach the standards. Some schools may also receive mandated academic standards but no guidelines for SEL standards. We have emphasized the importance of social-emotional development in the early childhood years, so as your team answers that first critical question of a PLC, What do we want all students to learn? (DuFour et al., 2016), think critically about the learning standards you may receive to ensure they address *all* the needs of young learners while still allowing you to answer the question in a way that makes your team confident it is setting students up to be successful in later years. Careful consideration of the standards will also set your team up for success. As you will see, much of the work of teams that we describe in the following chapters revolves around working with learning standards.

Curriculum

While learning standards for students usually come from a state or national entity, local divisions, such as school districts, typically determine the curricula teachers use to support teaching those standards. A *curriculum* is the design or plan for *how* to teach learning standards (learning objectives). Often, districts provide schools with resources to support the curriculum, such as textbooks, electronic devices, and curriculum pacing guides, but it is then the teachers' role to plan and work together to decide how to teach the curriculum on a monthly, weekly, and daily basis.

About curricula, the NAEYC (2018) states:

> A curriculum that draws on research assists teachers in identifying important concepts and skills as well as effective methods for fostering children's learning and development. When informed by teachers' knowledge of individual children, a well-articulated curriculum guides teachers so they can plan learning experiences that promote children's growth across a broad range of developmental and content areas. A curriculum also helps ensure that the teacher is intentional in planning a daily schedule that (a) maximizes children's acquisition of desired knowledge and skills through the effective use of time and materials and (b) offers opportunities for children to learn through play and through structured activities, individually and in groups, according to their developmental needs and interests. (p. 20)

Embedded in a well-designed and all-inclusive curriculum, you will find a combination of the learning content (developmental domains and learning standards), the pedagogy (the learning experiences, materials, approaches, and environment), and assessment. So, before your teams begin engaging in this process, be sure to take a big-picture look at your curriculum to ensure it has the necessary components to promote positive outcomes for all students.

After reviewing multiple documents (CASEL, n.d.; NAEYC, 2009, 2018, 2020; NAEYC & National Association of Early Childhood Specialists in State Departments of Education [NCAECS-SDE], 2003; NAEYC & National Council of Teachers of Mathematics [NCTM], 2010), we recommend an early childhood curriculum include the key components in figure 2.3 (page 40). To dig deeper into these vast components and learn more about specific features of each grade level, refer to the resources from NAEYC (www.naeyc.org).

Learning Domains	Learning Environment	Learning Experiences	Assessments for Learning
Social and Emotional Development Self-awareness, self-management, social awareness, relationship skills, and responsible decision making	**Physical Environment** Indoor and outdoor safe organized spaces for independent, social, active learning, and areas for rest	**Responsive Schedule** Routine and flexible with transitions, rest periods; balance of teacher and student-choice activities; and extended blocks for sustained play, investigation, exploration and social interaction	**Assessment Practices** Positive, developmentally appropriate, ongoing, and used to inform instruction
Physical Development Gross-motor and fine-motor skills	**Cultural Environment** Positive social-emotional climate with a focus on community building and family cultures, beliefs, and values	**Learning Activities** Rich, engaging, creative, and inquiry-based problem solving and is accessible to all students	**Assessment Methods** Observations, interviews, collection of work samples, and performance on authentic activities
Language Development Speech articulation, listening, and speaking (English language development)	**Learning Materials** Challenging, engaging, and promote exploration and experimentation Use of appropriate interactive technology tools	**Learning Formats** Teacher guided large- and small-group activities, play, and projects Student-guided learning centers and self-directed play and projects	
Cognitive Development Literacy, mathematics, science, social studies, art, music, physical education, health, and learning skills (executive function and so on)			

Source: Adapted from CASEL, n.d.; NAEYC, 2009, 2018, 2020; NAEYC & NCAECS-SDE, 2003; NAEYC & NCTM, 2010.

Figure 2.3: Key components for an early childhood curriculum.

As you can see from figure 2.3 there are many considerations in developing a complete multifaceted quality early childhood curriculum. Since each school and each team may be starting in a different place, we developed the tool in figure 2.4 to guide your conversation around the considerations and develop an action plan that will move you forward.

| Team members: |
| Grade level: _____ |

As a team, indicate which of the following components your early childhood curriculum includes.

Learning Domains	Learning Environment	Learning Experiences	Assessments for Learning
We have an established curriculum for the following learning domains. ☐ Social and emotional development 　☐ Self-awareness 　☐ Self-management 　☐ Social awareness 　☐ Relationship skills 　☐ Responsible decision making ☐ Physical development 　☐ Gross-motor skills 　☐ Fine-motor skills ☐ Language development 　☐ Speech articulation 　☐ Listening 　☐ Speaking (English language development) ☐ Cognitive development 　☐ Literacy 　☐ Mathematics 　☐ Science 　☐ Social studies 　☐ Art 　☐ Music 　☐ Physical education and health 　☐ Learning skills (executive function and so on)	The physical indoor environment has: ☐ Safe and organized spaces ☐ Independent learning spaces ☐ Social learning spaces ☐ Active learning spaces ☐ Areas for rest The physical outdoor environment has: ☐ Safe and organized spaces ☐ Independent learning spaces ☐ Social learning spaces ☐ Active learning spaces ☐ Areas for rest The cultural environment includes: ☐ Positive social-emotional climate ☐ Focus on community building ☐ Family values, beliefs, cultures, and language Learning materials are challenging and engaging and promote exploration and experimentation for: ☐ Play ☐ Mathematics ☐ Science ☐ Social Studies ☐ Art ☐ Music ☐ Physical education and health ☐ Technology	The daily schedule offers: ☐ Routines ☐ Responsiveness and flexibility ☐ A variety of transitions ☐ Rest periods ☐ A balance of teacher and student-choice activities ☐ Extended blocks for sustained play, investigation, exploration and social interaction Learning activities we use are: ☐ Accessable to all students ☐ Engaging ☐ Inquiry based and promote problem solving Teacher-directed learning formats include: ☐ Large-group learning ☐ Small-group learning ☐ Guided play ☐ Project learning Student-directed learning activities include: ☐ Play ☐ Student-guided learning centers with choice ☐ Project learning	Planned assessments for learning are: ☐ Positive and developmentally appropriate ☐ Used formatively and used to inform instruction ☐ Balanced and include a variety of methods—observations, interviews, collection of work samples, and performance on authentic activities

Source: CASEL, n.d.; NAEYC, 2009, 2018, 2020; NAEYC & NCAECS-SDE, 2003; NAEYC & NCTM, 2010.

Figure 2.4: Early childhood curriculum team-considerations tool.

continued →

Learning Domains	Learning Environment	Learning Experiences	Assessments for Learning
What steps or action plans does the team need to initiate to strengthen its early childhood curriculum?			
Who is responsible for initiating or maintaining the action plan (or plans)? What is the time line?			

*Visit **go.SolutionTree.com/PLCbooks** for a free reproducible version of this figure.*

Tips for **Administrators**	*Tips for* **Coaches**	*Tips for* **Teachers**
Clearly communicate to teams that they should focus on learning standards and use the curriculum as a resource. Assess the level of support teams require to understand the connection between play and academics and how to make them a part of daily instruction. Provide differentiated supports to teams as needed.	Facilitate team discussion around research, especially as it pertains to pedagogy, curriculum, and understanding of state or provincial standards Look for ways to support integration of cross-curricular thinking when teachers are learning a new curriculum. How can they incorporate multiple disciplines?	When choosing a curriculum, think about the pedagogy embedded in the materials you'll be using. If you are unclear on the best instructional approaches, ask questions of your team members, coaches, and administrators.

A Guaranteed and Viable Curriculum or the Educational Lottery?

When developing a curriculum, it is paramount for early childhood teams to avoid putting students in an educational lottery in which a student's learning outcomes depend more on the teacher he or she receives than the curriculum. Teams avoid this lottery by ensuring a guaranteed and viable curriculum (Eaker & Marzano, 2020). *Guaranteed* means that no matter which teacher a student learns from, he or she will learn the same essential standards. A curriculum is *viable* when there is enough instructional time available to actually teach the content and ensure students have time to learn it at variable rates. Does that mean all teachers have to teach in exactly the same way at exactly the same time? No.

The PLC process establishes a culture that is simultaneously loose and tight (DuFour et al., 2016). Tight elements of a PLC are nondiscretionary. These include being a member of a collaborative team that takes collective responsibility for every student, identifies essential standards, creates common formative assessments, and uses assessments to gather evidence of student learning to meet the intervention and extension needs of each student while informing individual and collective teacher practices. *Tight* means teacher collaboration is an expectation, not an invitation. *Loose* means that teams have the freedom to work within these defined parameters. For example, teams have the autonomy to decide which standards become essential, they create the assessments, and they use the data to decide how to intervene and extend the learning for students. Each teacher has the freedom to use an instructional pedagogy he or she believes works best to help students learn. Not all teachers are comfortable teaching in the same way, and schools that embrace the PLC process encourage educators to teach the most effective way for them and their students. These are all loose. However, what is tight, is that teams use data from team-developed assessments to determine which team members had the most effective practices on a particular skill. If the team as a whole was not successful on an assessment, they use this information to improve their collective practices and to identify professional development needs.

When a collaborative team adheres to the tight elements and answers the first critical question of a PLC, it is creating a guaranteed and viable curriculum. Educational researchers Robert J. Marzano, Tammy Heflebower, Jan K. Hoegh, Phillip B. Warrick, and Gavin Grift (2016) state the benefits of such a curriculum:

> A guaranteed and viable curriculum works to reduce variability in students' education. When the curriculum is viable, all the content can be taught in the instructional time available. Teachers do not have to make idiosyncratic decisions about what content to teach. Therefore, all teachers of a course or grade level deliver the same content to their students, guaranteeing the curriculum and creating consistency for all students. (p. 120)

While individual early childhood teachers will use different instructional styles and strategies, each student in the grade will benefit from not just the same intended curriculum but also the same implemented curriculum and attained curriculum. This ensures a curriculum is both guaranteed and viable.

Now, let's turn to the term *viable*, which is about ensuring common understanding of the curriculum among students. In Austin Buffum's (2019) presentation at the RTI at Work Institute, he humorously defines viable as "doable by a mere mortal." Teachers have raced through the curriculum for years by focusing on coverage of every single learning standard more than actually having students learn what's most important in the curriculum. Robert J. Marzano explains the impracticality of this approach, "To cover all of this content, you would have to change schooling from K–12 to K–22 . . . . The sheer number of standards is the biggest impediment to implementing standards" (as cited in Scherer, 2001, p. 15). In *Leaders of Learning*, Richard Dufour and Robert J. Marzano (2011) go on to say, "The Common Core standards have not solved the problem for the classroom teacher of developing standards that truly represent a viable curriculum—one that can be adequately addressed in the current time available to classroom teachers" (p. 93).

In the same keynote we cited here, Buffum (2019) said that Singapore schools have a motto—*teach less, learn more*. We are not saying to disregard the district or state curriculum—they are worthy of the school and teams' collective study—but teams must assess what elements within it are nice to know, important to know, and essential. Teaching nice-to-know and important-to-know elements can and does occur, but ensuring that students learn what teams have identified as essential ensures a viable curriculum.

What is the experience like for early childhood students when a curriculum is guaranteed and viable? As a mother of twins, Jacqueline placed her children together in the same preschool class, but they separated when they started kindergarten. During the first month of kindergarten, one child would excitedly share the new song, story, or skill she had learned only to have the other child complain, "That's not fair! I didn't get to do that!" As an educator and a parent, Jacqueline expects and appreciates the individual choices and instructional decisions the professionals who teach her children make. A school that operates as a PLC develops strong educators who are reflective practitioners and creative problem solvers capable of making informed decisions about how best to implement the curriculum to meet the needs of their students (a loose element of a PLC). If that means one teacher uses a book and song about ducks one twin loves so much she sings it over and over at home, bringing her twin brother to tears, that's OK. However, it's not OK if one teacher is using books with repeating rhyming patterns and songs that rhyme to draw students' attention to the phonological concept while the teacher across the hall is not doing anything to demonstrate that phonological concept. The latter leaves those students unprepared for early literacy, which is not acceptable.

If you are a parent, perhaps you remember that painful yet hopeful transition when handing your child off to his or her first teacher and wondering how that teacher will impact your child's future. Those first few years of schooling, parents hold their breath when opening the letter or email stating who their child's teacher will be, and then either sigh in relief their child got *that* teacher or cringe in dread because their child got *that* teacher. It's the educational lottery. A guaranteed and viable curriculum ensures no matter the teaching style, all teachers on a team must agree on the essential skills and standards for that grade or age level (a tight element).

Without this agreement, the educational lottery dictates that some students get the golden ticket and learn what is necessary to be successful in the primary grades and beyond while others may not be prepared for the next grade level because they didn't attain these essentials.

In fact, early childhood teacher teams in a school that embraces the PLC process will combine their collective expertise, sharing with their teammates the knowledge, skills, and dispositions they each have in order to meet the needs of all students—because the students are all "our kids." Until all early childhood educators embrace this philosophy, subpar teaching will continue to exist across the hall, and schools will have student winners and losers in the educational lottery. As teachers, even though our styles may differ and we maintain the autonomy to choose the best resources and instructional strategies for our class, we must ensure that we collaboratively determine what all students must know and be able to do. This ensures there is a plan and a way to assess high levels of learning for all students, eliminating the educational lottery. The next step in doing so is to identify and agree on the essential standards all students will master, which we explore in the next chapter.

Tips for **Administrators**	Tips for **Coaches**	Tips for **Teachers**
Clearly articulate guaranteed and viable curriculum expectations and the artifacts teams will produce as evidence.	Make time at collaborative planning meetings for reflection and sharing about the previous week's lessons. As teachers share successful resources or ideas, add them to the notes for that unit's curriculum so you have them for next year.	Communicating with your colleagues is very important. Is it OK to try out new ideas with your students that may not have been discussed as a team? Yes! But, if you discover your instructional practices or tools are successful, then it is your responsibility to share those ideas with your teammates so they can use them with students as well.
Highlight the wonderful things being done in each classroom with weekly photos in a staff newsletter. This shows you value teachers' creativity, unique teaching styles, and individual choice of instructional strategies while teaching the same curriculum and adhering to common pacing.	When individually coaching teachers, support both the pedagogy and content knowledge each needs to be successful with the curriculum.	Monitor your language. There should no longer be "my kids" or "his or her kids." Students are all "our kids."

Guiding Questions

Use the following guiding questions to learn together and build shared knowledge.

- Are all the teachers at each grade level using the same guaranteed and viable curriculum to ensure quality? If not, what steps can you take to make this happen?

- Are administrators learning alongside teachers, and is everyone focused on student learning? How do you know? Can you improve? If so, how? Make a list and discuss it at your next collaborative team meeting.

- Are all the teachers at each grade level using the same guaranteed viable curriculum to ensure equity? If not, what steps can you take to make this happen?

- How are you currently answering critical question one (What do we want our student to learn?), and what new thoughts do you have about next steps?

- Are the administrators supporting the work of teams by providing the resources teams need to be successful? If not, make a list of the resources teams need and create a plan for providing these resources.

Determining Essential Standards and Curriculum Mapping

What Do We Want Our Students to Learn?

In chapter 2, we discussed the components of a guaranteed and viable curriculum in relation to the first critical question of a PLC. At the center of these components are the learning standards that establish what students must know and be able to do, but just because they are called *standards* does not mean that every teacher's interpretation of them is standard and consistent. According to Marzano et al. (2016):

> Standards, as typically written, often include numerous subcomponents. One standard might encompass several individual elements that each require a separate proficiency scale. Alternatively, a standard might include some content that would be an appropriate target learning goal and some content that is simpler or foundational to the target. By breaking standards apart and rewriting their components as individual objectives, teachers can make the standards more useful and get a better sense of how much content there really is. (p. 120)

A teacher team may collaborate to develop their own set of learning standards or use a purchased curriculum, or it may receive mandated standards from a district, state, or other entity, such as the National Governors Association Center for Best Practices (NGA) & Council of Chief State School Officers (CCSSO; 2010a). One of the primary roles of the team is to collaboratively prioritize the most important skills and standards for its grade level and then make specific instructional decisions about what students must learn. For this reason, it is beneficial for teams to both select a set of *essential standards* (sometimes called *power standards* or *priority standards*) and then develop a *curriculum outline* to align those essential standards with the knowledge and skills students need to achieve those standards.

Because this can be challenging work, it is best supported when educators collaborate with a common set of goals and a common purpose. As figure 3.1 illustrates, this work is the foundation from which all early childhood teams produce their instruction. Therefore, in this chapter, you will learn more about the process for determining essential standards and using them to create a curriculum outline for early childhood instruction. With this information, teams can then develop daily schedules, an example of which we include at the end of the chapter. Before we proceed, however, consider the following vignette.

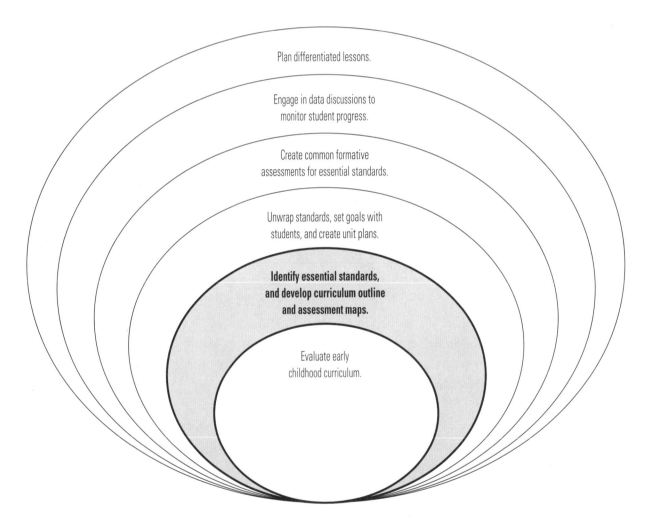

Figure 3.1: The work of early childhood teams in a PLC—Identifying essential standards and developing curriculum outline and assessment maps.

Vignette:

A Second-Grade Team Determines Essential Standards

When a team meets for the first time at the beginning of the school year to identify essential standards in language arts, members enter with the understanding that the essential standards they determine will form the anchor of all the work they do for the remainder of the year. They understand this work requires them to dedicate the necessary time to have deep discussions before coming to the final decisions about which learning standards are essential. This is a process that requires teams to go slow in order to go fast. When teams determine what students must know and be able to do in early childhood, they must take the time to discuss the standards (both SEL and academic) and ensure common understanding about *why* they are making the decision to deem a standard essential. The second-grade team in this vignette consists of a first-year teacher, an experienced teacher new to the school, a veteran teacher serving as the team facilitator, and the special education teacher who supports both second and third grade. Consider how the following conversation led to common understandings and helped them make critical decisions about essential standards so team members could be more efficient and their teaching more effective throughout the year.

Casey (team facilitator): Even though we have the reading pacing guide from the district, we still have to determine what we commit to being essential standards for our students, especially since we have a few new team members and the wording on a couple of the language arts standards have changed. I've printed out the standards and cut them apart so we can discuss them one by one.

Tessa (second-grade teacher): That's a lot of standards! Why don't we start getting in the mindset of what is most important by each taking a sticky note and writing three things we wish every new second-grade student who walks into our room this year would already know and be able to do?

Mauricio (second-grade teacher): I love this idea! I've often wondered how some of my students spent a year in first grade and left without some of the basic reading skills I think they need. This wish list should help us think about what is really important.

Zoey (special education teacher working with second and third grades): OK then. We should also take another sticky note and write three things we would want to guarantee that every student in our second-grade class will actually leave knowing and being able to do in reading before entering third grade. This way, we are thinking about it from both perspectives.

Tessa: Only three? That's tough! I teach them so many things in a year, but I guess it's a good idea for us to have a starting point for our discussion so we can see if we are in the same ballpark.

The team members then share their thoughts on sticky notes and find commonalities. When they can't agree on whether a standard is essential or not, they draw on research, their experience, and the chart they made using the criteria for determining essential standards they'd read about in AllThingsPLC Magazine (Many, 2016)—readiness, endurance, assessed, and leverage (R.E.A.L.). In doing so, the members determined the following questions for each R.E.A.L. component: Is it a prerequisite skill for learning next year, in third grade (readiness)? Will students need the knowledge and skill beyond a single assessment of unit in second grade (endurance)? Is it a concept students will encounter on high-stakes exams, such as the end-of-year state standardized assessment (assessed)? Will students be able to apply the standard in more than one subject, such as an informational reading standard in social studies (leverage)? The conversation continues as Tessa holds up one of the printed standards.

Tessa: I'm glad we have these R.E.A.L. criteria to keep referring to. I don't think I've ever considered this nonfiction standard essential before, but it does give students leverage in social studies and science.

Zoey: I'm not sure I can agree that's essential though, because can we really say all students are going to master it? What about my friends in special education with Individualized Education Plans?

Mauricio: I went to a conference this summer, and they said when we are talking about having the same high expectations for all students we should define *all* as any student expected to live independently as an adult.

Zoey: Well that helps, but I'm still not sure some of the students will get there.

Casey: They may not have gotten there in the past, but if we are agreeing this standard has leverage and is essential, then we've got to put the additional time and support in place to get them there this year. That means looking at what we're doing during intervention time and maybe making some shifts to focus more on these essential standards and less on other skills we might have erroneously spent too much time on last year.

Mauricio: But that makes me worry that we are going to spend all our time on these standards and ignore the ones we are deciding are not essential. Some of those are still important even if they don't meet the R.E.A.L. criteria we agreed to follow.

Casey: It does feel a little scary, but remember, we still teach all standards. We just are going to spend our collaborative time unpacking, sharing practices, developing common formative assessments, and designing interventions only for the essential standards.

Mauricio: OK. I feel like we should write what you just said on a poster that we'll see in our team meetings, so we remember that this time is meant for collaborating about the essential standards!

Tessa: I know Mauricio was worried we may ignore the standards we are deciding are not essential, but I am feeling kind of overwhelmed at how many standards we are saying are essential. There are so many already, and we're not even done. The Common Core standards we are using for reading are separated into Reading Informational Text, Literature, and Foundational Skills. Can't we just focus on Reading Informational Text and Reading Literature since the standards for Foundational Skills would have been essential last year in first grade?

Casey: Well, every year, we have students who need interventions on those foundational skills, so if the essential standards are the ones we agree we'll assess, reteach, and develop interventions for, then even if the foundational skills standards were taught last year, we have evidence they weren't learned by all. I think we'll have students with holes in those areas if we don't include them as essential.

Tessa: OK, but I wish there was a magic number of essential standards we're supposed to have so I'd know if we're picking too many or too few.

Casey: No magic. Just the power of our collaborative discussion, the R.E.A.L. criteria, our knowledge of what the research says, our experience with our students, and the input we'll get from first- and third-grade teachers when we share our list of standards with them after we finish today.

Tessa: I forgot they'd have a chance to review this. That makes me feel more confident that we'll catch any gaps or overlaps. OK, next standard . . . ?

The team continued to sort the standards they decided were *need-to-know* (essential) standards and *nice-to-know* (nonessential) standards into two circles arranged side-by-side on the table. Standards that members felt could fall into both categories they put in the middle, between the circles. For these standards, the team determined members would discuss further or get input from first- or third-grade teachers before finalizing the decision about which group in which to place each standard. This same process can be applied to other grade levels. Figure 3.2 illustrates how a preschool team sorted their paraphrased Texas state standards using customized dot notation. The standards in the overlapping area the preschool team plans to discuss with the kindergarten team to make a final decision.

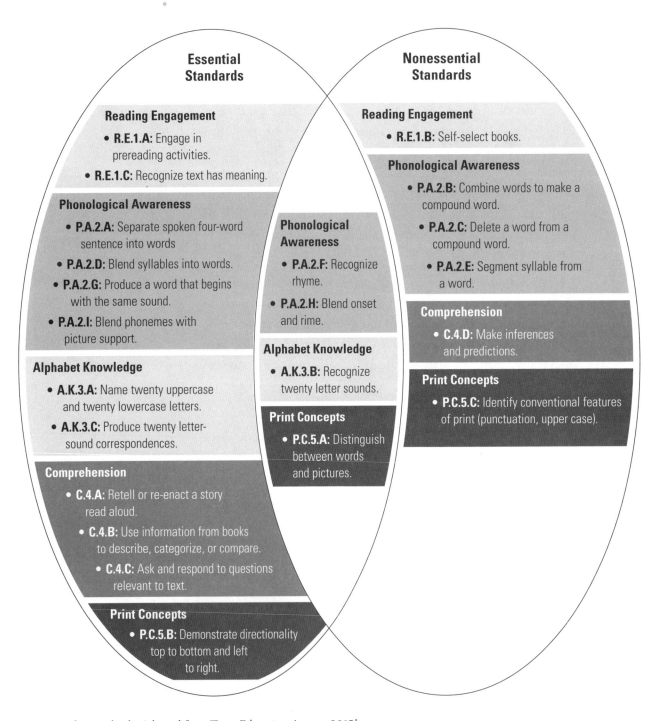

Source for standards: Adapted from Texas Education Agency, 2015b.

Figure 3.2: Teams work to determine essential standards.

Some teams find this sorting of essential standard to be enough to get them headed in the right direction, but the preschool team in this example decided to take it a step further. They looked at all of the essential standards in the Venn diagram and decided to split the essential standards even further into *need-to-know essential standards* and *important-to-know essential standards*. Taken together, the important- and need-to-know standards will drive the team's unit planning, and it will convert them into student-friendly learning targets. However, the team's common formative assessments and Tier 2 interventions (see page 167) will focus only on the need-to-know learning standards.

During the process of identifying the essential standards, one teacher created an electronic document to house all the standards for reading, as figure 3.3 shows. At a later team meeting, they replicated the process for each of their content areas.

Reading Engagement		
Essential Standards (Need to Know)	**Essential Standards (Important to Know)**	**Nonessential Standards (Nice to Know)**
R.E.1.A: Engage in prereading activities	**R.E.1.C:** Recognize text has meaning.	**R.E.1.B:** Self-select books.
Phonological Awareness		
Essential Standards (Need to Know)	**Essential Standards (Important to Know)**	**Nonessential Standards (Nice to Know)**
P.A.2.D: Blend syllables into words. **P.A.2.F:** Recognize rhyme. **P.A.2.G:** Produced a word that begins with the same sound.	**P.A.2.A:** Separate spoken four-word sentence into words. **P.A.2.I:** Blend phonemes with picture support.	**P.A.2.B:** Combine words to make a compound word. **P.A.2.C:** Delete a word from a compound word. **P.A.2.E:** Segment a syllable from a word. **P.A.2.H:** Blend onset and rime.
Alphabet Knowledge		
Essential Standards (Need to Know)	**Essential Standards (Important to Know)**	**Nonessential Standards (Nice to Know)**
A.K.3.A: Name twenty uppercase and twenty lowercase letters. **A.K.3.B:** Recognize twenty letter sounds.	**A.K.3.C:** Produce twenty letter-sound correspondences.	

Figure 3.3: A team prioritizes curriculum standards.

continued →

Comprehension		
Essential Standards (Need to Know)	**Essential Standards (Important to Know)**	**Nonessential Standards (Nice to Know)**
C.4.A: Retell or re-enact story read aloud. **C.4.C:** Ask and respond to questions relevant to text.	**C.4.B:** Use information from books to describe, categorize or compare.	**C.4.D:** Make inferences and predictions.
Print Concepts		
Essential Standards (Need to Know)	**Essential Standards (Important to Know)**	**Nonessential Standards (Nice to Know)**
P.C.5.A: Distinguish between words and pictures.	**P.C.5.B:** Demonstrate directionality top to bottom and left to right.	**P.C.5.C:** Identify conventional features of print (punctuation, upper case).

Source for standards: Adapted from the Texas Education Agency, 2015b.

Identification of Essential Standards

As you reflect on the process illustrated in this chapter's vignette, think about how much clarity both the second-grade team and the example of the preschool team will have as teachers approach each unit. Through this process, members came to know what to focus on, not only with their planning and instructional time but also with their common formative assessments, reteaching, and interventions. Keep these factors in mind as you read the rest of this chapter and learn about identifying essential standards and curriculum mapping to support your team's work.

To begin, let's talk about the value of making certain standards a priority. Why would it be important to take all the possible learning standards for a grade level and work as a team to value some standards over others? If teachers deem certain standards essential, does that mean they forget about the rest of them? Must they teach all the standards? To be clear, teams should teach to *all* standards. However, rather than leaving it up to individual teachers to prioritize some standards over others, teams take collective responsibility to determine essential standards for the following reasons.

- Teams can frame collaborative-planning time and teacher learning about standards, and team members can dig into the content and pedagogy, determining how to best teach standards.

- Teachers can spend more instructional time teaching essential standards.

- Teams can create common formative assessments and common end-of-unit assessments on essential standards to consistently determine which students have mastered them and which need further support.

- Teams can use the data they collect to create student interventions or extensions driven by the essential standards.

Figure 3.4 illustrates the prioritization of learning standards.

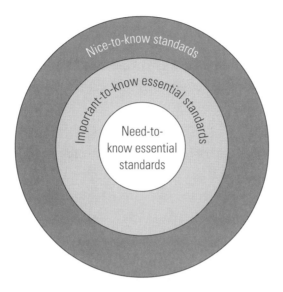

Source: Adapted from Schuhl, Kanold, Deinhart, Lang-Raad, Larson, & Smith, 2021.
Figure 3.4: Prioritization of learning standards.

Although the vignette for this chapter depicts a teacher team working collaboratively to determine essential standards, you may be in a state or province that has already determined essential standards for the schools in your district. We believe that because teachers are the ones actually teaching the standards, they are in the best position to decide which standards are essential for the students in their school. They know their students and know what they can guarantee those students will master during the school year. Therefore, all teams could use the district document of priority standards (if there is one) as a guideline, but the process we describe, which develops common understanding among teams, must be done at the school and team level using research-based criteria. If, at the beginning of the year, teachers do not have full understanding of and agreement around their essential standards, then they will end up with variances in what Robert Marzano (2003) refers to as their intended curriculum and their implemented curriculum. A teacher team must own the process to be confident team members have established a guaranteed and viable curriculum. Further, when teacher teams join together for vertical articulation, the teachers in the grade above and below can offer insight that helps the team take a wider view to understand which standards are not essential and which ones are absolutely necessary for success in the next grade. This ensures there are no gaps.

To guide the group decision-making process as to whether a given standard is essential, Douglas B. Reeves (2005) and Thomas W. Many (2016) suggest teams consider the following criteria.

- **Readiness:** Is it a prerequisite skill for learning in the next course or grade level? For example, *Retell a story read aloud* in preschool is a necessary step to building reading comprehension in kindergarten.

- **Endurance:** Will students need the knowledge and skill beyond a single test, unit, or course? For example, *Identify whether the number of objects in a group is greater than, less than or equal to another group* is a counting and cardinality skill in kindergarten that has endurance when students compare larger numbers and learn fractions in later grades.

- **Assessed:** Is it a concept that students will encounter on high-stakes exams? For example, an end-of-year benchmark assessment to determine if a second-grade student can *Read and comprehend literature and in the grade level text band proficiently* may contribute to the decision to ensure that teams deem certain comprehension standards for literature as essential.

- **Leverage:** Will students be able to apply the standard in more than one subject? For example, *Participate in shared research* is a literacy skill needed in social studies and science.

Often, team members disagree about whether a standard is really a need-to-know item or just a nice-to-know item. Or, teachers might agree that a particular standard is, in fact, essential, but they may struggle to determine if it is *a need-to-know standard* or an *important-to-know standard*. That disagreement is a valuable part of the collaborative process because, in sharing their different viewpoints, teachers are coming to a common understanding of what each standard really means and the level of rigor they expect to consider students proficient. When there is team disagreement, it is important to use the R.E.A.L. criteria to frame the discussion so it is not about opinions or preferences but how a standard prepares students for success in one or more of the four criteria.

In the following sections, we provide further guidance for early childhood teams on how to choose essential standards and ensure they have time to facilitate collaborative discussions.

Choosing Essential Standards

A team of kindergarten teachers we worked with met at the start of the school year to have a rich discussion about mathematics standards using their own prior teaching experiences and mathematics research, along with the R.E.A.L. criteria to determine essential learning standards for the year from the Common Core State Standards (NGA & CCSSO, 2010b). Using the protocol in figure 3.5 for identifying essential standards allowed them to be efficient in their decision making and confident their decisions were sound. No matter the grade level of the team or the source for standards, following this protocol will help teachers successfully collaborate around this task.

1. Use R.E.A.L. criteria (readiness, endurance, assessed, leverage) to determine priorities.

2. Consider additional criteria to identify the relative importance of the standard, such as blueprints from your state assessment, current research, and so on.

3. Separate standards into two initial lists, delineating essential standards from supporting nice-to-know standards.

4. Using your list of essential standards to determine which are need-to-know essential standards that will shape your interventions for every student and which are important-to-know essential standards that, when combined with the need to know standards, will shape your learning targets and unit planning.

Figure 3.5: Team protocol to identify essential standards.

*Visit **go.SolutionTree.com/PLCbooks** for a free reproducible version of this figure.*

Figure 3.6 shows an example of the standards in the mathematics reporting category *Counting and Cardinality* from the kindergarten CCSS mathematics standards. The team looked at all the standards in each of the mathematics reporting categories and determined which mathematics standards were need-to-know essential standards, important-to-know essential standards, and nice-to-know nonessential standards. As you can see from the figure, the team took a different approach to recording their essential standards than the preschool team in this chapter's vignette (page 49). They simply annotated next to the standard instead of copying them into a new chart.

Counting and Cardinality*
Know number names and the count sequence:
K.CC.A.1: Count to 100 by ones K.CC.A.1: Count to 100 by tens.
K.CC.A.2: Count forward beginning from a given number within the known sequence (instead of having to begin at 1).
! **K.CC.A.3: Write numbers from 0 to 20. Represent a number of objects with a written numeral 0–20 (with 0 representing a count of no objects).**
Count to tell the number of objects:
K.CC.B.4: Understand the relationship between numbers and quantities; connect counting to cardinality.
K.CC.B.5: Count to answer "how many?" questions about as many as 20 things arranged in a line, a rectangular array, or a circle, or as many as 10 things in a scattered configuration; given a number from 1–20, count out that many objects.
Compare numbers:
K.CC.C.6: Identify whether the number of objects in one group is greater than, less than, or equal to the number of objects in another group, e.g., by using matching and counting strategies. K.CC.C.7: Compare two numbers between 1 and 10 presented as written numerals.

*All essential grade-level standards (bold type); need-to-know essential standards (★); important-to-know essential standards (**!**); nice-to-know grade-level standards (not bold).

Source for standards: NGA & CCSSO, 2010b.

Figure 3.6: Essential mathematics standards for kindergarten.

Creating Collaborative Time

One of the questions we often hear is, "How can we find time to determine priority standards for an entire curriculum?" The reality is, there is no one right way, and teams can adopt a variety of methods to do this work. Two effective approaches include using a staff-development day—where all stakeholders are present, and there can be vertical articulation between teams—or breaking this work up and using parts of weekly team planning meetings at the beginning of the school year.

Table 3.1 shows two examples of how teams can identify standards together during the school day. If your team is part of a self-contained preschool (that isn't in the same building with kindergarten) or if your kindergarten team is in an elementary school (and not in the same building with the preschool), consider developing a partnership with a feeder school (where many of your students come from or go to) for vertical articulation at the early childhood level. Communication doesn't always have to be in person, so virtual collaboration works well in these instances.

Table 3.1: Ways for Teams to Find Time to Identify Essential Standards

Staff Development Day	Weekly Team Planning Meetings
1. Grade-level teams meet to identify essential standards in one subject area (schools often choose to do mathematics or reading first and use it as a model for teams to continue this process for other content areas at another time). Members use printed standards and physically sort the standards into essential or supporting piles, or use an electronic document and highlight or annotate the standards they deem essential.	1. Prior to the weekly collaborative meeting, each team member independently reviews and highlights his or her own list of possible essential standards for a particular content area.
2. Members from the grade-level team consult with teacher teams in grade levels below and above and share their product in a gallery walk. Together, the vertical teams look for gaps to ensure essential standards align across grade levels.	2. At the team meeting, all teachers have a collaborative discussion and share their ideas with one another and eventually come to consensus on the essential standards of learning they will be teaching as a team. The team then records their essential standards and shares the document with vertical teams above and below the grade level via an electronic document.
3. Each team considers the feedback from the grades above and below and makes revisions. Then, the whole staff comes back together to ensure there are no gaps.	3. For the first few minutes of the following team meeting, team members devote time to compare their essential standards with that of the grade levels above and below to ensure vertical alignment and no gaps. The team considers the written feedback from the vertical teams and adjusts their essential standards, if needed.

Notice how in each of these examples the *team* decides what is essential. Teachers are not just receiving a list of essential standards from another school or district that already determined them, nor from just one team member or school team leader coming up with a list and distributing it to the team. The value in doing this work together is learning together. Time is a commodity, and your team may find it tempting to accept the standards without going through this process. However, not only do the rich team discussions about essential standards lead to better understanding and teaching of those standards, but this process also provides teams the opportunity to connect vertically and work with the teachers in the grades above and below to bring clarity and purpose to the work. This is not something teams engage in frequently, but it is an important use of time at the beginning of the school year, before teams move on to the other team tasks in figure I.2 (page 11). Where teams are in the PLC process (just starting out or well into the work), will determine how frequently they need to meet to adjust and revise their essential standards.

The ultimate goal is to create a guaranteed and viable curriculum at your school, which means all teams take collective responsibility for student learning across the years. Determining essential standards is the foundation for this to happen. Having the conversations that lead teams to good decisions at this point in the process actually saves time and makes the teams more efficient and effective throughout the entire school year.

Tips for **Administrators**	*Tips for* **Coaches**	*Tips for* **Teachers**
Team by team and as a whole staff, prioritize and find time for teachers to identify essential standards. Providing for whole-staff collaboration allows vertical teams to look at the identified standards to discover gaps or overlaps. This is the anchor of the rest of the work teams will engage in and a worthy investment of team time. Provide content experts and resources to assist teams with this work. Allow teams to make difficult decisions about which standards are essential, and resist the urge to tell them what is essential. There is no magic number, and teams may need to adjust based on the information the process provides. Instead of relying on or being subjected to mandates, teams learn by doing and should continuously reflect on and modify their work using district guidelines as guides to assist them.	Think about the strengths of each team you work with, and provide choices for members to identify essential standards. Options include sharing the standards electronically or having teams physically work with them by highlighting, cutting and pasting, or using printouts members physically cut and sort. In any case, print and post the final essential standards for team members to see and access throughout the year, especially in team meetings. Ask guiding questions that challenge teachers to think about what the research says about a potential essential standard as they make decisions.	Share your background knowledge and expertise with teammates based on what you've experienced in the classroom, and ask clarifying questions of your teammates rather than rushing to complete this process. How you pace the year, determine every common formative assessment, and develop systems of interventions and extensions are based on these essential standards decisions. If you are not sure if a standard meets the R.E.A.L. criteria, be transparent and ask for help. This is a sign of strength, not weakness.

Year-Long Curriculum Outlines

Once teams identify the standards essential for students to learn, they need to think about which standards, when taught together, support students in building concepts and practicing skills. Then, teams need to determine how much time to devote to teaching the standards and when they will teach them. Clearly, teams will devote more time to essential standards than nonessential supporting standards, but there needs to be designated time for teaching all the standards. An effective way to accomplish this is for the team to map out the curriculum and develop a year-long *curriculum outline*. Figure 3.7 uses the mathematics standards from figure 3.6 (page 57) to illustrate a typical year-long curriculum outline. Notice how this curriculum outline includes *all* the grade-level standards for mathematics. Traditionally, teams map out and develop separate year-long curriculum outlines for each content area, although it is possible to integrate content areas and develop interdisciplinary teacher tools, as we discuss and highly recommend later in this chapter.

Time	Units of Study	Grade-Level Standards (Essential standards in bold)
Weeks 1–6 (August–September; 28 days)	Unit 1: Building Routines and Counting	Know number names and the count sequence **K.CC.A.1, K.CC.A.2, K.CC.A.3** Count to tell the number of objects **K.CC.B.4 (A, B, C), K.CC.B.5**
Weeks 7–11 (October; 25 days)	Unit 2: Data and Counting and Comparing	Classify objects and count the number of objects in each category **K.MD.B.3** Compare numbers **K.CC.C6**, CCSS.K.CC.C.7 *Previously taught:* Know number names and the count sequence **K.CC.A.1, K.CC.A.2, K.CC.A.3** Count to tell the number of objects **K.CC.B.4 (A,B,C), K.CC.B.5**
Weeks 12–16 (November–December; 26 days)	Unit 3: Operations and Algebraic Thinking (Part 1)	Understand addition as putting together and adding to, and understand subtraction as taking apart and taking from **K.OA.A.1, K.OA.A.2** *Previously taught:* Know number names and the count sequence **K.CC.A.1, K.CC.A.2, K.CC.A.3** Count to tell the number of objects **K.CC.B.4 (A,B,C), K.CC.B.5**
Weeks 17–21 (January–February; 27 days)	Unit 4: Measuring and Counting and Comparing	Describe and compare measurable attributes K.MD.A.1, **K.MD.A.2** *Previously taught:* Know number names and the count sequence **K.CC.A.1, K.CC.A.2, K.CC.A.3** Count to tell the number of objects **K.CC.B.4 (A,B,C), CCSS.K.CC.B.5** Compare numbers **K.CC.C6**, K.CC.C.7

Weeks 22–26 (February–March; 26 days)	Unit 5: Operations and Algebraic Thinking (Part 2)	Understand addition as putting together and adding to, and understand subtraction as taking apart and taking from **K.OA.A.3**, K.OA.A.4, **K.OA.A.5**
		Previously taught:
		Understand addition as putting together and adding to, and understand subtraction as taking apart and taking from **K.OA.A.1**, **K.OA.A.2**
		Know number names and the count sequence **K.CC.A.2**, **K.CC.A.3**
		Count to tell the number of objects **K.CC.B.4 (A,B,C)**, **K.CC.B.5**
Weeks 27–32 (March–April; 28 days)	Unit 6: Geometry	Identify and describe shapes K.G.A.1, **K.G.A.2**, K.G.A.3
		Analyze, compare, create, and compose shapes K.G.B.4, K.G.B.5, **K.G.B.6**
		Previously taught:
		Classify objects and count the number of objects in each category **K.MD.B.3**
Weeks 33–36 (May; 18 days)	Unit 7: Number and Operations In a Base-10 System	Work with numbers 11-19 to gain foundations for place value K.NBT.A.1
		Know number names and the count sequence K.CC.A.1 (count to 100 by tens)
		Previously taught:
		Know number names and the count sequence **K.CC.A.1 (count to 100 by ones)**
		Count to tell the number of objects **K.CC.B.5**
		Understand addition as putting together and adding to, and understand subtraction as taking apart and taking from **K.OA.A.3**, K.OA.A.4

Source for standards: NGA & CCSSO, 2010b.

Figure 3.7: Year-long curriculum outline for kindergarten mathematics standards.

*Visit **go.SolutionTree.com/PLCbooks** for a free reproducible version of this figure.*

As you reflect on figure 3.7, here are a few things for teams to consider when developing a year-long curriculum outline.

1. **Cluster standards within each of the content strands:** Start off by grouping standards within content strands. Based on pedagogical content knowledge, determine if multiple standards should be taught together and simultaneously. Begin by forming some initial clusters of common standards that connect and may help students build deeper conceptual understanding within a content strand.

2. **Identify standards that connect across strands:** Look across the content strands and determine which standards the team should teach together to help students build deeper connections between multiple concepts and strands. In particular, look for how you might be able to connect need-to-know essential standards across strands in more than one unit of study so students have multiple opportunities to learn essential standards throughout the year.

3. **Form units of study:** Look at the standards you clustered together, and determine if the team can order them in a way where they might build on one another to form a strong unit of study. A strong unit of study has a balance of standards that require both higher and lower levels of cognitive demand. Each unit of study should contain several essential standards, and the essential standards should spiral throughout the curriculum and during the school year. Also, be sure you have included all grade-level standards (essential and nonessential) within the curriculum.

4. **Order units of study:** When making decisions about the placement of units the team will teach during the school year, team members might consider starting the year with units that include concepts students will be developmentally ready for or that students might have some background knowledge about from previous years. In general, your units of study should build on each other and throughout the year.

5. **Determine the duration of each unit of study:** Begin to form some general ideas about how long teachers will need to teach the concepts and skills within each unit of study, and determine the total number of instructional days available within the year for teaching each unit of study. As a team, decide which concepts in the units of study might take more or less time for students to learn based on their rigor, if the concepts are completely new for students, or if components of them have been previously touched on. Then, decide how many instructional days to allot for each unit of study.

Notice how the kindergarten team we featured in figure 3.7 (page 61) clustered several essential standards together in many of the units and how many of the need-to-know essential standards *spiral and will be consistently revisited and taught throughout the course of the year.* For example, the counting and cardinality concepts and skills are foundational building blocks for kindergarten students. Therefore, you will notice how several of the counting and cardinality standards are not only deemed essential, but they also spiral throughout the entire school year and many of them appear in six out of the seven kindergarten mathematics units of study. Also, in unit 2, "Data and Counting and Comparing," it makes sense that students would have opportunities to sort objects and then count what they sort as well as compare the number of objects in each group.

School districts often provide year-long curriculum outlines and other various instructional tools to support teachers. While they can be extremely useful, it is still important for team members (the experts on their students) to look at the instructional tools they receive and make adjustments to ensure there is enough time for teachers to instruct the essential standards during the school year. Teams should use district tools as *guidelines* as they go through the process of identifying and sequencing *the team's* essential standards. Teams should not skip the important, job-embedded professional development that comes from members' collaborative discussions while analyzing standards and building these necessary and important instructional tools early in each school year.

Befitting the flexible nature of collaborative work in a PLC, there are a variety of options teams can explore to support and supplement or replace their approach to mapping out the curriculum and developing the useful instructional tools that will work for the team's unique needs. In the following sections, we explore two of these instructional planning tools: assessment maps and integrated curriculum maps.

Assessment Mapping

An important next step for teams is to determine when all end-of-unit assessments will occur throughout the year. To facilitate this, teams might add specific assessment dates into the curriculum year-long outline or develop an *assessment map* that shows when within-unit common formative assessments and end-of-unit assessment will occur. Having this sort of assessment plan assists teams with pacing out assessments and allows them to ensure timely discussions (data-discussion meetings) around the assessment results to intervene and extend for students and to use results to share effective practices amongst teachers. Figure 3.8 (page 65) illustrates one type of assessment map; notice how it correlates with the sample kindergarten year-long outline in figure 3.7 (page 61).

It is all too easy to get bogged down in what must be accomplished week by week, but this kindergarten team wisely began the year laying out a plan that will help them ensure they are headed in the right direction month by month to reach the desired result of high levels of learning. To achieve this, its team members developed this map at the beginning of the school year, after deciding to use a calendar to establish when all end-of-unit common assessments would occur. This type of *backward design*, which refers to the process of starting with the end in sight, prompts teams to consider how and when they will collect evidence of learning *before* teaching the first lesson. Leadership experts Jay McTighe and Greg Curtis (2019) explain the importance of backward design to curriculum development, "We find that the intentional use of backward design for curriculum planning results in more clearly defined goals, more appropriate assessments, and more purposeful teaching" (p. 37).

In figure 3.8, the kindergarten team has twenty-five instructional days to teach the concepts and skills within unit 2. Each week, team members engage in weekly team meetings and decide the lessons and common formative assessments they will use with students throughout the unit. Teams can use part of or all of these team meetings to discuss results from the common formative assessment, to intervene and extend for students, and to share effective practices. Following the end-of-unit common assessment, the team conducts a data discussion to analyze students' results, determine what students have learned and what they still need to learn, plan for necessary interventions and extensions, and again, be prepared to share effective practices between teammates (as the calendar shows this team will do on November 6). This particular kindergarten team also consistently uses a project-based learning approach to their instruction and decided to also place all project dates on the calendar at the start of each new unit of study. All of the curriculum planning tools this team uses are electronic, so they can save them in a common location that all team members can access. This also allows the team to reflect on their plans year to year and make revisions easily.

To avoid having multiple instructional tools, teams may decide to put the end-of-unit assessment on their year-long curriculum outline. Some teams may prefer the idea of backward design and start with a blank calendar, first thinking about what common end-of-unit assessments the team will use and when it will administer them. After selecting assessment dates and putting them on the assessment map, teams may want to use this same calendar template during their planning meetings. Teams list out the standards they will be teaching each day along with the common formative assessments they will be using during the week. If one team decides to list only the end-of-unit assessments and data discussions on an assessment calendar while another decides to list out the specific dates on the yearly curriculum outline (thus limiting the number of tools in use), that is OK. As we wrote previously, teams can make choices about the instructional tools that best meet the needs of the team.

Often it is easy to push formative assessment dates back and keep teaching a particular concept, hoping the students will eventually master the concept through reteaching. The trouble with delaying assessments is that teams often take too long to teach a concept and then run out of time at the end of the year to cram in remaining essential standards, or they continue teaching lessons without informative data to make good instructional decisions based on students' specific needs. While teachers don't want units to stretch into extra weeks, they also cannot say, "It's time to move on" if students don't get the concept the first time around. If learning is constant and time is the variable, how do teams balance pacing with student achievement? Chapter 5 (page 109) and chapter 6 (page 137) discuss how to reach this balance through the use of common end-of-unit assessments and data discussions

Unit: Data and Counting and Comparing (unit 2)

Duration: Seven to eleven weeks (twenty-five days)

OCTOBER				
Monday	**Tuesday**	**Wednesday**	**Thursday**	**Friday**
September 29 Unit 2: Data and Counting and Comparing Start date	September 30 Common preassessment (Observe students counting a set of objects during mathematics workshop and while at play.) →	31	1	2 Team meeting to discuss common preassessment data
5	6	7	8	9
12	13	14 Common formative assessment (performance assessment): Rote Counting 1–100 (during the mathematics workshop)	15 →	16 Team meeting to discuss common formative assessment results
19	20	21	22	23
		DATA-COLLECTION PROJECT: RECYLING		
26	27	28	29 Unit 2: Data and Counting and Comparing—Common end-of-unit assessment →	30
	DATA-COLLECTION PROJECT: RECYLING			
November 2 Unit 3: Operations and Algebraic Thinking (part 1) Start date	November 3	November 4	November 5	November 6 Team data-discussion meeting about Unit 2: Data and Counting and Comparing; common end-of-unit assessment

Figure 3.8: An assessment map.

Integrated Curriculum

If your team teaches content in distinct time blocks when mapping units, it makes sense to develop separate curriculum outlines for each content area. For example, it is common for a teacher to get a sixty-minute block to teach mathematics, a ninety-minute block to teach language arts, a forty-five-minute block to teach science and social studies, and a forty-five-minute block for a specials subject area (music, art, physical education, and so on). In that case, teachers identify standards in each subject area and create separate curriculum outlines. However, some schools integrate the various subject areas throughout the day and also map them into the same curriculum outline. How could a team take this approach and integrate all its essential standards and skills into the available months, weeks, or days? What would that look like?

If your district provides curriculum outlines already, your team has a clear place to start. However, if your district does not provide these tools, your team must examine which approach it will use to integrate the curriculum. Susan M. Drake (2012), an expert on integrated curricula development, explains the need and importance of using an integrated curriculum approach. She also explains that education for the 21st century expects learners to make real-life connections to the world around them and use and practice the skills across curriculum areas. Figure 3.9 illustrates a continuum we developed showing various methods to integrate curriculum. In the following sections, we describe the different learning approaches within each method of integration and show what an integrated curriculum outline looks like.

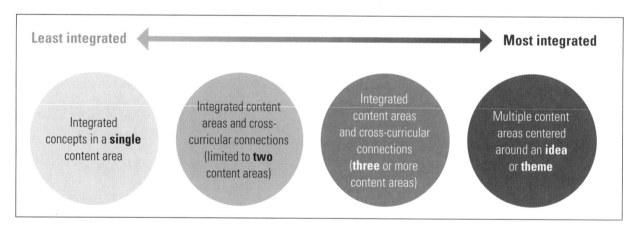

Figure 3.9: Integrated curriculum continuum.

Integrated Concepts In a Single Content Area

In this approach, the learning focuses on one single content area, such as mathematics, but it integrates standards across multiple strands that connect to an overarching concept or group of related skills for which it makes sense to practice simultaneously. For example, teams might connect and teach together preschool mathematics standards from various strands (number sense, geometry, and data collection). In this scenario, preschool students might engage in a learning experience where they are first sorting a set of objects, then counting the objects in each set, and then using an object graph to represent their sorting categories. This learning experience could occur at learning centers, in small teacher-guided groups and student-directed groups, or through the use of a multiday whole-class project. No matter the learning experience, the teacher has taken the integrated concept approach and moved student learning forward in the strands of number sense, geometry, and data collection, instead of addressing them in three separate units.

Integrated Content Areas and Cross-Curricular Connections

In this approach, which is further along the continuum toward fully integrating curriculum, teams integrate learning from across multiple content areas. Teams may connect standards both within content strands (such as in the previous approach) and between multiple content areas (such as literacy and social studies) with relationships established between them. This approach could integrate just two content areas or multiple areas, including SEL. For example, teams could connect and teach preschool standards from mathematics, science, literacy, and visual arts simultaneously over a particular period. In this scenario, preschool students might engage in learning experiences that focus on standards from each of those content areas relating to similarities and differences, classification, and the sorting of objects. Specific learning experiences may include students sorting shapes for mathematics; collecting leaves, twigs, acorns, and so on for science and also using those materials to make an art project; sorting lower- and uppercase letters, letters and numbers, objects that either sink or float, and so on; sorting and classifying object, such as liquids, solids, and gases; identifying shapes from consumable and recyclable items (such as paper towel roll, plastic containers, and used boxes); and reusing items to make an invention or art project. All these learning experiences could occur at learning centers or in small teacher-guided or student-centered groups or within a multiday project.

Multiple Content Areas Centered Around an Idea or Theme

In this approach, the learning focuses on standards within multiple content areas that center around one theme or idea. For example, students may engage in a multiday project and learning experience with a theme about the importance of recycling. This might involve the students in creating their own classroom recycling system. During this time, they might engage in science learning that focuses on ideas around conservation and reusing and recycling items. They might learn about social studies concepts that focus on standards about what people do in their communities to support recycling and use citizenship skills (problem solving and sharing thoughts, ideas, and opinions as they work collaboratively). Students might focus on mathematics standards about sorting objects and, as they collect recyclable items, they develop their own system for sorting the objects into categories. The teacher might read books about recycling and use literacy skills to compare and contrast information learned in books, and he or she could use a combination of oral communication, writing, and visual arts skills students could employ while making classroom recycling signs and presentations.

Regardless of the specific approach, teams then produce a curriculum outline.

Integrated-Curriculum Outline

The process of creating an integrated-curriculum outline and corresponding assessment maps is mostly the same as we explained in the Year-Long Curriculum Outlines section (page 59), which focused on developing a curriculum outline for a single content area. For an integrated-curriculum outline, your team still engages in backward design by thinking about the end goals of the project-based learning or theme and determines when and how to assess the essential learning standards in multiple content areas for each unit. Table 3.2 compares the curriculum-outline process for a single content area and an integrated curriculum.

Table 3.2: Integrated Curriculum Outline Process

Single Content-Area Curriculum	Integrated Curriculum
1. Cluster standards within each of the content strands. 2. Identify standards that connect across strands. 3. Form units of study. 4. Order units of study. 5. Determine the duration of each unit of study.	1. Choose enough themes, ideas, or projects to ensure all essential standards are taught and learned. 2. Identify standards across content areas that connect to each idea, theme, or project. 3. Form units of study. 4. Order units of study. 5. Determine duration of each unit of study

If integrating curriculum content is new for your team, it can begin by considering just two content areas to merge for a unit (table 3.3). In this example, team members combined mathematics with science and literacy with social studies. By doing so, they've freed up time daily for more opportunities for extended learning through play.

Table 3.3: Integrating Two Content Areas to Increase Play Time

Single Content-Area Learning	Integrated Content Learning
Morning meeting (teachers and students) and SEL time	Morning meeting (teachers and students) and SEL time
Literacy	Literacy and social studies
Lunch and recess	Lunch and recess
Mathematics	Mathematics and science
Social studies	Block available for self-initiated and teacher-guided *play*; teams decide what play looks like for each grade level.
Science	

Integrating the curriculum not only adds more time for teacher-guided and student-initiated play, it is also highly engaging and allows for more connections to real-world and project-based learning.

Daily Schedules

As your team outlines its curriculum, its pedagogy and structures (such as the daily schedule), influence how teachers teach and assess throughout the school year. We close this chapter with a detailed sample of a kindergarten daily schedule featuring an integrated curriculum (see figure 3.10). This one-day snapshot reflects how a team begins to consider how it will integrate SEL and academic content into every block of the day, including arrival, dismissal and transitions.

Time	Primary Content Area and Focus	Integrated Content Focus	Example of Learning Activities
9:10 a.m.– 9:25 a.m.	Daily arrival with self-directed independent or cooperative play	SEL	Students interact with magnet-shaped building blocks and snap-together bricks. Students interact with playdough, letter-shaped molds, and number mats
9:25 a.m.– 9:35 a.m.	Morning meeting	SEL, mathematics, and literacy	Students and teachers greet and welcome each other, often through a song. There are opportunities for sharing and asking questions, a community-building activity, and reading a morning message from the teacher describing the day ahead.
9:35 a.m.– 9:37 a.m.	Transition	Literacy and oral language	After students have been sitting during the morning meeting, teachers ask them to get up and go on a one-minute letter hunt around the classroom to look for objects that start with the letter sound *d* (*desk*, *door*, and so on). Before sharing out in a whole-group setting, students turn and talk with a partner about all the things they found.
9:37 a.m.– 10:58 a.m.	Literacy (reading focus lesson) Reading stations Writing workshop	Language and social studies or SEL	Teachers model during a five- to ten-minute whole-group focus lesson. Students participate in interactive read-aloud or shared reading incorporating phonological awareness, phonics, vocabulary and reading fluency, and comprehension. Teachers work with small groups while other students engage with self-selected books, independently or with a partner. Students use multisensory materials for letter or word work and writing.
10:58 a.m.– 11:00 a.m.	Transition	SEL and mathematics	Teachers ask students to come to the carpet and engage in calm breathing exercises while simultaneously using counting skills. As students are walking to the cafeteria, teachers ask them to look for patterns they see in the hallways.
11:05 a.m.– 12:05 p.m.	Lunch and recess		Teachers provide outdoor play toys for students (basketballs, soccer balls, chalk, outdoor sand and water tables, and so on).

Figure 3.10: Sample kindergarten daily schedule with emerging curriculum integrations.

continued →

Time	Primary Content Area and Focus	Integrated content Focus	Example of Learning Activities
12:10 p.m.– 12:25 p.m.	Rest time		After students return from recess, teachers keep the lights low in the classroom while playing quiet music.
12:25 p.m.– 12:27 p.m.	Transition	Mathematics and physical movement	After the rest period, teachers want to get students' blood flowing to their brain to help energize them; so, they ask students to engage in physical movements while identifying various numbers and engaging in counting movement activities (for example, six jumping jacks, four toe touches, and so on).
12:30 p.m.– 1:28 p.m.	Mathematics (focus lesson) Mathematics learning stations (choice time)	Science and SEL	Teachers conduct a whole-group mathematics focus lesson embedded with the use of engaging manipulatives, visuals, auditory elements, and (or) kinesthetic learning techniques. Teachers provide opportunities to answer problems and questions at various cognitive levels and give students opportunities to use oral language skills, such as turning and talking with their peers to explain their thinking and process, their ideas, and so on. Students engage in small-group learning opportunities with a teacher, as well as partner or small-group student-directed learning at stations with engaging tasks, games, technology, and mathematics manipulatives. Frequent integration of science concepts and skills into mathematics instruction should occur.
1:28 p.m.– 1:30 p.m.	Transition	SEL	After the mathematics workshop and before going to a specials class, teachers ask students to turn and talk to a partner about an activity or strategy that helps calm them when they are frustrated or upset (for example, listening to music, jogging, playing a sport, drawing, and so on).
1:35 p.m.– 2:35 p.m.	Specials (music, art, physical education, library)	Academic areas and SEL	Before leaving the classroom, teachers ask students to guess what number they think they will land on if they start counting silently in their brain from the time they leave their classroom until they reach their next destination. When they get to their destination, teachers allow a few students to quickly share their results aloud or with a nearby peer to see if they got close to their estimate.
2:40 p.m.– 2:45 p.m.	Snack	SEL with specific content focus	After returning from specials, students have a snack and engage in a rest period or calm activity, such as listening to soft music, watching a short instructional learning video, participating in a teacher read-aloud, reading silently, or quietly socializing with peers at their table sets.
2:45 p.m.– 3:15 p.m.	Science and social studies cooperative learning, experimentation, and exploration	SEL	Students participate in a large- or small-group learning experience that may involve guided play or project learning.

3:15 p.m.–3:40 p.m.	Self-directed and teacher-guided play (materials available for discovery, exploration, and imaginative thinking)	Guided play to support social skills, oral-language skills, mathematics skills, and so on	Students receive play materials: dramatic play tools (puppets, play foods that partition into fractional parts for fair sharing, cash register, and so on) or physical consumable objects for creative building and constructing (tape, scissors, empty paper towel rolls, empty boxes, string, and so on). During this time, teachers may also facilitate guided play with individual or small groups of students.
3:45 p.m.–3:50 p.m.	Daily reflection and closing circle	SEL and literacy	Students come to the carpet, sit in a circle, and reflect on various periods of their day. They use the turn-and-talk structure to engage with their peers and use oral-communication skills. Teachers also take a moment to highlight sequencing during the daily reflection, such as emotions students may have felt during various parts of the day, and highlight the next day's activities to allow students time to reflect and prepare for things that may evoke feelings of worry (things that may be challenging) or things that generate excitement (and possible over stimulation).
3:50 p.m.	Dismissal	SEL and mathematics	Teachers conduct a closing circle to allow students to share reflections on the day. Then they play games using the number of each bus that arrives and count and group the number of students left after each announcement.

As you reflect on the information in this sample schedule, there are a lot of components to consider, including arrival and dismissal, morning meetings, transitions, learning experience and student-choice time, academic content areas, SEL, and play. Each of the following sections briefly explores these components.

Arrival and Dismissal

Arrival and dismissal can be challenging for many of our young learners, creating "big feelings" as they transition from two very different environments (from home to school and vice versa). To support this transitional period and students' social-emotional needs, teachers may consider starting or ending students' school day with periods of play. During this time, students have an opportunity to work on their communication and social-emotional skills while they are at play with their peers.

Morning Meetings

Morning meetings can focus on multiple learning areas simultaneously and they can shift throughout the week. For example, teachers might ask students to read a morning message that focuses on big feelings and then ask them to locate particular sight words, capital letters, or spelling patterns they have been learning located within the morning message. During the greeting and sharing, students are building vocabulary and practicing SEL skills, and there is often a song, dance, or opportunity to build working memory by repeating a pattern while building a positive classroom community.

Transitions

Think about the overall flow of the school day and how it impacts students, and be sure to balance it with built in periods of active learning and periods of rest. Purposeful planning of transitions can support students social-emotional, behaviorial, and academic needs in small ways, and teams should use several transitions throughout the school day. Thinking about when to incorporate longer transitions between the learning of content areas and before or after more active or less active parts of a students' school day are important things to think about when developing the daily schedule. Although teachers use frequent transitions throughout their day, sometimes spontaneously, this schedule reflects those bigger, purposefully planned transitions.

Learning Experiences and Student Choice Time

Provide a balance of indoor and outdoor student self-directed and teacher-guided engaging learning activities and experiences throughout the day. Allowing students the opportunity to make choices about their own learning and interests is important and typically results in students having more impactful levels of engagement. Teams can build choice time into play periods throughout the day or during academic learning blocks. For instance, give students a choice about the mathematics learning stations they interact with. This requires teachers to have efficient routines and procedures for students to engage them in on-task learning.

Academic Content Areas

A balance of large- and small-group learning should occur during academic learning blocks (literacy, mathematics, science, and social studies). A workshop model allows teachers to work with small groups of learners and provide guided instruction. With smaller student-teacher ratios comes more opportunity for frequent use of oral language. This learning format also provides opportunities for small student groups to either work cooperatively with peers using social skills (active listening, conflict resolution, decision making, and so on) or independently by focusing on multiple executive functions (task initiation, attention, organization, time management, and so on).

SEL

Teams should integrate SEL throughout the school day and infuse it into academic and nonacademic focused areas. Often, teachers use the morning meeting time as a place to focus on social-emotional skills. At the end of the day, teachers also find that a daily reflection or closing circle is another great time to talk about what happened throughout the day and connect it to students' feelings and emotions. Transitions are another great opportunity to teach social and self-regulation skills and strategies. Keep in mind students also need time to practice their new SEL skills during nonacademic blocks, such as lunch, recess, and rest periods.

Play

It is important that teams designate sustained periods of play that are both self-directed and guided within the daily schedule. Note that, in a preschool setting, play periods may occur daily and in shorter periods throughout the day. For older students (K–2), play may occur for longer periods that occur several times a week.

Guided play can occur during designated academic blocks or during the designated play block. Teachers engage with small groups of students while at play and pose careful questioning techniques. Teachers choose to rotate between groups of students or engage with individual students. Choice of play materials is crucial to making these play periods productive. For example, imagine that sometime during the week, a teacher reads books by Mo Wilems to students and then provides pig and elephant puppets during play. Thinking critically about the choice of play materials can spark student imaginations or may even engage them in play scenarios where they are using and practicing literacy and mathematics skills. Provide engaging materials that might promote imaginative play, peer interaction, and self-discovery. Puppets and costumes often invoke dramatic peer play, use of shapes and magnetic building blocks may prompt students to use and practice learned mathematics skills, and so on.

When making choices about play materials, think about incorporating a balance of materials that support varied forms of play. Play materials may look different in a preschool setting than in a first-grade elementary classroom. For example, dramatic play tools may include dolls or costumes in a preschool setting, but in a first-grade classroom, it's a felt board with book characters (in the form of manipulatives) for acting out the story and a working cash register.

Guided teacher playgroups contain approximately three students at a time for fifteen to twenty minutes and allow teachers to engage with all students in the guided-play situation across a week. Figure 3.11 illustrates a model for scheduling guided play and formally observing students at play that integrates opportunities for learning science and social studies content.

	Monday	**Tuesday**	**Wednesday**	**Thursday**	**Friday**
2:45 p.m.–3:05 p.m.	Guided play, group A: Nate Allison Gib	Guided play, group C: Kyle Emily Kirstin	Conduct ten-minute small-group rotations for teacher-guided science experiments or social studies projects while other students engage in self-directed play.	Guided play, group E: Anthony Ashley Rory	Guided play, group G: TJ Kathleen Allie
3:05 p.m.–3:25 p.m.	Guided play, group B: Griffith Mimi Rick	Guided play, group D: Tessa Pat Signe		Guided play, group F: Bu Tommy Becky	Assessment: Observe students at play and collect data.
3:25 p.m.–3:45 p.m.	Whole-group science or social studies lessons or project learning			Whole-group science or social studies lessons or project learning	

Figure 3.11: Sample guided-play schedule.

No matter your approach, integrating the curriculum on any level allows students to make important connections between the various content areas, and it allows more time in the schedule for periods of play.

Tips for **Administrators**	*Tips for* **Coaches**	*Tips for* **Teachers**
Set the expectation for teams to start with the end in mind by developing or discussing the common formative and end-of-unit assessments at the beginning of the unit before teams begin planning lessons. Using backward design ensures all team members have common knowledge, common language, and common understanding. Assess your allocation of resources to support each team's work. Is there enough time for teams to work collaboratively? Are there human resources in the best places to help teams accomplish their work and support students' needs?	Help create a place to electronically store the work from collaborative meetings, so all teachers have access to the dates set for common formative assessments and unit resources. Because teachers often want more time, support them in completing assessments by agreed-on dates, but keep the big picture in mind. Be sure teams always go back to the original standard as written when determining essential standards. Support teams in creating curriculum tools so as not to lose sight of the rigor originally expected, which can sometimes happen when teams use shorthand and just put a few keywords next to the standard number.	Brainstorm ideas at your team meetings, share the workload, and have team members leave meetings with action steps the team decides and agrees on. This way, your team won't spend the whole meeting generating one idea and one final product. Instead, team members generate many ideas and designate the person responsible to follow up on each. This allows them to return to subsequent meetings with multiple products ready to present for final consensus. Look through your current daily plans, and make note of how you are already integrating some SEL into content areas or transitions. Share with teammates, and make note of how you can do it more routinely and purposefully next week.

Guiding Questions

Use the following guiding questions to learn together and build shared knowledge.

- 💬 Have teacher teams agreed on essential standards, and are members collaborating on the right work? If not, what are some steps you can take to move them in this direction?

- 💬 How do you provide time for teams before school starts for them to frontload the important work of understanding their curriculum outline and assessment maps in order to pace the year well from the start?

- 💬 Where would your team place most of its instruction along the continuum of integrated curriculum, and what could be some next steps to better integrate the curriculum (academic and SEL) for young learners?

- 💬 Why is your daily schedule set up the way it is? Is your team making decisions based on what is best for early childhood students or what is comfortable for the adults?

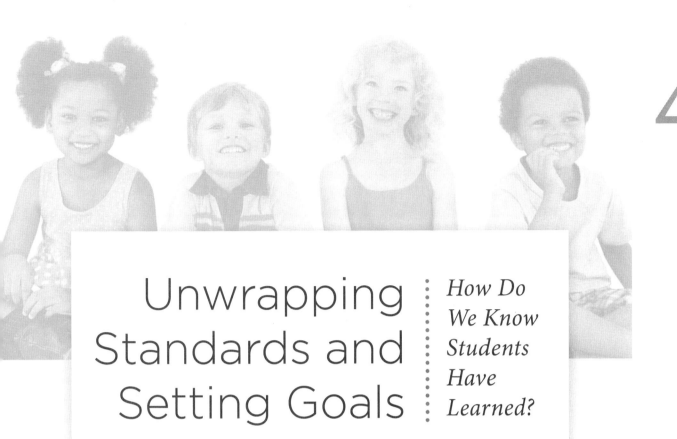

Unwrapping Standards and Setting Goals

How Do We Know Students Have Learned?

Once a team has done the work at the beginning of the year to determine essential standards and map curriculum for the year (as we describe in chapter 3), it is time for students to start actually learning. Many teachers only think of assessment when they consider how they might answer the second critical question: How will we know if each student has learned it? (DuFour et al., 2016); however, this chapter focuses on an equally important precursor to creating assessments—unwrapping standards, developing learning progressions, and setting goals with students (see figure 4.1, page 76).

To know if students have learned, teams have to accomplish three steps: (1) break the standards down into specific learning targets that clarify for both teachers and students exactly what students are learning, (2) develop learning progressions that clarify the steps toward proficiency, and (3) communicate those steps to students by goal setting with them. Not only does this process create common understanding for team members as they sharpen their pedagogy while unwrapping standards into learning targets, it also creates common understanding between teachers and students as both groups use those learning targets to set goals that address the needs of the whole child.

To show how teams transition from answering the first critical question, this chapter begins with a vignette that illustrates how a preschool team turned its focus

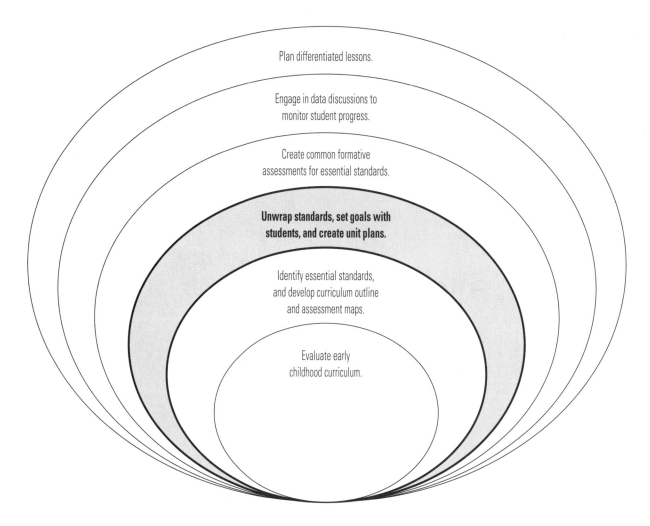

Figure 4.1: The work of early childhood teams in a PLC—Unwrap standards, set goals with students, and create unit plans.

to student social-emotional needs by developing a plan to address the second critical question of a PLC as part of a whole child approach to learning, rather than one focused purely on academic growth. After reading and reflecting on this vignette, you might find yourself asking questions like the following.

- "How often does my team take time to work collaboratively to unwrap standards and think about student proficiency?"

- "How do students and teachers use goal cards? Does the team create learning progressions and a student goal card for each essential standard?"

- "How can my team collaborate to create common formative assessment tools on academic or SEL skills? What might that look like? How can we better integrate academic and SEL skills and concepts into our unit plan?"

Throughout the rest of this chapter, we answer those questions and explain how early childhood teams can begin to answer the question of what students have learned by unwrapping essential standards, developing learning progressions, setting student goals for learning, and planning units using pacing guides. In doing this work, teams position themselves to design more effective units and assessments (which we cover in chapter 5, page 109), and just as important, they position students to answer the second critical question for themselves rather than relying on their assessment score or their teacher to tell them if they have learned. Students who know what their specific learning goals are and how they're progressing are empowered to take ownership of their learning and expand their social-emotional development.

Vignette:

A Preschool Team Creates a SEL Progression

Research confirms that the social-emotional development of early childhood learners is just as important as their understanding and development of academic concepts and skills. Research from Jones and colleagues (2015) shows substantial links between social-emotional skills in kindergarten and positive outcomes in young adulthood. In fact, many social-emotional skills are necessary for young learners to access academic standards in the classroom. Durlak and colleagues (2011) state SEL increases student achievement, improves teacher-student relationships, and improves student behavior. The next question becomes, "What are the SEL skills teams need to teach, and how do we effectively and appropriately teach them?" In their review of research, Rosemarie O'Conner, Jessica De Feyter, Alyssa Carr, Jia Lisa Luo, and Helen Romm (2017) find the best way to teach these skills is by integrating them into students' daily learning.

In the previous chapters, we used vignettes of teacher teams planning mathematics and language arts curriculum to think about students' academic learning development and to determine what students should know and be able to do. In this vignette, a preschool team reflects on how it is supporting students' social-emotional skills and how the state's standards for SEL connect with the academic standards the team identified as essential. The team's goal this year is to find additional ways to integrate its curriculum across content areas, particularly with regard to incorporating SEL *and* play into the content areas. The research of Sheldon Berman, Sydney Chaffee, and Julia Sarmiento (2018) clarifies the team's approach:

> Regardless of the specific competencies selected, the key to fostering social and emotional development is a continuing loop in which we first help students understand why the skills are important and how they can be used effectively, then create opportunities for students to practice those skills, and finally provide feedback and time for reflection. (p. 13)

The team began in the fall of a new school year by identifying and annotating a set of essential SEL standards from the Illinois State Board of Education strands (Illinois Early Learning Project, 2013; see figure 4.2). If your state or province, district, or school does not have SEL standards and is interested in learning more, the Collaborative for Academic Social and Emotional Learning (CASEL, n.d.) is one resource to consult.

Preschool Social-Emotional Standards*
Goal 30: Develop self-management skills to achieve school and life success and develop positive relations with others.
Learning standard 30.A: Identify and manage one's emotions and behaviors.
30.A.ECa: Recognize and label basic emotions.
30.A.ECb: Use appropriate communication skills when expressing, needs, wants, and feelings.
30.A.ECc: Express feelings that are appropriate to the situation.
30.A.ECd: Begin to understand and follow rules.
30.A.ECe: Use materials with purpose, safety, and respect.
30.A.ECf: Begin to understand the consequences of his or her behavior.
Learning standard 30.B: Recognize own uniqueness and personal qualities.
30.B.ECa: Describe self using several basic characteristics.
Learning standard 30.C: Demonstrate skills related to successful personal and school outcomes.
30.C.ECa: Exhibit eagerness and curiosity as a learner.
30.C.ECb: Demonstrate persistence and creativity in seeking solutions to problems.
30.C.ECc: Show some initiative, self-direction, and independence in actions.
Goal 31: Use social-awareness and interpersonal skills to establish and maintain positive relationships.
Learning standard 31.A: Develop positive relationships with peers and adults.
31.A.ECa: Show empathy, sympathy, and caring for others.
31.A.ECb: Recognize the feelings and perspective of others.
31.A.ECc: Interact easily with familiar adults.
31.A.ECd: Demonstrate attachment to familiar adults.
31.A.ECe: Develop positive relationships with peers.
Learning standard 31.B: Use communication and social skills to interact effectively with others.
31.B.ECa: Interact verbally and nonverbally with other children.
31.B.ECb: Engage in cooperative group play.
31.A.ECc: Use socially appropriate behavior with peers and adults, such as helping, sharing, and taking turns.
Learning standard 31.C: Demonstrate an ability to prevent, manage, and resolve interpersonal conflicts in constructive ways.
31.C.ECa: Begin to share materials and experiences and take turns.
31.C.ECb: Solve simple conflicts with peers with independence, using gestures or words.
31.C.ECc: Seek adult help when needed to resolve conflict.

Goal 32: Demonstrate decision-making skills and behaviors in personal, school, and community contexts.
Learning standard 32.A: Begin to consider ethical, safety, and societal factors in making decisions.
32.A.ECa: Participate in discussions about why rules exist.
32.A.ECb: Follow rules and make good choices about behavior.
Learning standard 32.B: Apply decision-making skills to deal responsibly with daily academic and social situations.
32.B.ECa: Participate in discussions about finding alternative solutions to problems.

*All essential grade-level standards (bold type); need-to-know essential standards (★); important-to-know essential standards (❗); nice-to-know grade-level standards (not bold).

Source for standards: Illinois Early Learning Project, 2013.

Figure 4.2: Social-emotional standards annotated to indicate preschool team-identified essential standards.

Once the team established this knowledge, team members turned their attention to answering the second critical question of a PLC—specifically, How would they approach unwrapping standards to establish a learning progression to help both the teacher and students in the learning of these important skills? The following exchange depicts this process.

> **Han (team facilitator):** It's been a busy beginning of the school year, but we need to talk about what we want our preschool students to specifically learn in regard to the social-emotional essential standards we identified and figure out how we'll determine if students are actually learning and developing essential social-emotional skills. We don't have time to unwrap all the standards at once, so what skills should we focus on today?

> **Shawna (counselor):** Based on the issues we've been having, I think we should look at the area of developing self-management skills to achieve school and life success and develop positive relations with others. I think students will better be able to relate to their peers' feelings and emotions after they can first identify their own feelings and basic emotions.

> **Han:** What does everyone else think? We identified three essential standards in that area: (1) recognize and label basic emotions, (2) express feelings that are appropriate to the situation, and (3) use materials with purpose, safety, and respect. First, let's figure out how we could describe these concepts to students and put them into student-friendly language.

> **Nisha (preschool teacher):** I've used *I can* statements with my students for years. Maybe we could try to create one? But, I think the standard about "express feelings that are appropriate to the situation" is tough to put into words the students would understand. Maybe we could use statements like, "I can use words to share my feelings"?

Han: So, what would we specifically expect a preschool student to be able to do?

Shawna: I would want students to be able to describe the things that make them mad, for example, if someone is teasing them, someone is getting in their personal space, or if they're not getting a turn during a game.

Han: OK, our students are at varying stages of being able to do that, so let's think about it like a learning progression or continuum of skills. What does a student need at the earliest stages to understand these concepts?

Jairo (preschool teacher): I think that before students can describe their own feelings and emotions, they first must recognize and label different types of feelings and basic emotions, which is one of our essential standards.

Han: That makes sense. Does everyone think that's where we should begin? What would come next in our SEL progression?

Nisha: I noticed that many of my students get frustrated and sometimes really angry about situations, but when I try to talk with them, they have a hard time even listening to what I'm saying because they have become so overwhelmed.

Shawna: Once students can identify basic emotions and feelings, we need to teach them to describe their feelings and identify what might trigger their emotions. I have many students who struggle with self-regulation. I wonder if there are specific tools or strategies we could teach them to help?

Jairo: What would the tools and strategies be that students could actually use?

Shawna: When a student gets mad or angry, a strategy that might help them cool down would be to take deep breaths, count to ten, visualize a happy place, and so on. We need to specifically teach these types of self-regulation strategies to our students.

Erin (special education teacher): Some of our students with special needs might also have specific strategies and tools to help them self-regulate. We have some students that use weighted objects or fidgets to help them with self-regulation. I wonder if other students could use tools like fidgets to help with self-regulation? At our next meeting, I can bring a few calming tools we made so that you can take a look at them, and I can explain how we might use them with students.

Shawna: I know the kindergarten teachers have spent a lot of time teaching their students how to use *I* statements to express their feelings and emotions. This would be important for us to start using this same language with our preschoolers as well.

As a result of this meeting, the preschool team took fifteen minutes to develop a SEL progression based on the skills and concepts they discussed. Figure 4.3 shows the learning progression they produced.

Skill 1	Skill 2	Skill 3	Skill 4
The student can identify feelings and basic emotions (happy, surprised, sad, angry, proud, afraid, and so on).	The student can identify his or her own feelings.	The student can use tools and strategies to help in managing his or her feelings and emotions.	The student can express his or her feelings and emotions with appropriate words or actions.

Figure 4.3: Learning progression for the self-awareness and self-management essential standard.

Using this learning progression, the team decided to create a student-friendly goal card that teachers could use with students to help them in learning these social-emotional concepts. Figure 4.4 illustrates this goal card.

Figure 4.4: Student goal card for self-awareness and self-management skills.

*Visit **go.SolutionTree.com/PLCbooks** for a free reproducible version of this figure.*

At a follow-up meeting, the school counselor provided the team with relevant SEL research, and the team members had a rich discussion about the specific concepts related to student self-awareness and self-management skills. This included the following quote from researchers Stephanie M. Jones and Jennifer Kahn (2017) on the importance of including SEL skills with academic learning:

> First, some skills act as building blocks, serving as a foundation for more complex skills that emerge later in life. For example, regulating and managing one's emotions is fundamental to resolving complex social conflicts, and identifying basic emotions in oneself is essential to being able to regulate

them effectively. This suggests that children must develop
certain basic social, emotional, and cognitive competencies
before they can master others. (p. 8)

This conversation affirmed work the team had previously done regarding the
learning progression (figure 4.3, page 81) and goal card (figure 4.4, page 81) for
this standard. In particular, the team felt the learning progression represented in
the goal card would help determine if students are actually learning the essential standard. The teachers know social-emotional skills are developmental, and
students are not all starting at the same place. The counselor shared that some
students might be able to appropriately express their feelings and emotions with
words and actions on some days but not every day. When it comes to SEL, the
learning progression is never about mastery; it is a tool to help guide teaching practices. It assists teachers in knowing what skills the student is currently
using and uses that information to support students' overall needs, as well as
help teachers determine what skills they can teach, model, coach, and praise
(O'Conner et al., 2017). Since SEL is developmental, educators teach, wait, and
watch for growth instead of pushing. The student goal cards are then useful
visual instructional tools to help students in that learning and growing process.
The team in this vignette recognizes they should not use goal cards to evaluate
or label students in any way. Instead, they become part of the SEL learning.

Unwrap Standards to Ensure Common Understanding

As we note in the chapter introduction, this chapter's vignette involves a lot of
moving parts, and you likely have questions. Throughout this section and chapter,
we show how your team can do this important work. We start by examining how
teams unwrap essential standards.

For the purposes of this book, we use the term *unwrap* to describe the process
of breaking down standards, but it's common to describe it as *unpacking* or *decon-
structing* standards. Whichever term your school uses, be consistent about your language across teams so everyone has clarity about the process and its importance.
Unwrapping standards is essential before creating assessments because it leads teams
to discover the types of questions necessary for their assessment so they can assess to
what level of proficiency students know and are able to do what teachers expect relative to each essential standard. By building shared knowledge and learning together,
teams will help more students achieve at higher levels (DuFour et al., 2016). When
teams collaborate to do this work, they engage in important professional development and they learn by doing.

In the rest of this section, we examine a process for unwrapping standards. While
teams could unwrap standards at any point in the year, it is often most useful to

designate time a week or two before beginning a new unit to unwrap the essential standards for that unit. This ensures everyone on the team has clarity and common understanding as they collaboratively build the unit and assessments for learning.

Author and consultant Larry Ainsworth (2015) breaks down the process of how teachers can unwrap essential standards. He recommends teams begin with rereading their essential standard exactly as written in the original form (in their state or CCSS document) and complete the following steps (Ainsworth, 2015).

1. Underline the teachable concepts within each standard. These are the important *nouns* and *noun phrases* telling what students should know.

2. Circle the skills, which are the *verbs* or *actions students should be able to demonstrate*.

In the vignette at the start of this chapter, the preschool teacher team took time at the beginning of the school year to determine SEL standards members agreed were the most important and of highest priority to student learning. Team members designated these *essential standards*, then devoted some of their planning time to dig in and unwrap these standards into learning targets using student-friendly *I can* statements as Ainsworth (2015) recommends.

Figure 4.5 (page 84) shows a more detailed example based on a similar document a second-grade team at Blytheville Primary School in Arkansas used as they completed the unwrapping process. In 2018, this team adapted a template from *School Improvement for All* (Kramer & Schuhl, 2017) to include prerequisite skills, key vocabulary, and proficiency levels. They included prerequisite skills to ensure that they were constantly considering what students would need to know to access new learning and to appropriately scaffold instruction. They also discovered that there were key vocabulary words embedded in standards that could be difficult to interpret. So, they included these to ensure all team members had the same definition and could explain the vocabulary correctly to all second-grade students. Finally, they included proficiency levels on what they would expect for mastery of the standard. These levels derived from conversations about the depth of knowledge (DOK) students must show evidence of when meeting each standard (Webb, 1997, 1999). Erik Francis (2017), in his blog, "What is Depth of Knowledge" explains:

> Depth of knowledge designates *how deeply* students must know, understand, and be aware of what they are learning in order to attain and explain answers, outcomes, results, and solutions. It also designates *how extensively* students are expected to transfer and use what they have learned in different academic and real world contexts.

This is important because all team members must have a common understanding of what learning looks and sounds like in their classroom instruction, assessments, and expectations for students. Ultimately the DOK level (1–4) describes the kind of *thinking* a task requires, not whether or not the task is difficult. A higher DOK level indicates more demanding thinking. As you review this form, think about what concepts and skills the preschool team in this chapter's vignette would have unwrapped in a similar way. What concepts and skills might your team unwrap from its curriculum?

Essential Standard to Unwrap

RF.1.2a: (Distinguish) long from short <u>vowel sounds</u> in spoken <u>single-syllable words</u>.

Prerequisite Skills
Understand concepts of beginning, middle, and end (initial, medial, final) to describe where the vowel sound is
Master letter-sound relationships
Be able to segment the sounds in words
Know that vowels can make more than one sound (short vowel and long vowel)

Content (Nouns) What students need to know	**Skills (Verbs)** What students need to be able to do	**DOK**
Syllables	Segment one-syllable words. (Finger spell)	1
Vowels	Identify the initial, medial, and final sounds.	1
Long and short sounds	Distinguish (label) long- and short-vowel sounds.	1–2

Key Vocabulary
Phonemes (each unit of sound in a word)
Variant vowels (different spelling patterns for long-vowel sounds)

Learning Targets
I can segment one-syllable words into sounds. (Finger spell)
I can identify the vowel sound in a syllable.
I can tell if the vowel in a word is a long-vowel sound or short-vowel sound.

Criteria for Mastery of Standard: How Might Students Demonstrate Mastery?
Students can hear and say the initial, medial, and final sounds in each syllable of a multisyllabic word. Students can tell the difference between long- and short-vowel sounds in each syllable of a spoken word.

Proficiency Levels With Standard	
4 **(Exceeds proficient)**	Student can segment the initial, medial, and final sounds in each syllable of a multisyllabic word and determine if the vowel in each syllable of a spoken word is a long- or short-vowel sound.
3 **(Proficient)**	Student can hear and say the initial, medial, and final sounds of a one-syllable spoken word and identify the vowel as a long- or short-vowel sound.
2 **(Partial)**	Student can segment a one-syllable spoken word to isolate the vowel sound but cannot accurately identify the sound as a long- or short-vowel sound.
1 **(Minimal)**	Student may or may not hear and say the initial, medial, and final sounds in a one-syllable word and is still solidifying letter sound knowledge, especially for similar sounding short vowels such as *e* and *i*.

Source for standard: NGA & CCSSO, 2010a.
Source: Adapted from Kramer & Schuhl, 2017.

Figure 4.5: Unwrapping an essential standard.

*Visit **go.SolutionTree.com/PLCbooks** for a free reproducible version of this figure*

After teams are familiar with unwrapping standards and have created a document to capture the information shown here, in future years, they may be able to make unwrapping part of the unit-planning process. To facilitate this combined process, experienced teams can use the essential standards chart shown in figure 4.6 to guide their conversations and document their work. Keep in mind the value is not about filling out a form but in the process of teams gaining clarity and commitment. Use or adapt these examples to fit the needs of your team (or teams), but be sure to discuss each component of the chart.

What We Expect Students to Learn						
Grade: _____	Subject: _____	Team Members:				
Description of Standard	Example of Rigor	Foundational Skills	Prerequisite Skills	Extension of the Standard	When to Teach	Common Assessments
What is the essential standard students must learn? Describe the standard using student-friendly vocabulary.	What does proficient student work look like? Provide an example or description.	What does a student need in the earliest stages to access this content?	What prior knowledge, skills, or vocabulary does a student need to master this standard?	What will we do when students have already learned this standard?	When will we teach this standard? How often will we spiral back to this standard?	What assessments will we use to measure student mastery?

Source: Adapted from Buffum, Mattos, & Weber, 2012.

Figure 4.6: Essential standards chart template.

You'll notice columns on the essential standards chart for foundational and prerequisite skills necessary for students to access the grade-level standard, as well as a column for how to extend for students who have already mastered it. Response to intervention (RTI) experts Austin Buffum, Mike Mattos, and Janet Malone (2018) differentiate between *foundational skills* (those building blocks from previous years' instruction) and *prerequisite skills* (more immediate skills from prior units in the same school year). It is crucial for teacher teams to have conversations that reach this level of depth on the essential standards, so each member leaves understanding how to differentiate for all the students in his or her classroom. Teams use the essential standards chart template to lead them to a deeper understanding of what they are expecting all students to learn, develop a deeper commitment to be sure every student learns it, and use the information in the chart to plan the instructional unit. Figure 4.7 (page 86) shows a filled out essential standards chart using the kindergarten mathematics standards for counting and cardinality shown in figure 3.6 (page 57).

Using the essential standards chart as a tool to study essential standards naturally leads early childhood teachers to think about each student's learning path for a

Grade: Kindergarten	Subject: Mathematics	Team members: General education kindergarten teachers, a special education teacher, an English language teacher, a technology specialist, and a mathematics specialist				
		What We Expect Students to Learn				
Description of Standard	**Example of Rigor**	**Foundational Skills**	**Prerequisite Skills**	**Extension of the Standard**	**When to Teach**	**Common Assessments**
What is the essential standard students must learn? Describe the standard using student-friendly vocabulary.	What does proficient student work look like? Provide an example or description.	What does a student need in the earliest stages to access this content?	What prior knowledge, skills, or vocabulary does a student need to master this standard?	What will we do when students have already learned this standard?	When will we teach this standard? How often will we spiral back to this standard?	What assessments will we use to measure student mastery?
K.CC.B.5: Count to answer "how many?" questions about as many as 10 things in a scattered configuration; given a number from 1–20, count out that many objects. I can count up to ten things even when they are all mixed up. I can count up to twenty things when they are all set up or arranged in a line or in a shape pattern (circle, rectangle, and so on).	Students match one number word with one and only one object being counted. Student have a system for keeping track of what they are counting when there is a group of up to ten scattered objects. Student can count larger sets up to twenty when they are all set up or arranged in a line or in a shape pattern (circle, rectangle, and so on). Students have foundational understanding in counting and quantity. (Core counting principles)	**K.CC.B.4.A:** When counting objects, say the number names in the standard order (stable order principle), pairing each object with one and only one number name and each number name with one and only one object. (1–1 correspondence principle)	**K.CC.B.4.B:** Understand that the last number name said tells the number of objects counted. (Cardinality principle) The number of objects is the same regardless of their arrangement or the order in which they were counted. (Conservation of number) **K.CC.B.4.C:** Understand that each successive number name refers to a quantity that is one larger. (Hierarchical inclusion principle)	Students can count a set of up to fifty objects using a system for organizing and keeping track of the count. **CCSS.1.NBT.A.1:** Count to 120, starting at any number less than 120. In this range, read and write numerals and represent a number of objects with a written numeral. **K.CC.A.1:** Count to one hundred by ones and tens.	Weeks 1–6 (August–September; 28 days) We will spiral back and work on these skills and concepts again in units 2–5 and unit 7. We will have students practice counting skills during transitions and in learning stations with games, tasks, and activities, and during guided and self-directed play. Interventions will be ongoing as needed and determined based on students' needs.	**Performance Assessments: Student Interviews** Ask students to count a set of seven blocks to "Tell how many" are in the scattered set. Observe if they are using 1–1 correspondence, and ensure they are not miscounting or double counting. Ask the question immediately after, "How many blocks are there?" (to see if they have cardinality). After students count the set of seven objects, rearrange them and again ask, "How many?" (to see if they can conserve numbers). Ask students to give you ten blocks (observe for all counting principles). Put sixteen counters in a line, and ask the student, "How many?" (observe for all counting principles).

Source for standards: NGA & CCSSO, 2010b.

Source: Adapted from Buffum, Mattos, & Weber, 2012.

Figure 4.7: Kindergarten team-developed mathematics essential standards chart—Counting and Cardinality.

Visit go.SolutionTree.com/PLCbooks for a free reproducible version of this figure.

particular concept or skill. As teachers engage in this process, they share their own professional experiences and knowledge of the content and pedagogy; however, they can also rely on information from a variety of resources that provide research into early childhood learning, such as the following.

- International Literacy Association (www.literacyworldwide.org)

- The Collaborative for Academic, Social, and Emotional Learning (CASEL; https://casel.org)

- National Association for the Education of Young Children (NAEYC; www.naeyc.org)

- National Council for the Social Studies (NCSS; www.socialstudies.org)

- National Council of Teachers of English (NCTE; https://ncte.org)

- National Council of Teachers of Mathematics (NCTM; www.nctm.org)

- National Science Teaching Association (NSTA; www.nsta.org)

These resources will help teams develop appropriate assessments while answering the second critical question of a PLC.

As we move into the next section on learning progressions, what's important to understand about these tools is that they are not required. Teams may opt to use something entirely different, something they tailor to their specific needs. The important thing is the *process* of doing this work together. When Mason Crest received the 2016 DuFour Award as a model of all model PLC at Work schools throughout the world, we had visitors in the hundreds coming to observe our teams, and they often wanted copies of our tools and documents. We were (and are) happy to share these, but only after these visitors observed a team engaged in the work did they understand that the tool may change next year, next month, or even next week. What is important is for the team to adapt its tools in ways that help accomplish their goals.

Develop Learning Progressions to Support Essential Standards

Because not all students will be working at the same level at the same time, the NAEYC and NCTM (2010) position statement explains how mathematics experts define learning paths for students ages three to six, and literacy specialists describe a children's development continuum in early reading and writing (International Reading Association [IRA] & NAEYC, 1998). Since students of the same age will exhibit a range of typical skills (Dodge, Heroman, Charles, & Maiorca, 2004), the goal is for teams to meet each student where he or she is and move him or her forward to proficiency with essential standards. Teams can successfully determine an ideal path for this learning by developing learning progressions for each essential standard.

Learning progressions are common in education, but not every school or district refers to them the same way. You may see learning progressions referred to as *learning paths*, *skill ladders*, or *proficiency maps*. According to researchers Carol L. Smith, Marianne Wiser, Charles W. Anderson, and Joseph Krajcik (2006), *learning progressions* are "based on research synthesis and conceptual analyses and describe successively more sophisticated ways of reasoning in a content domain that follow one another as students learn" (p. 2). Learning progressions allow teams to see the steps that students are taking toward proficiency and ensure every student is showing growth, whether they began with foundational holes in that area or were already functioning at the grade-level benchmark. In this way, teams must broaden their concept of how they determine when a student has learned an essential standard beyond using a single score on a common assessment.

Let's look at how the preschool team in this chapter's vignette approached developing a learning progression later in the school year—after team members realized they had been integrating the district's standards for oral communication and literacy in their instruction but did not have a way of measuring student growth in listening comprehension. The team had already designed assessments for most of the district's required standards, including assessments for identifying letters, sounds, and rhyme, but now they needed to develop an assessment for listening comprehension. The team was clear about how to help students make progress in these areas, but there were a few essential standards members needed to really dig into. Table 4.1 lists the essential standards they were currently integrating in their unit, with the standards the team had yet to address in boldface.

As the team reflected on these standards, they asked questions like the following.

- "Does 'Answer questions about what is read' mean simple yes-or-no questions or questions demanding higher levels of oral communication?"

- "Can students use the book to point to their answers, or do they need to answer from memory?"

The team knew it needed to develop common understanding to have common expectations for students; so, after clarifying their understanding while discussing the standard, they decided to create a learning progression to break down the skills students needed at the foundational and prerequisite levels. This enabled team members to ensure they hit a learning target for this standard during their instruction. Looking at their essential standards, the members grouped two oral-communication standards with two literacy standards that also focus on similar skills. The team decided to think about the learning progression for comprehension and create a common formative assessment using the following four essential learning standards.

Table 4.1: PreK Language Arts Essential Standards

Category	Standards
Oral Communication	**Describe actions.**
	Express ideas and needs.
	Listen and speak to peers and adults.
	Follow one-step oral directions.
	Engage in retelling and acting out familiar stories.
Literacy	Identify words that rhyme.
	Recognize first names.
	Identify twelve uppercase and nine lowercase letters.
	Identify four sounds and match to letters.
	Identify beginning consonant sound with a picture.
	Answer questions about what is read.
	Identify a character and two events of a story.

Source for standards: Adapted from Virginia Department of Education, 2013.

1. Answer questions about what is read. (Literacy)

2. Engage in retelling or acting out familiar stories. (Oral communication)

3. Identify a character and two events in a story. (Literacy)

4. Describe actions (Oral communication)

The preschool teachers, including the classroom and special education teachers, met once during each grading period of the school year with a literacy specialist and a mathematics specialist and used that time to create a common formative assessment to encompass all four essential standards. To ensure vertical alignment on comprehension that set up students for success at the next grade level, the team then asked a kindergarten teacher from the building to give feedback on the rigor the team expected. That teacher's input was especially valuable in helping the preschool team think about what extension would look like for students who could already answer questions about what they read.

During the initial discussion, the mathematics specialist noticed the connection between the literacy standard that prepared students to show comprehension through retelling—"Identify a character and two events of a story" (Virginia Department of Education, 2013)—and one of the team's identified mathematics standards— investigating the passage of time and sequencing and the use of time vocabulary (that is, *morning*, *noon*, and *night*). The team decided by including this mathematics standard in the common formative assessment, members would not only be assessing oral-communication and literacy skills but also mathematics skills. This integrated approach eliminated the need to create a separate mathematics assessment and saved teachers instructional time.

In reflecting on this example, think back to the beginning of the chapter, when we asked if your team has taken time to determine essential SEL standards and how members might incorporate these standards into academic units. Whether combining standards from more than one academic content area or combining academic standards with SEL standards, it's beneficial to integrate standards whenever possible if it can minimize the number of different assessments and maximize instructional time.

To develop a learning progression, the preschool team used its essential standards chart and thought about the foundational and prerequisite skills students need for retelling events of a story. Team members broke down their essential standards chart into the knowledge students need about *retelling or sequencing* and *story or books*, and included both in the learning progression in figure 4.8.

Foundational	Prerequisite	Grade-Level Benchmark	Extension
Retell real-life events: "First I _____, then I _____." When the teacher asks a simple question during read-aloud, the student responds on topic about the book.	The student can sequence events such as the life cycle of a butterfly or seasons in science. The student understands stories have a *who* (character) and *what* (events and actions).	The student can retell two events of a familiar story using characters, actions, and time vocabulary (*morning*, *next*, and *then*).	The student can retell main events from the beginning, middle, and end of a new story using specific vocabulary from text.

Figure 4.8: Preschool comprehension learning progression.

Once the team had its learning progression, members could then develop a quick-and-easy common formative assessment. The assessment asked students questions after a read-aloud, and teachers used students' responses to determine where each student currently was on the learning progression. This allowed the teachers to appropriately differentiate instruction for each student in order to move all students forward.

Remember, the most important aspect of the processes in this section is *educators must value team collaboration and ensure collective understanding regrding every procedure or end product.* The method teams use to get there is immaterial, as long as it is effective and efficient. For example, an alternative way of approaching this work would be for the preschool team to start with samples of student work, sort the work into groups (students doing similar work), and then come up with descriptors for each group to form a learning progression.

In this case, after watching students build a tower with blocks or paint a picture, a teacher could ask students to tell him or her what they did first, next, and after that. The teacher would record their responses to see where each student is with the skill of sequencing. Some students might not respond on topic at all, some might only tell the last thing they did, others might describe multiple actions they performed (not necessarily in order), and others might give a blow-by-blow description. When teachers start by thinking about the actual students in front of them, it allows them to more easily group students by need and determine what to teach each group to move students to the next step on a learning progression. If you line up the steps on the progression, you'll form a "ladder" that describes how the learners in your class move up as they increase their skill on an essential standard. Teams can then take these learning progressions and put them into student-friendly language using *I can* statements, making them powerful tools to help students keep track of their own learning by setting their own goals (see the next section).

To be clear, as teams engage in the process of determining where students are along a learning progression, they are not labeling students, but rather, labeling *each student's skill level at a moment in time*. Teachers must maintain the mindset that no matter a student's current skill level, he or she is fully capable of learning at high levels. It is the teachers' job and the work of the whole team to support and help all students reach grade-level mastery.

Tips for **Administrators**	*Tips for* **Coaches**	*Tips for* **Teachers**
In concert with guiding coalition and leadership teams, monitor products that come from the work of teacher teams. The essential standards charts and unwrapping documents are two products that administrators should expect to come from the work of the teams' collaborative efforts.	Support individual teachers and teams in the process of looking at standards through a vertical lens. Know what current early childhood research says about how standards correlate within each grade level and how the standards vertically align with the grade levels before and after them.	After the team has engaged in the unwrapping process and had rich discussions about the unit's essential standards, revisit the standards and associated documents and reflect on them again as a team. This ensures instruction and assessment for the unit stay true to the team's understandings developed when unwrapping the essential standards for the unit.
In concert with guiding coalition and leadership team, come up with a timeline for teacher teams to complete team products.	Share the work of one team with that of the grade level above and below them to help them think through prerequisite skills and extensions at each end of the learning progression. For example, when the first-grade team is unwrapping a standard, be prepared to show them the kindergarten and second-grade teams' unwrapping document on their similar standard.	Remember, by unwrapping standards at the start of a new unit, teams may identify essential standards connected to multiple units of study.
Be tight about the unwrapping process and the deep discussions that the essential standards chart provides. This is nondiscretionary, or is what is called a *tight* aspect of the work. Teachers cannot opt out of this critical process. This work is what ensures the team has a common understanding and leads to creating a guaranteed and viable curriculum.		

Set Student Goals for Learning

Consider this question: If it is vital for teachers to unwrap essential standards and know the learning targets, isn't it just as important for students to also know these same learning targets? Once a team knows what foundational, prerequisite, and grade-level skills students need to know and be able to do, members have the following choices.

- Work themselves into the ground trying to push students to achieve those goals.

- Make students partners in the process by ensuring they also know and understand the goals they must meet.

Rebecca DuFour often shared a favorite quote from assessment expert Rick Stiggins, "Students can hit any target that they can see and that holds still for them" (Stiggins et al., 2004, p. 57). If teachers don't explicitly share the goals with students, how do students know what they are aiming for, and why should they bother engaging in lessons? According to Stiggins and colleagues (2004), teachers should transform the learning targets into student-friendly *I can* statements, like those you've seen throughout this book. This process not only helps teacher teams come to a common understanding about what students need to actually know and do to demonstrate proficiency on standards but also clarifies for students what they are trying to accomplish in terms they understand. *I can* statements are also a great resource for parents to get clarity on what teachers expect of their children (DuFour et al., 2016). Most important, *I can* statements empower learners as central partners in their own learning. In fourteen different studies, Robert J. Marzano (2010), cofounder and chief academic officer of Marzano Resources in Denver, Colorado, finds the practice of students tracking their own progress associates with an average 32 percentile-point gain in their achievement.

It is important that *I can* statements are authentic to students who are engaging in the learning. If a team has followed the unwrapping process and has used the essential standards chart to deepen their understanding of the essential standard from the first part of this chapter, they are ideally prepared to turn their learning targets and learning progressions into effective *I can* statements. However, there is limited impact in teachers just posting words or visuals on the board or on classroom walls, where the statements effectively end up becoming wallpaper with limited connection to daily learning. One way to avoid this pitfall is to orally use the *I can* statements and integrate them into the daily work of students. For example, when teachers are explaining a task or a game, they can orally state the *I can* statement with picture supports, which can then serve as a label on the task or game students are engaging in.

Once teachers use *I can* statements to ensure students know what teachers expect of them, team members face the following questions.

- How do the students and teachers monitor students' progress?

- How can teachers make this progress monitoring manageable for both themselves and for their students, particularly students in preK and kindergarten, who are not yet reading or may not be independent enough to manage a tool, such as a data notebook (what upper grades often use)?

An effective way to answer these questions is to use goal cards as an avenue for helping students get to know their learning targets and keep track of their own learning. Goal cards, like those in figure 4.9, figure 4.10 (page 94), and figure 4.11 (page 94), can help any student track his or her progress in a meaningful way. Effective goals cards for early childhood learners typically utilize picture support to make them meaningful.

Figure 4.9: Student goal card with stand-alone goals.

*Visit **go.SolutionTree.com/PLCbooks** for a free reproducible version of this figure*

Figure 4.10: Student goal card for mathematics progression.

Visit go.SolutionTree.com/PLCbooks for a free reproducible version of this figure

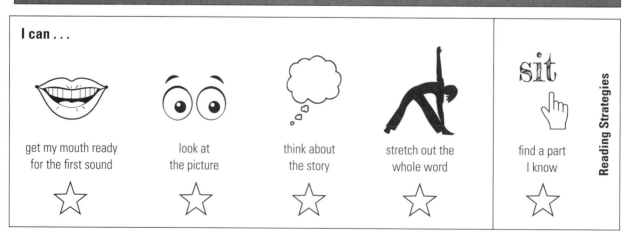

Figure 4.11: Student goal cards for reading progression.

Visit go.SolutionTree.com/PLCbooks for a free reproducible version of this figure

As students master their goals, they can (in conference with their teacher) check off or hole punch the stars on the goal cards. This allows students to know their current learning goals and celebrate what they have already learned, which sets a platform for a *positive growth mindset* (Dweck, 2006). This refers to a mindset that learning ability is not fixed and that all students can grow as learners.

When turning learning progressions into goal cards, keep in mind that learning may vary from one content area or standard to another, so the format of goal cards should also vary. In our experience, as some teams at Mason Crest got deeper into goal setting with students, team members realized that measuring progress toward goals in social-emotional skills and literacy could often be different than in mathematics. For example, in mathematics, students can become completely proficient on a goal (like *counting numbers one to five*) and never practice that skill again as they move on to more complex numbers. Contrast this with literacy learning, in which students might master a goal (like *describe characters with detail*) using a simple six-page book, but then they need to continually practice and improve their skill as the length and complexity of the texts increase.

While it may be tempting to download or pay for a resource of premade goal cards, it's a positive experience for teams to go through the productive struggle it takes to collectively figure out how to present goal cards to students in ways that motivate them, match their teaching language, and make the targets explicit. The work some Mason Crest teams put into developing goal cards resulted in a variety of different formats, including the one in figure 4.12 (page 96). This goal card allowed teachers to monitor student *progress* (with tally marks in the boxes) rather than *mastery* (by punching a star under each reading strategy they observed). The team determined this better fit student's needs for this particular goal, but as you'll start to see from the variety of goal cards shown in the chapter, there is no one correct or best template to use. The best approach is for the team to ensure they have a deep understanding of the learning progression in order to make their first goal card and then be willing to change and adapt it over time as team members learn how students respond to using the goal card.

Figure 4.13 (page 96) presents another way teams can adapt goal cards to meet their individual needs. This student goal card is for counting twenty objects, and it connects to the kindergarten team-developed mathematics essential standards chart illustrated in figure 4.7 (page 86). The teachers thought up this design when some team members began to use the team-created common formative assessment for counting and noticed many students were only able to count a set of five or ten objects. After making a learning progression, the team decided it was important to set smaller scaffolded goals that would help students progress to counting a set of twenty objects, which is the grade-level expectation. Notice how figure 4.13 has two sections. The first section includes skills and concepts taught in kindergarten, while the second section includes skills and concepts taught at the first-grade level.

I can . . .

get my mouth
ready for the
first sound

look at
the picture

think about
the story

say the whole
word slowly

find a part
I know

Reading Strategies

Figure 4.12: Revised student goal card for reading with room to add tally marks when the teacher observes the behavior.

*Visit **go.SolutionTree.com/PLCbooks** for a free reproducible version of this figure*

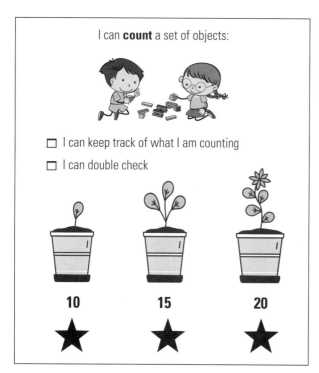

Figure 4.13: Differentiated student goal cards for mathematics.

*Visit **go.SolutionTree.com/PLCbooks** for a free reproducible version of this figure.*

Teachers differentiated the full series of team-developed goal cards for each learner, resulting in multiple entry points. At Mason Crest, each kindergarten student got a goal card to use throughout the unit. When the teacher observed a student meeting a goal, the teacher checked off that goal on the student's card. The teacher also differentiated how students interacted with the cards. Teacher A told students they could monitor their own learning, and, when they were able to reach a goal (like counting a set of fifteen objects), they could come and show her. Teacher B allowed students to get stickers from the class sticker bin on the back table and place a sticker on the individual goals each student met on his or her goal card. Teacher C shared that when a student in her class finally reaches counting a set of twenty on his or her goal card, she will have the whole class stand up and give a little cheer for that student. Teacher D told students when they complete a goal card, she would send the card home, so parents or guardians could not only see the content their child has been learning but also how their child was setting and accomplishing goals for him- or herself.

You might thinking, *Do goal cards lead to issues with competition between students? What about those students who struggle with just counting a smaller set of objects?* Keep in mind, one of the three big ideas of a school that functions as a PLC is creating a collaborative culture, and that doesn't just mean among the staff. Community building plays an important role in the classroom, so all students and adults should develop the mindset that all students can and will learn and that every student will reach grade-level goals. Yes, some students may need a scaffolded goal card to include smaller numbers, but the goal card most certainly will include not just that smaller goal but all the smaller goals that lead up to the grade-level benchmark. A team that can do this, as well as have goal cards for students working beyond grade-level expectations, is showing true differentiation at its finest and cultivating a classroom community that encourages students to support and celebrate each other's *progress* in learning instead of competing for top *proficiency* scores. Getting to the level of differentiation in the last example is a process; it doesn't happen immediately.

In reading this section, you may being saying to yourself, *This sounds great, and our team would love to do it, but where would we start, and how would we—as a school or team—create goal cards?* We again want to emphasize that it's a process, and the examples derived from teacher work at Mason Crest show that this process can be messy. Teams should see *messy* as a powerful part of the process that leads to deep understanding and commitment to goal setting. You still may be saying to yourself, *OK, we are fine with messy, but we still don't know how and where to begin in creating goal cards.* In *Time for Change*, best-selling authors Anthony Muhammad and Luis Cruz (2019) share that one of the reasons people resist change is because they don't know how to implement the change being asked of them. They have not been given the proper time, training, tools, or support to move forward with the change. In essence, they have a rational reason to resist because of an unmet need. In no way do we want your needs or the needs of your team to be unmet, so we created a five-step template for collaboratively developing team goal cards. See figure 4.14 (page 98) and figure 4.15 (page 99) for two examples of using this template. In each of these templates, you will notice five sections, each with corresponding questions that lead from start to finish.

Learning standards: What are the standards we are using to create the student goal card?

We will use the following SEL standards.

- Students will recognize and label basic emotions.
- Students will express feelings that are appropriate to the situation.

Learning targets: What are the specific learning targets, and what are their content-focus and grade-level designations?

- **SEL (PreK):** Students identify basic feelings and emotions (happy, surprised, sad, angry, proud, afraid, and so on).
- **SEL (PreK):** Students identify their own feelings and emotions.
- **SEL (PreK):** Students use tools and strategies to manage their feelings and emotions.
- **SEL (PreK):** Students express their feelings and emotions with words or actions.

Learning progression: How can we arrange learning targets in a progression? What performance descriptors will we use? Do students have to demonstrate every skill to show proficiency?

Skill 1	Skill 2	Skill 3	Skill 4
The student can identify feelings and basic emotions (happy, surprised, sad, angry, proud, afraid, and so on).	The student can identify his or her own feelings.	The student can use tools and strategies to manage his or her feelings and emotions.	The student can express his or her feelings and emotions with appropriate words or actions.

Student goal card: How can we use the learning progression to develop a goal card with student-friendly language (*I can* statements) and appropriate grade-level visuals?

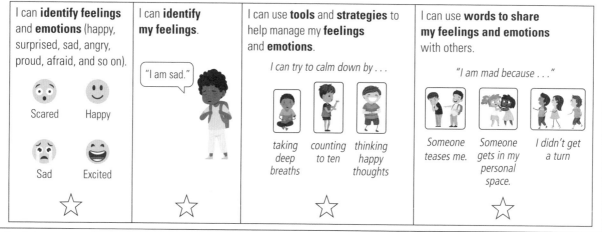

Students' goal-setting system and plan: When and how will teachers specifically use and communicate goal cards with students? How will teachers store goal cards, ensuring easy access for both students and teachers?

Teachers will place a large goal card on the whiteboard and use it during whole-group learning (morning meeting) and refer to it during daily instruction. Individual goals (such as *I can identify feelings and emotions*) will be displayed on smaller goal cards and visible to students at small-group teacher and student-guided learning stations and during play.

Figure 4.14: Collaborative team goal-card template—Social-emotional.

*Visit **go.SolutionTree.com/PLCbooks** for a free reproducible version of this figure.*

Learning standards: What are the standards we are using to create the student goal card?

We will use three standards, one for second grade (grade level), one for first grade, and one for third grade.

- **W.1.1:** Write opinion pieces in which they introduce the topic or name the book they are writing about, state an opinion, supply a reason for the opinion, and provide some sense of closure.
- **W.2.1:** Write opinion pieces in which they introduce the topic or book they are writing about, state an opinion, supply reasons that support the opinion, use linking words (e.g., because, and, also) to connect opinion and reasons, and provide a concluding statement or section.
- **W.3.1:** Write opinion pieces on topics or texts, supporting a point of view with reasons.

Learning targets: What are the specific learning targets, and what are their content-focus and grade-level designations?

We will use the following second-grade writing targets.

- Introduce the topic and state an opinion about it.
- Give reasons to support the opinion.
- Use linking words to connect reasons to opinion.
- Provide a concluding sentence that restates the opinion.

Learning progression: How can we arrange learning targets in a progression? What performance descriptors will we use? Do students have to demonstrate every skill to show proficiency?

Foundational	Prerequisite	Grade-Level Benchmark	Extension
The student states an opinion.	The student states an opinion and gives one reason to support it.	The student states an opinion and uses linking words to connect more than one reason to support it. The student begins with an introduction and ends with a conclusion.	The student introduces the topic and develops his or her point of view by linking several reasons to support his or her opinion. The student's conclusions articulate a point of view.

Student goal card: How can we use the learning progression to develop a goal card with student-friendly language (*I can* statements) and appropriate grade-level visuals?

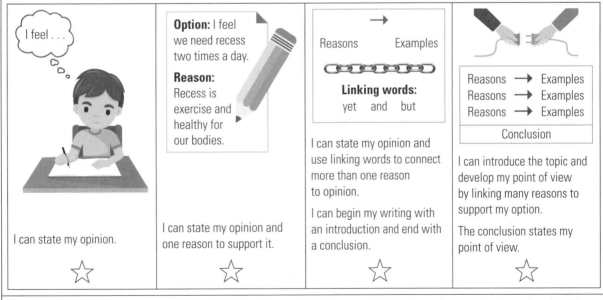

Students' goal-setting system and plan: When and how will teachers specifically use and communicate goal cards with students? How will teachers store goal cards, ensuring easy access for both students and teachers?

Students will keep their goal cards in their writing folders. During teacher and peer conferencing, they will evaluate their writing. When they meet each goal, they get to punch a start into that goal on their goal card.

Source for standards: NGA & CCSSO, 2010a.

Figure 4.15: Collaborative team goal-card template—Literacy.

*Visit **go.SolutionTree.com/PLCbooks** for a free reproducible version of this figure.*

At this point, you may be beginning to see how the team tasks we describe in chapter 3 (page 47) all connect and build on one another. The learning that occurs through each process assists teams in creating effective unit plans with common assessments (which we will talk about in chapter 5, page 109). Figure 4.16 illustrates this. In the next section, we cover how to use pacing guides and other tools to develop a unit plan.

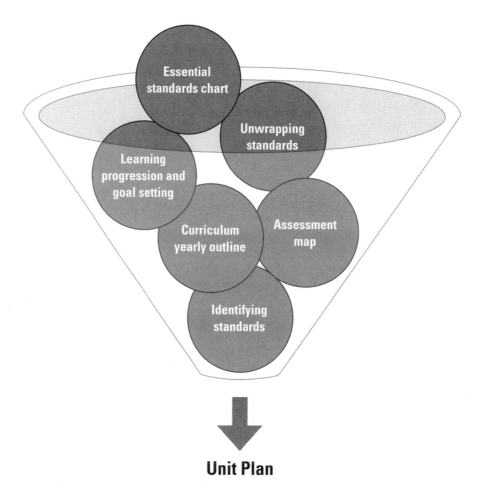

Unit Plan

Figure 4.16: Progressing toward a unit plan.

Pacing Guides and Unit-Planning Tools

Sometimes districts go beyond providing teachers with just a suggested timeline for when to teach particular standards in each of the developmental domains and instead give teachers a more-in-depth tool to plan a unit of study. This teacher tool may or may not include the key elements needed for developing an effective unit of study. Whether teams receive a minimal or more in-depth tool from their district, it is the job of the team to turn that teacher tool into a team tool. If teams do not receive any resources to assist them in the planning of a unit, they can use as a starting point their year-long curriculum outline, which includes the standards in each unit and the instructional timeline.

What do teams need to do to plan an effective unit of study? During the process of identifying standards, teams determine what standards are essential to student learning. When they work through the essential standards chart together, they learn what students need to know at the grade level and what skills and concepts come prior and come next. They identify important vocabulary and think about how to assess essential standards. When this work is complete, it is important to take all that information and put it into one team resource that all team members can easily refer to throughout the unit and use during the daily lesson-planning process. It is also important for teams to have conversations about essential understandings and big conceptual ideas they want students to learn within the unit. This helps the team decide the potential teaching practices, strategies, and tools to use with students. This ripple effect will then guide the team in generating or choosing highly effective learning resources (tasks, activities, games, and so on) needed to support the learning of skills and concepts. Figure 4.17 shows an example of a kindergarten team's district-provided unit-planning tool. The team enhanced this tool by working together to fill out the chart in figure 4.18 (page 103). We recommend creating electronic unit-planning tools where various instructional resources or lessons could possibly be linked electronically to the document.

Unit 1: Building Routines and Counting
Weeks 1–6 (August–September, 28 days)

Instructional considerations when teaching this unit of study: It is important for our earliest learners to engage in a variety of counting experiences where they can think flexibly about numbers and their relationships in order to develop important counting principles.

Counting principles:

- **1-to-1 correspondence:** Match only one counting word with only one object when counting.

- **Stable-order principle:** There is a set of words used when counting, and the word order does not change.

- **Cardinality:** When counting a set of objects, the last word said tells how many are in the set.

- **Conservation:** The number of objects doesn't change no matter how they are arranged, moved, or hidden.

- **Hierarchical inclusion:** Know that all numbers proceeding a number are included in the value of the next number.

These concepts should be developed with the use of concrete items (blocks, buttons, stickers, and other various collections) and with tools, such as number tracks and hundreds boards. Students should explore counting in a variety of contexts, including real-life situations and objects. Students should participate in problem solving and engaging activities that require them to focus on number relationships and practice these number and counting skills. They should also receive opportunities to practice number and counting concepts connected to other cross-curricular areas. Subitizing (learning small quantities by instant recognition without counting) is a foundational skill that connects with a variety of other counting and computation concepts, therefore, teachers need to plan specific activities and use specific tools (dice, five and ten frames, fingers, and so on) to foster this skill.

Figure 4.17: District-provided pacing guide for Kindergarten mathematics—Unit 1.   continued →

Kindergarten Mathematics Grade-Level Standards*	Correlated Mathematics Standards

Know number names and the count sequence:
 	
 K.CC.A.1: Count to 100 by ones
 	
 K.CC.A.2: Count forward beginning from a given number within the known sequence (instead of having to begin at 1).
 	
! K.CC.A.3: Write numbers from 0 to 20. Represent a number of objects with a written numeral 0–20 (with 0 representing a count of no objects).
 	
Count to tell the number of objects:
 	
 K.CC.B.4: Understand the relationship between numbers and quantities; connect counting to cardinality.
 	
   + **K.CC.B.4.A:** When counting objects, say the number names in the standard order, pairing each object with one and only one number name and each number name with one and only one object.
 	
   + **K.CC.B.4.B:** Understand that the last number name said tells the number of objects counted. The number of objects is the same regardless of their arrangement or the order in which they were counted.
 	
   + **K.CC.B.4.C:** Understand that each successive number name refers to a quantity that is one larger.
 	
 K.CC.B.5: Count to answer "how many?" questions about as many as 20 things arranged in a line, a rectangular array, or a circle, or as many as 10 things in a scattered configuration; given a number from 1–20, count out that many objects.
 	
Compare numbers:
 	
 K.CC.C.6: Identify whether the number of objects in one group is greater than, less than, or equal to the number of objects in another group, e.g., by using matching and counting strategies.
 	
K.CC.C.7: Compare two numbers between 1 and 10 presented as written numerals
	PreK
	
	Know number names and the count sequence:
	
	   • Pk.A.1: Rote Count to 20
	
	Count to tell the number of objects:
	
	   • Pk.B.2: Count a collection of up to ten objects using one-to-one correspondence.
	
	   • Pk.B.2: Count to answer "how many?" questions about as many as 10 objects.
	
	Compare numbers:
	
	   • Pk.C.1: Create sets of objects with same and different amounts
	
	First Grade
	
	Extend the counting sequence:
	
	   • CCSS.1.NBT.A.1: Count to 120, starting at any number less than 120. In this range, read and write numerals and represent a number of objects with a written numeral.
	
	Compare two-digit numbers with symbols:
	
	   • CCSS.1.NBT.B.3: Compare two two-digit numbers based on meanings of the tens and ones digits, recording the results of comparisons with the symbols >, =, and <.

*All essential grade-level standards (bold type); need-to-know essential standards (★); important-to-know essential standards (!); nice-to-know grade-level standards (not bold).

Source for standards: NGA & CCSSO, 2010b.

As mentioned earlier, there is no one right way to do this important work. To learn more about other unit-planning processes and tools, refer to the *Mathematics Unit Planning in a PLC at Work, Grades PreK–2* (Schuhl et al., 2021) and *School Improvement for All* (Kramer & Schuhl, 2017). In chapter 7 (page 179) we devote more time to discuss how to use this unit guide to plan meaningful daily lessons. For now, let's take a moment to think back about the work of the kindergarten team in this chapter and chapter 3 (page 47).

Team Unit Pacing Guide

Content area: Mathematics

Unit: 1

Dates and Grade-Level Standards	Grade-Level Instructional Strategies and Tools	Grade-Level Instructional Resources	Supports, Scaffolds, and Extensions	Grade-Level Formative Assessments	Integrated Curriculum
What are the instructional dates? What standards will students be learning? In what order will they be taught?	What instructional strategies, practices, and tools will we use with students?	What learning activities (tasks, games, projects, and so on) will students be using to learn?	What differentiation practices will we put in place for students who need their learning supported or extended?	What formative assessments (observations, interviews performance tasks, exit tickets, and so on) will we use with students?	What content areas (SEL, social studies, science, mathematics, literacy, and so on) can we integrate?
Weeks 1–3 Know number names and the count sequence: ★ **K.CC.A.1: Count to 100 by ones** ★ **K.CC.A.2: Count forward beginning from a given number within the known sequence (instead of having to begin at 1).** **!** **K.CC.A.3: Write numbers from 0 to 20. Represent a number of objects with a written numeral 0–20 (with 0 representing a count of no objects).**	Counting strategies: Musical instruments with counting to teach one-to-one concepts (hit drum and place object in the jar) Materials: Numeral cards, number tracks and hundreds charts, ten and twenty frames when counting concrete collections (farm animals, dinosaurs, cars, blocks, and so on), and computers or tablets Subitizing: Finger images, dice, five and ten frames, and assorted subitizing pattern cards	Literature books (focus on the numbers 1–20): • *How Many Snails* by Paul Giganti Jr. (1988) • *Chicka Chicka 1, 2, 3,* by Bill Martin and Michael Sampson (2004) Water and sand table-counting discovery station (finding hidden objects and counting them) Counting bags activity Matching number cards with counting sets game Collect, count, and build Calendar counting (morning meeting) Kinesthetic counting (transitions)	**Scaffolds and Supports** Literature books (focus on the numbers 1–10): • *Ten Black Dots* by Donald Crews (2010) • *The Very Hungry Caterpillar* by Eric Carle (1987) • *Anno's Counting Book* by Anno Mitsumasa (1986) Materials: • Number tracks and charts with numbers up to five and ten • Writing tablet app	**Performance Assessments** Listen to students rote count aloud up to one hundred by ones. Ask students to start at different numbers. ("Start counting at six, and I will tell you when to stop.") Ask students to do the following. 1. Count a set of eight objects to see if they are using counting principles. (One-to-one correspondence.) 2. Immediately after, ask, "How many blocks are there?" (Cardinality)	**Science Standards** S.A.5: Observe, investigate, and classify things in nature (include objects from nature in counting collections). **Visual Art Standards** V.Arts.C.1: Use motor skills (cutting, molding, tearing, and so on) to create art. Have students use playdough and clay to create their own counting sets, and use numerals to represent the quantity in their sets. Have students create pictures (drawing or painting) using specific quantities or have them count items in famous paintings.

continued →

Figure 4.18: Team Unit-Planning Tool—Kindergarten mathematics, unit 1.

*Visit **go.SolutionTree.com/PLCbooks** for a free reproducible version of this figure.*

Dates and Grade-Level Standards	Grade-Level Instructional Strategies and Tools	Grade-Level Instructional Resources	Supports, Scaffolds, and Extensions	Grade-Level Formative Assessments	Integrated Curriculum
Count to tell the number of objects: **K.CC.B.4:** ★ **Understand the relationship between numbers and quantities; connect counting to cardinality.** **K.CC.B.5: Count to answer "how many?" questions about as many as 20 things arranged in a line, a rectangular array, or a circle, or as many as 10 things in a scattered configuration; given a number from 1–20, count out that many objects.**		Jack Hartmann counting videos Computer- or tablet-based counting apps Subitizing: • Quick images • Kinesthetic subitizing activity and associated computer or tablet computer activities	**Extensions** Literature book: *Let's Count to 100* by Masayuki Sebe (2011) Materials: • Numeral cards, number tracks, and charts with numbers up to 120 (students can use hundreds charts when counting larger sets or collections up to 50) • Tablet apps for counting and writing larger numbers	3. After students count the set of eight objects, rearrange them and again ask, "How many?" (Conservation) **Observations** Observe students counting sets at learning stations and during play. (Look for development of counting principles.) **Goal Cards** Issue student goal card focused on standard K.CC.B.5.	**Social-Emotional Standards** **!** **31.B.ECb: Engage in cooperative group play.** ★ **31.A.Ecc: Use socially appropriate behavior with peers and adults, such as helping, sharing, and taking turns.**

Weeks 4–6		Scaffolds and Supports	Performance Assessments (Tasks)	Literacy Standards
Know number names and the count sequence: **! K.CC.A.3: Write numbers from 0 to 20. Represent a number of objects with a written numeral 0–20 (with 0 representing a count of no objects).** Compare numbers: **★ K.CC.C.6: Identify whether the number of objects in one group is greater than, less than, or equal to the number of objects in another group, e.g., by using matching and counting strategies.** • *K.CC.C.7: Compare two numbers between 1 and 10 presented as written numerals* **Note:** Continue instruction of previously taught concepts (KCA.1, K.CC.A.2, KCC.A.3, K.CC.B.4, and KCC.B.5) and integrate them with writing numbers and comparing standards.	Missing number tracks or blank number tracks and missing number or blank hundreds charts Concrete counting collections Ten and twenty frames Computers or tablets Student-counting book activity Roll, count, and write activity Writing number strips Counting and comparing collections Compare card game; compare dice game	Tracing-numerals activities Mats or large circles as place holders when counting and comparing sets. Tablet number-tracing app **Extensions** Write numbers beyond 20 up to 120 (board puzzles up to 120, missing-number charts up to 120). Use writing number strips starting and stopping at different numbers up to 120. Count and compare larger collections (up to 120 or more); introduce symbols (less than, equals, greater than).	Provide a writing numbers task (record missing numbers on a one to twenty number track). Ask students to count a set of nine objects and record their count using written numerals. **Observation (During Play or as a Task)** Have students count two collections and compare the sets. Student can use written numbers to record amounts, use number cards to represent quantities, or use vocabulary words (*more, less, same,* or *equal*) when comparing.	RF.K.1.D: Recognize and name all upper- and lowercase letters of the alphabet. Have students sort upper- and lowercase letters from a set and count and compare using visual numerals or by writing numerals. Or, have students sort numbers from letters, count and record the quantities in each group, and compare their results.

Source for standards: NGA & CCSSO, 2010b.

*Visit **go.SolutionTree.com/PLCbooks** for a free reproducible version of this figure.*

At the beginning of the school year, the team took time to identify the essential mathematics standards (see figure 3.6 page 57). Next, they created a curriculum outline for the entire year (see figure 3.7 page 61). After that, the team unwrapped the essential mathematics standards and used the essential standards chart (figure 4.7, page 86) that specifically related to their unit of study. Then, the team created a counting learning progression (figure 4.8, page 90) and used it to create a variety of student goal cards, which all team members committed to using with their students throughout the school year. The kindergarten team's next step is to develop a plan for assessing the counting standards in unit 1, which you will learn about in the next chapter. Eventually, the team uses use the accumulated knowledge gained through all of these processes to create an effective unit of study on counting and cardinality (as illustrated in figure 4.18, page 103). Table 4.1 shows a basic timeline for when this kindergarten team found time to do all of this important work utilizing teacher workdays at the start of the school year (before students arrived) and through their team meeting time during the school year.

Table 4.1: Kindergarten Team Tasks Timeline

When	What	See
Teacher workdays before school starts in August	Identified essential standards in mathematics and language arts at the kindergarten level Met with vertical teams for conversations about the essential standards in both mathematics and language arts taught in preK and first grade	See Identification of Essential Standards (page 54) and figure 3.6 (page 57)
	Created year-long curriculum outline	See Year-Long Curriculum Outlines (page 59) and figure 3.7 (page 61)
Teacher workdays before school starts in August	Unwrapped as a team grade-level standards for counting; used the essential standards chart to deepen collective understanding of the standard	See Unwrap Standards to Ensure Common Understanding (page 82) and figure 4.17 (page 101)
	Created a learning progression for counting	See Develop Learning Progressions to Support Essential Standards (page 86)
	Drafted a student goal card for counting	See Set Student Goals for Learning (page 92) and figure 4.13 (page 96)
Team meeting during week 1 (September)	Finalized student goal card for counting	See Set Student Goals for Learning (page 92), Vignette: A Kindergarten Team Assesses Mathematics Learning, and figure 4.13 (page 96)
	Created common formative assessments and data-collection tool for counting	See chapter 5 (page 109), figure 4.17 (page 101), and figure 4.18 (page 103)
Team meeting during week 2 (September)	Developed a unit-pacing guide for counting	See Pacing Guides and Unit-Planning Tools (page 98)

Tips for **Administrators**	*Tips for* **Coaches**	*Tips for* **Teachers**
Build shared knowledge by sharing research, articles, and evidence as to why student goal setting is so important to the mission of high levels of learning for all.	Support teachers in building pedagogy, and provide teams with relevant research on best instructional practices.	Start off trying goal setting in just one subject area, and build a working system for your team and your students.
Set the expectation that student goal setting is tight and nondiscretionary.	Provide teams with resources to help them build their content knowledge around the progression of learning in different content areas, including social-emotional development.	Think about how your team will organize its work. Consider using electronic resources, which provide access to all team members and can be added to from week to week or even year to year.
Continue to clarify key terms to ensure consistent understanding in order to move forward as one.		

Guiding Questions

Use the following guiding questions to learn together and build shared knowledge.

- If your early childhood team is new to having deep discussion about and unwrapping essential standards, what content area will the team attempt first: literacy, mathematics, or social-emotional and behavior standards?

- If a team member misses a team meeting, how will you ensure that teacher deeply understand the learning targets, learning progression, or other knowledge from the meeting?

- Once you create goal cards that align with a learning progression, how will you explain to students the *I can* statements, and how will you use the goal cards?

- How can you utilize your team's *I can* statements to communicate with parents?

- Where will your early childhood team keep the curriculum tools and artifacts it creates so everyone has access and can continually reference, adapt, and modify resources?

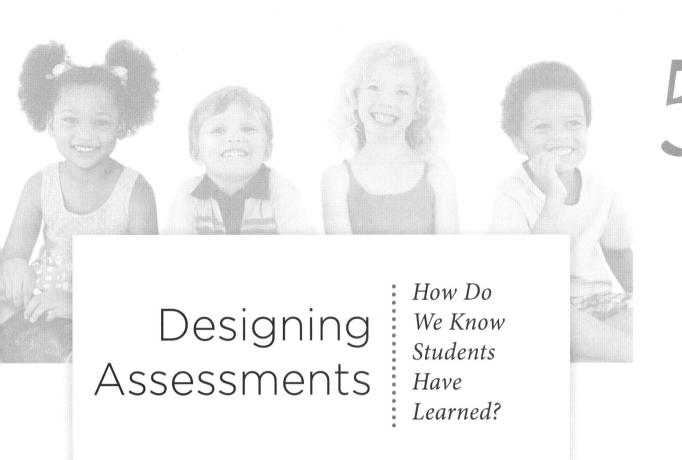

Designing Assessments

How Do We Know Students Have Learned?

The early 21st century has been an era of high-stakes assessment in education, and those teaching during this time have all heard colleagues at every level lament, "All I ever do is assess, and I never have time to teach!" Early childhood educators have the additional concern that some of the types of assessments their province, state, or district ask them to do are not developmentally appropriate for preK–2 learners and may give false information about what students actually know and are able to do. For example, through play, a preschooler shows he can actually maintain conservation of number, but the anxiety of performing on demand in a one-to-one assessment situation with the teacher causes him to shut down. A kindergarten student demonstrates he can isolate the beginning sound of a word, but, when taking the standardized assessment on the computer, he just clicks on the first box that pops up each time because it's fun. A proficient second-grade reader can orally summarize a story to show comprehension, but when the teacher asks her to write a summary of what she read, the physical task of writing becomes too laborious, so she leaves out major events and supporting details. For these reasons and more, assessments may need to look different in the preK–2 years than what teachers are familiar with using in later grade levels.

This is, in part, why the work of creating common formative assessments for essential standards comes after teams identify and unwrap essential stndards and create learning progressions. See figure 5.1.

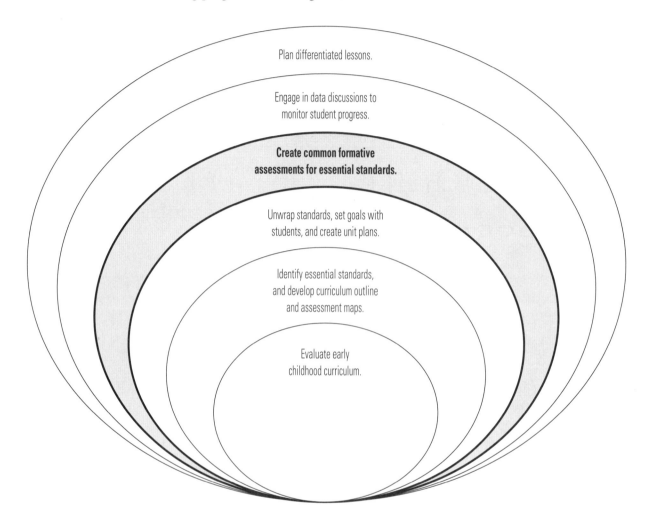

Figure 5.1: The work of early childhood teams in a PLC—Creating assessments.

The important thing to remember is teams don't just create common formative assessments to come up with a score. Answering the second critical question of a PLC, How do we know if students have learned it? (DuFour et al., 2016), means teams need appropriate ways to gather useful data that allow them to know if each student has indeed learned the essential curriculum. Implementing common formative assessments is the linchpin of the PLC process because they do two important things.

- They allow teams to know which students did or did not master the standard in order to determine appropriate interventions and extensions based on that data (the third and fourth critical questions).

- They are a critical tool for teachers to compare results, not to sort and select, rank, evaluate or identify the best teacher. In other words, they highlight which teachers demonstrated effective practices based on the results of the assessments. This is a great opportunity for team members to learn from and with each other based on the evidence of irrefutable results. If no teacher on the team showed effective practices based on the results of the assessment, then the team would need to engage in action research outside of their immediate knowledge base to put more tools and strategies in their toolkit.

In *Learning by Doing*, DuFour et al. (2016) state that teams working in high-performing PLCs develop one or more common formative assessments for each unit of instruction to:

- Promote efficiency for teachers
- Promote equity for students
- Provide an effective strategy for determining whether the guaranteed curriculum is being taught and more importantly, learned
- Inform the practice of individual teachers
- Build a team's capacity to improve its program
- Facilitate a systematic, collective response to students who are experiencing difficulty
- Offer the most powerful tool for changing adult behavior and practice (p. 149)

To help your team achieve these goals, this chapter offers multiple examples of how to create useful team-developed common formative assessments for preK–2 learners. You'll see how some assessments look different than those for students in upper-elementary grades. You'll also learn about different assessment techniques, assessment tasks, and data-collection tools effective with early childhood students. To set up this exploration, first consider the following story of a kindergarten team that needed to determine an ideal approach to assessing students' mathematics skills.

Vignette:
A Kindergarten Team Assesses Mathematics Learning

A kindergarten team must determine how they will assess learning for the mathematics standard:

> Count to answer "how many?" questions about as many as 20 things arranged in a line, a rectangular array, or a circle, or as many as 10 things in a scattered configuration; given a number from 1–20, count out that many objects. (K.CC.B.5; NGA & CCSSO, 2010b)

First, team members spent fifteen minutes of their weekly mathematics meeting unwrapping the standard and filling out the essential standards chart (see figure 4.7, page 87) and then proceeded to have the following discussion about how they would answer the second critical question of a PLC. At this school, they've made sure the master schedule allows for the special education teacher who supports kindergarten to be available for weekly team meetings, and the four classroom teachers rotate who facilitates the weekly meetings each quarter.

Juanita (current team facilitator): Now that we unwrapped this essential standard, I'm clearer about what we're teaching, but what would be the best assessment tool to capture students' learning of this concept?

Rose (kindergarten teacher): What if we have a pencil-and-paper task that has a picture of twenty frogs on it, and students have to count them? We provide them with three answers to choose from, and the students would have to select the correct answer.

Latisha (kindergarten teacher): I like this idea. This task would allow us to tell who is able to correctly count a set of objects and who is not, but I'm not sure it would tell us what specific counting errors students are making as they count. I'm not sure I would know how to specifically support students on their counting if I didn't actually watch them count a set of physical objects.

Rose: Maybe we should think about doing an interview with each student. What if we have an actual set of twenty cubes, and we watch students count them?

Bobby (kindergarten teacher): Yes, but maybe instead of cubes we have them count the little frogs we have in our sorting set?

Carmine (special education teacher): I'm sure students would rather count little frogs over cubes, but if we use the interlocking cubes, they could snap them together, and it might help them keep track of their counting.

Juanita: OK, so we have a few ideas on the table. Maybe we should come to consensus on a few things. Does anyone have any other ideas? If not, should we use a pencil-and-paper task or a student interview, and do we want to use frogs or cubes?

Bobby: I think we can all see we'll get more useful information from the interview, right? And Carmine's idea that the cubes set up the students for success by helping them keep track does sound good. Agreed?

Carmine: What if we posed the questions to students while they are at play in the building blocks center? Could we give them a set of twenty cubes, and ask them "How many?", observe them count, and then leave them with an open-ended verbal prompt, like, "I wonder what a house would look like using these twenty cubes?"

All five teachers agree.

Juanita: OK, so what should we be looking for as we are watching them count? What do we want students to be able to do? Should we refer to the document we made when we unwrapped the counting standards?

Latisha: Well, they need to have one-to-one correspondence and match each object to a number. We need to observe that students don't double count any of the cubes. One of our related standards says, "When counting objects, say the number names in the standard order, pairing each object with one and only one number name and each number name with one and only one object." Also, the set of twenty needs to be arranged in a pattern and not scattered.

Bobby: So, it would help to see if students have an organized system for keeping track of their counting. Are they sliding each cube, stacking them, connecting them together, etcetera?

Juanita: Speaking of organizing, how are we going to organize and keep track of all the data we collect?

Carmine: What if we make a checklist? On the checklist, we have our class list of students' names and, in the first column, it says, "Student accurately counts a set of twenty objects using one-to-one correspondence," and we record either *yes* or *no* next to that student's name. Then, in the next column it says, "Student has an organized system for keeping track of counting," and again, we either record *yes* or *no*.

Juanita: What about our students who can't count past ten?

Bobby: If a student is struggling to count the set of twenty, why don't we limit the set to ten to see if they can count a set of ten? If they can't, then we give only five. We can either write this information in the Notes section or have a separate column on our checklist that shows if they can just count a set of ten or five.

Latisha: As we were filling out the essential standards chart, we also talked about how students have to be able to understand that the last number name said tells the number of objects counted. So, after the students say how many cubes there are, what if we immediately rearrange the twenty cubes, and ask them again, "How many cubes are there?" We can watch to see if the students can immediately recall the same number they just said without recounting the cubes. Do they know that the last number they said represents the whole set of counters they just counted?

Rose: Yes, great idea!

Latisha: So, there are three standards that all connect together, and we would be assessing all three in this one task. Instead of just recording our data on a paper checklist, I am wondering if we should make an electronic checklist so we can easily sort the data. It would help us group students for reteaching or extension.

Bobby: Yes, but I also think we should include a space on the checklist to write notes. So, maybe a student has one-to-one correspondence and is matching every object with a name but skips one of the teen numbers. I want to be able to record a note that says this student needs to work on rote counting, focusing specifically on the teen numbers.

Rose: That makes sense, Bobby. I can make an electronic checklist based on everything we just discussed, and I can bring it to our next planning meeting. You can all give feedback, and we can make any necessary modifications to it.

Juanita: Thank you, Rose, for taking the lead on that. I'm thinking we may also need a rubric to go along with the common formative assessment to help us think about differentiation in our classrooms. For example, if we create a 3–2–1 rubric to see if they accurately count all twenty cubes correctly using one-to-one correspondence, we'll need to have an organized system for keeping track of their counting and whether they can rearrange the set of twenty cubes without recounting to know that there still are twenty cubes. It's clear that a rubric score of 3 would be considered mastery, but what would a score of 2 and 1 look like?

Bobby: We've got ten minutes left. I'll create a rubric template on my computer and start filling it in while we talk about descriptors for a level 2 and level 1 score on the assessment. Let's see if we can walk out of here with it ready to be electronically shared with everybody.

Developmentally Appropriate Common Formative Assessments in Early Childhood

If you are a preschool teacher reading this chapter's vignette, you may be thinking, "We have a curriculum, but we don't explicitly assess students. Could this process work for my team too?" Conversely, a district or state may require many elementary teachers to do so much standardized testing that they do not collaborate to create team-developed common formative assessments. In that case, you may also be asking, "Can this process work for my team?" The answer in both cases is, "Yes! Absolutely!"

Whether you are new to creating a common formative assessment with your team or simply hoping to refine and improve your collaborative processes, this chapter helps explain how teams can answer some the following guiding questions.

- Which learning targets from the essential standards should the team address in the assessment? (Social, emotional, and communication learning targets are just as valid as mathematics or reading content learning targets.)

- Which assessment technique is most appropriate for students for this standard? Should teams have more than one way of assessing student learning?

- What if a student does not have foundational skills to access the content on the grade-level assessment?

- What tools will the team use to collect data, and how should it organize the data?

We start in this section with an examination of developmentally appropriate common formative assessments for preK–2 learners. Through this examination, you'll see how some of the assessments look different than those for students in upper-elementary grades. First, it's important to understand what *common formative assessment* means and why those three words are so powerful. So, let's examine each word.

- **Common:** Assessments for essential standards must be *common*, meaning teachers give the assessment in the same way at around the same time so the team can use accurate data together purposefully. While individual teachers will check for understanding in multiple ways during every lesson and may choose to do some individual assessments in each of their classrooms, during each unit of instruction, teams must agree to and develop common assessments for the essential standards.

- **Formative:** Assessments must be *formative*, meaning the assessments actually measure the impact of each teacher's daily instruction (as opposed to some district- or state-required assessments, which do not necessarily align with what teachers have taught). Formative assessments are assessments *for* learning (Stiggins et al., 2004). They inform about the student learning happening, but when teams collaboratively analyze results and share the practices that led to those results, formative assessments inform and improve teach teacher's instructional practice.

- **Assessment:** As redundant as it may sound, assessments must actually be an *assessment* of learning and not just a teacher's general idea of what he or she thinks a student can do. While assessments in early childhood embrace the fact that students demonstrate stronger skills through play (Bohart & Procopio, 2018), teachers can interview, do performance assessments, use observation checklists, and collect work samples during play that give data about learning that is just as valid as a score on a paper-and-pencil assessment. These data allow teams to have discussions that are not subjective and based on an individual teacher's overall impressions of the student.

Figure 5.2 shows how these three aspects of assessment align with the three big ideas of a PLC. Notice how teachers focus on *collaboration* rather than isolation, *learning* rather than teaching, and *results* rather than intentions.

Common = **Collaboration**

Formative = **Learning**

Assessment = **Results**

Figure 5.2: How common formative assessments embody the three big ideas of a PLC.

Some teachers shy away from the term *assessment*, thinking it means putting students at a desk with paper and pencil or computer to answer questions that test their knowledge in developmentally inappropriate ways. In reality, assessment in early childhood can reflect a variety of formats, including simply observing, which is a specific way of watching students that every early childhood teacher engages in every hour of every day to check for understanding. In fact, observation is an integral part of teaching in preK–2, from students lining up for snack time to free play. Teachers can also assess during a conversation with students; for example, when the teacher asks a student to draw something or sort manipulatives. Yes, assessment can also involve the teacher giving a student a pencil and paper to answer a question or work out a problem in a more traditional way.

Once teams move past the anxiety of the term *assessment*, they need to tackle the *common* aspect of common formative assessment. In chapter 2 (page 31), we write about eliminating the educational lottery by collectively deciding on essential standards (and go into more depth about those essential standards in chapter 3, page 47). How do teams know if students have mastered these standards without measuring the student learning that happened? Teaching without learning is just talking (Angelo & Cross, 1993), so when teams of teachers agree to teach common essential standards, they must also agree on how they will gather evidence of learning, thus, *common assessment*. For example, what would happen if your team determines identifying twelve uppercase letters is an essential standard and asks each teacher on the team to assess his or her students and share the data? However, the team has not developed a common assessment. Consider the following questions that come from not having common assessments and how each case might lead to a curriculum that offers students no guarantees about learning.

- What if one teacher shows his or her students the letters in alphabetical order and asks students to name them while another teacher shows the letters on individual cards out of order?

- What if another teacher's cards have a picture on them of something that begins with the sound a letter makes?

- What if the next teacher presents students with twelve magnetic letters and names the letter the teacher wants the students to hand her?

- What if the final teacher gives students two magnetic letters at a time and asks them to point to the letter the teacher says?

The rigor in each example in this list is completely different—sometimes the field of responses varies, and some of the letter-identification assessments are asking students to actively identify the letters, while other students are responding to a teacher prompt. This example of the importance of determining a consistent set of common formative assessments as a team before teaching the standard hits home. As education author and consultant Mike Schmoker (2004) observes, "Clarity precedes competence" (p. 85).

Students experience monumental development in early childhood. According to researchers Timothy T. Brown and Terry L. Jernigan (2012), the preschool years represent a time of expansive psychological growth and blossoming brain development, with the most dynamic and elaborative anatomical and physiological changes happening in the early childhood years. Students develop at different rates, and preschoolers come to school with various experiences. So, when teams design instructional practices and assessments, they need to consider each student's cognitive, behavioral, social-emotional, and communication needs, as well as his or her cultural background and unique life experiences. This requires teams to have a variety of assessment types at their disposal.

What types of assessments are most appropriate for early childhood learners? In a policy information report, "State Pre-K Assessment Policies: Issues and Status," writers Debra J. Ackerman and Richard J. Coley (2012) evaluate the trend of collecting assessment data in preschool settings across the United States and note the following as the most effective methods.

- Direct assessments

- Observation checklists and scales

- Samples of students' work

- Combinations of these methods

The preschool programs in this report not only vary in the specific types of assessments they use with students but also how often teachers administer them. Ackerman and Coley (2012) did find an overall preference for comprehensive observation-based assessments over direct assessments. They conclude the reason for this preference might be that teachers can better capture the development of students' learning in multiple ways during a school year by assessing everyday activities in their learning environment more so than by asking students direct questions or having them perform discrete tasks that may not be connected to what they are learning or doing at a particular time.

Just because there is not a one-size-fits-all assessment for preK–2 students does not mean common formative assessments are any less important than they are for the upper-grades students. It means teachers must have powerful discussions with their teammates as the team makes decisions about how to assess. Teams should also heed the warning from the National Research Council (Snow & VanHemsel, 2008) that young learners, and especially those from nondominant cultures, are at greater risk than older students of suffering negative consequences as a result of the misuse of assessment. Teams need to recognize the limitations of any one assessment.

The NAEYC (2009) position on assessment for early childhood learners outlines many important considerations to help teams when designing, implementing, and using the results of early childhood assessments. We summarize several of its findings about assessments under the following two categories.

1. **Assessment methods:**

    - Are ongoing, strategic and purposeful with a focus on progress toward important goals in all developmental domains

    - Include feedback from families and students in addition to the teacher

    - Consider carefully a student's cultural and linguistic context

    - Allow students to demonstrate competence in different ways through a variety of developmentally appropriate methods (observation, interview, work samples, performance activities)

    - Connect experiences to what is assessed (for example, occurs during small-group participation or at play)

    - Assess what a student can do independently and with scaffolding from adults

2. **Assessment results:**

    - Are only used for the intended purpose and produce reliable and valid information

    - Are housed in a system developed to collect and use data

    - Are used to improve teacher practice

- Are used to inform curriculum planning for responsive instruction and interactions with students

- Are communicated to families along with their purpose and process

- Are used to determine a student's skill level based on multiple sources of information, never a single or one-time assessment

Everything we discussed in chapters 2–4 was in the service of answering the first two critical questions: What do we want our students to learn? and How will we know if each student has learned it? (DuFour et al., 2016). If assessments do not validly measure learning in early childhood, then all the work of teams up to this point was for naught. To self-assess your team's, school's, or district's assessment practices, we developed the tool featured in figure 5.3. After discussion about using this tool, teams rate the extent to which they systematically and consistently embrace each of the considerations when developing, using, and sharing data from early childhood assessments.

Team members:
Grade level: _____
Directions
1. Individually, then as a team, reflect on which of the following considerations (assessment methods and assessment results) are incorporated in your current assessment practices.
2. Discuss and rate your current practices for each consideration using the following symbols.
X = We do not yet systematically incorporate this consideration.
! = We inconsistently incorporate this consideration.
★ = We consistently and systematically embrace this consideration.
3. Create an action plan and timeline to improve assessment practices.
Assessment Methods
_____ Are ongoing, strategic, and purposeful with a focus on progress toward important goals in all developmental domains
_____ Include feedback from families and students in addition to the teacher
_____ Consider carefully a student's cultural and linguistic context
_____ Allow students to demonstrate competence in different ways through a variety of developmentally appropriate methods (observation, interview, work samples, performance activities)
_____ Connect experiences to what is assessed (for example, occurs during small-group participation or at play)
_____ Assess what a student can do independently and with scaffolding from adults

Figure 5.3: Team evaluation of early childhood assessment considerations.

continued →

Assessment Results
____ Are only used for the intended purpose and produce reliable and valid information
____ Are housed in a system developed to collect and use data
____ Are used to improve teacher practice
____ Are used to inform curriculum planning for responsive instruction and interactions with students
____ Are communicated to families along with their purpose and process
____ Are used to determine a student's skill level based on multiple sources of information, never a single or one-time assessment
What steps or action plans need to be initiated to strengthen your early childhood assessments?
Who is responsible for initiating or maintaining the action plan(s)? What is the timeline?

Source for assessment methods and results: Adapted from NAEYC, 2009.
*Visit **go.SolutionTree.com/PLCbooks** for a free reproducible version of this figure.*

Assessment Methods

After teams ensure they are incorporating important assessment considerations into their practices, they can begin to think about the best method and tools to use to assess any given essential standard. As teams engage in the use of common assessments and determine how to best assess each essential standard, they answer the following questions around assessment techniques, assessment tasks, and data collection and evaluation.

1. **What assessment techniques will the teacher be using?** Observing students is the least intrusive and most student-directed technique in early childhood. Asking questions in an interview or having a conference is a productive teacher-directed technique. Expecting students to provide an independent response is the most direct form of assessment technique, but teachers can also use a combination of these techniques in one assessment.

2. **What will the students actually do to show their learning?** Teams need to decide what tasks students will use to demonstrate their learning. The tasks could be performance-based actions (such as reading a passage from a book), physical product-based work students produce (such as posters, pencil-and-paper problem solving, and persuasive writing), or a blend of actions and products.

3. **What tools do we need in order to collect and evaluate student data?**
   In the upper grades, it is most common for teachers to get their data
   when students turn in an assessment they completed independently,
   either on pencil and paper or on a computer. However, early childhood
   teams need to use a variety of tools for data collection. By this point,
   the team has already made determinations about the techniques and
   tasks it will use to assess any given standard, and the tools the team
   uses or develops will derive from these determinations. While the data-
   collection tool could be a paper and pencil or electronic assessment, it
   could also be a checklist, chart, conference notes, photograph or video,
   work-sample analysis, rubric, continuum, or recording form the team
   procured from an outside source or developed itself.

Figure 5.4 illustrates the progression teams undertake when making decisions
(such as the kindergarten team did in this chapter's vignette) about which assessment techniques, tasks, and tools they use to assess each essential standard. In the
following sections, we go into specific detail about each of these considerations.
We then conclude this topic with an examination of the decisions teams make
about assessment.

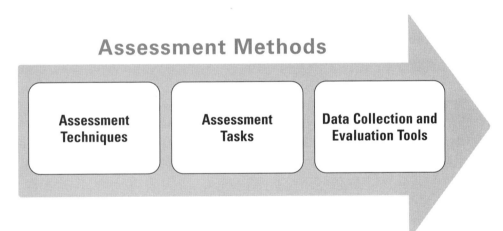

Figure 5.4: Team decisions about assessment methods.

Assessment Techniques

In the vignette at the beginning of this chapter, the first decision the team made
when developing a common formative assessment was to determine which assessment technique they would use to collect data on students' learning. There are three
different techniques early childhood teams often use for this purpose.

1. **Teacher observation:** The teacher observes students (at play,
   performing a specific task, presenting a project, and so on) and records
   data about their learning. This is not casual observation but purposeful
   observation during a specific time frame. It occurs after the teaching

of an essential standard to collect evidence of learning about the knowledge or skills that students demonstrate during the observation.

2. **Teacher and student interview or conference:** The teacher generates questions for students and asks them to respond orally as the teacher records data about their learning. All questions can be predetermined, or the questioning can be open ended and flow like a conversation, with the teacher getting the necessary information after just a question or two. In some cases, teachers conduct more follow up, asking additional clarifying and probing questions to assess a student's learning.

3. **Student independent response:** The teacher generates questions, prompts, or problems and students work independently to record their own responses. What differentiates this technique (from observation or interview) is that the teacher is not part of the response process and assesses students' learning by looking at their response products *after* they produce it.

We discuss specific strategies for using each of these techniques later in the chapter, but for now, think more generally about when and why your team might choose to use one of the techniques over the others (or a combination of more than one technique). When thinking about how to best assess an essential standard, teams ensure the act of assessing does not get in the way of young learners showing what they truly do know and are able to do. Have you worked with a student who realized he or she was being assessed, and the unfamiliar situation caused him or her to freeze up? Or, have you had a student choose to answer some questions but not be interested at the time of the assessment in answering other questions, even if you have reason to believe from the student's in-class behavior that he or she does know the answer? At times, this means the best technique is to purposefully select the materials, tools, toys, or resources available to students and then select the assessment technique of teacher observation as the student engages with, manipulates, and uses the materials without direct guidance, interference, or direction from the teacher.

Some preschool students may already have the communication and metacognitive skills necessary to communicate their thinking and ideas to engage in a more formalized assessment through a student interview or conference. However, before using this approach, it is important to consider cultural norms for each student. One of the greatest dangers in assessing young students is to associate developmental status with the dominant cultural norms in the community (National Research Council, 2001b) because this leads to misunderstanding of some students' functional abilities.

Teachers need to be cognizant of each student's home culture expectations about child-adult communication when deciding the best instructional strategies and assessment tools to use with him or her. The National Research Council's (2001b) ethnographic research shows striking differences in how adults and children interact verbally in different cultures. In some homes, parents begin questioning games with their children from infancy, such as "Where is teddy bear? Ah, there he is!" This sets students up to be comfortable answering teacher questions. However, cultural expectations in other homes may or may not be in line with this type of interaction. For example, some cultures may expect children to learn by observing adults as compared to engaging in questioning games. As a result, not all students will be comfortable with teacher questioning techniques, which is something teams should consider when choosing assessment techniques.

If the team determines a student can accurately show what he or she knows and can do through oral communication, then, to set up the student for success, members should also consider the environment where the assessment will take place. Teachers can conduct interviews and conferences in the classroom setting or in a quiet setting outside the classroom, depending on the classroom environment and the student's needs. Student interviews and conferences are also more successful when the teacher has a relationship with the student. A teacher can start to build this rapport and trust by first asking an individual student nonrelated questions about the subject area. Or, the teacher could allow the student to play with the tools he or she will be using during the student interview. In addition to establishing trust, these steps allow the student to feel comfortable in the testing environment.

When teachers do prompt, question, or interact with a student, then the technique changes from an observation to an *interview* or *conference*. This is a more direct form of assessment and may allow teachers to gather more data more quickly. Sometimes, teachers script the interview questions, and sometimes the questions are inductive and based on how the student responds to previous questions. For example, if you give a student colored bears and ask him or her to sort them and the student groups them by color, you may ask, "Can you sort them a different way?" It is equally important to assess if the student understands the word *sort* as you don't want a lack of vocabulary to affect the validity of the assessment. From this prompt, a student might group the bears by size, make a colorful pattern of bears in a parade, or get stuck. Your next question will depend on how the student responds to the prompt of sorting by more than one attribute.

Finally, the most direct assessment technique is when the student *independently* records his or her answers or shows his or her thinking. For example, in addition to physically sorting the bears into two piles, the student represents his or her thinking by either coloring in the bears on paper to show what is in each pile or drawing circles around the correct response to show if he or she sorted by color, shape, or size.

As students grow and develop their writing skills, they will begin to communicate their ideas in writing more and more; therefore, the emergence of collecting data through student independent response becomes increasingly relevant and important during the early childhood years. By first and second grade, many students have developed their writing skills and the use of some pencil-and-paper assessment items can become more appropriate. When giving students these assessments, some teachers find it helpful to observe them in a small-group setting, which allows teachers to both observe students and have an opportunity to ask students questions about what they are doing on an as-needed basis. The teachers' prompts and questioning are still quite necessary and appropriate in early childhood education as is having full use of appropriate tools and manipulatives while using independent response assessment techniques.

Assessment Tasks

After a team chooses an assessment technique to measure student learning of the standards, team members make decisions about the assessment tasks the students will receive. There are two broad categories of assessment tasks teams can use as evidence of student learning.

1. **Actions:** Assessment tasks that involve performance-based actions such as sorting a set of objects, reading aloud, giving a presentation, or choosing the colored block that continues the pattern are common in early childhood learning. If a team chooses the assessment technique of observation or interview, they are likely to collect data based on an assessment task the student performs.

2. **Products:** As students get older, producing a physical product of their learning becomes more common. The product could be a single paper such as a vocabulary quiz or mathematics problems solved, it could be a portfolio or collection of student work samples over time, or it could be in the form of a project. The product could also be electronic, accessed by the teacher through technology rather than a physical product handed in. If a team chooses the assessment technique of independent response, often their next step is to create a product-based assessment task.

It bears noting that, through products, teachers begin to build a portfolio of each student's learning. Such portfolios are a collection of student work teachers collect over time and organize in a way to reflect a student's learning of a concept or multiple skills. According to Ann S. Epstein, Lawrence J. Schweinhart, Andrea DeBruin-Parecki, and Kenneth B. Robin (2004):

> Portfolios are most commonly thought of as an assessment approach appropriate in elementary and secondary schools. Yet they have long been used in preschools to document and share children's progress with parents, administrators and others. For portfolios to be used for program accountability, as well as student learning and reflection, the evaluated outcomes must be aligned with curriculum and instruction. (p. 7)

At any point in time during a student's elementary experience, teachers can use a formalized and teacher-managed portfolio to capture student learning. For portfolios to be considered common formative assessments, the teacher team must work collaboratively to decide on the criteria for the samples included in the portfolio and work together to determine how the team will analyze student evidence in a common way.

It is important to note many early childhood teams create common formative assessments that often consist of a combination of both actions and products. This is because the act of learning and the act of assessing should not be separate. Students do not have to stop their learning for teachers to take time out of instruction to perform assessments. If they are actively engaged in learning tasks, then teachers can observe their actions without interfering (the observation assessment technique) or ask them about their learning (the interview assessment technique). At the same time, the student continues what he or she is doing (an action-based assessment task). Later in the chapter, we give scenarios of teachers doing this kind of assessment, but at this point, the best way to think about the types of assessment tasks is to consider how they align with the decisions the team made about assessment techniques to form the most developmentally appropriate assessment method for a given learning target.

Data-Collection and Evaluation Tools

In the upper grades, when teams conduct electronic assessments and receive results they can sort and analyze by standard or by student, it is easy to color-code data and see at a glance the percentage of students who mastered a given standard. This makes it possible for teams to collectively focus on how to intervene or extend based on the data. In the primary years, when data may more often come from teacher observation or interview while students are engaged in an assessment task, the data are not as easily collected and evaluated. When considering student performance data and pictorial or verbal explanations of student thinking, the process of evaluating the data may look slightly different than compiling the scores on a multiple-choice test. However, there are still many tools from which to choose, which we classify in the following three categories.

1. **Student recording tools for data collection:** These include tools students use to independently record their learning using pencil and paper or using a computer-based format.

2. **Teacher recording tools for data collection:** These tools include teacher checklists, look fors, charts, and other team-created recording forms and templates.

3. **Data collection and evaluation tools:** These tools include learning progressions and rubrics as well as student self-evaluation tools, such as goal cards and assessment wrappers.

In many U.S. states, the third-grade year is when students begin standardized state testing, and many of these tests are computer-based assessment tasks in which the product of student learning is captured electronically. If the assessments are computer based, the tools are often online. Although computerized testing may offer many benefits, physical manipulatives and tools are important for early childhood students. So, before using technology for a team-developed assessment task, teachers should carefully consider if students have the necessary computer skills to engage in a computer-based assessment. In particular, consider if they will be able to show their thinking in an authentic way without the physical materials used in daily learning.

Team Decisions About Assessment

When teams work together to plan for assessment by considering the most appropriate assessment techniques, tasks, and tools to use with their students, they ensure their assessment methods are developmentally appropriate for their students and yield reliable data to inform instruction. Would it be appropriate to give a pencil-and-paper multiple-choice assessment to preschool students? Most likely, no! As students' ability to show their thinking orally and in writing develop, so do teams' options for assessments.

The teacher's role in the assessment process changes and evolves as students become more independent and develop their communication, written, and cognitive skills. While observation and interview assessment techniques tend to give way to student independent response as students age (since it is more efficient), some second graders may still struggle with the physical act of writing with pencil and paper that such tasks demand. As a result, those assessments may not provide valid data about what the student knows and can do. *Responsive teaching* means teachers always start with thinking about the unique needs of their students when making instructional decisions. This also includes making decisions about the effectiveness of their instruction. Figure 5.5 illustrates and summarizes the steps we recommend teams discuss when making decisions about creating and using common assessments.

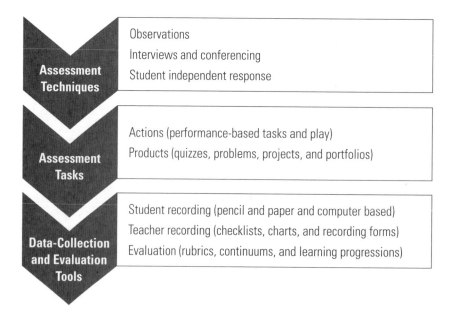

Figure 5.5: Team decision-making process when choosing assessment techniques, tasks, and tools.

Finally, remember not all students learn the same way, and not all students need to be assessed the same way. When determining the best assessment techniques, tasks, and tools to use with preK–2 learners, think about the following for *each* student.

- Does the student have the developmental verbal-communication and social-emotional skills necessary to communicate their ideas in more formal teacher-student interviews? If not, how can the teacher gather student data in a way that is embedded within the learning environment?

- Does the student have the cognitive and written skills necessary to communicate their ideas on paper? If not, how else might a teacher record the information?

- Does the student have the technology and self-regulation skills necessary to take an assessment on the computer, and can the teacher capture the students' ideas via the technology? If not, what accommodations or scaffolds could the teacher put into place?

Tips for Administrators	Tips for Coaches	Tips for Teachers
Empower teams to determine the best way to assess their students. Allow teachers to have the flexibility of creating the number of common formative assessments that appropriately gives them the information needed to make decisions. Implement a system for holding teams accountable for having timely data to inform instruction.	Push teams to consider the types of assessment techniques or tasks they are not currently using. This way, students have a variety of ways to show their learning, and teachers broaden their ideas about assessment.	Think about what your assessment environment looks and sounds like in your classroom. What are you doing as the teacher, and what are the expectations for your students?
Communicate with parents about developmentally appropriate assessment practices, so they understand why and how teachers assess their children at young ages—even if the parents don't see traditional graded assignments.	Guide the team in making decisions about common scoring practices.	Determine what procedures and structures you need in your classroom to allow you to assess students in small groups or individually.
To help staff learn more about the comprehensive nature of assessment, the Assessment Center at Solution Tree is a powerful resource (visit www.SolutionTree .com/assessment-center).	Highlight possible opportunities for teachers to assess multiple content-area skills with one assessment.	Decide how you are going to store and organize the assessment tools you are using with students.
	Think about how to support the team in creating or choosing quality assessment tools through which all students have entry points and access to the assessments teams are using.	

Sample Assessment Scenarios

To get a better idea of what it looks like to assess young learners in a variety of ways, the following scenarios show how two early childhood teams—one preK and one second grade—used the team decision-making process summarized in figure 5.5 (page 126) to develop very different yet equally strong assessments in the same content area (mathematics).

Preschool Scenario

In this scenario, a preschool team already worked together to unpack the mathematics essential standard for identifying and copying patterns. As a result, it determined the following.

- **Prerequisite skills:** Students must be able to sort a set of objects by one attribute.

- **Grade-level skills:** Students must be able to identify and copy AB patterns.

- **Beyond grade-level skills:** Students must be able to extend patterns and create patterns beyond just AB patterns.

The teacher team first decides they will not use student interviews as an avenue for collecting data because it is early in the school year, and they are still building rapport with students. Instead, teachers will observe a performance-based task while students are at stations. The stations are set up to help students identify patterns, nonpatterns, and copy patterns with bracelet-making materials, stickers, and ice cube trays prefilled with one row of colorful materials in a pattern and one row empty for students to copy the pattern.

Figure 5.6 illustrates the resources teachers supply for each station. They have differentiated the three stations and included materials to assess both grade-level skills of AB patterns and extensions with non-AB patterns as part of the assessment task. If a teacher observes any students struggling with the grade-level standard of identifying or copying the patterns at any of the stations, then he or she will pull those students aside and ask them to sort the materials by color (gauging if each student has this prerequisite skill). If, after three to four days, a teacher has evidence that some students can copy a pattern but doesn't have evidence they could extend or create patterns, he or she would specifically ask those students to create and extend a pattern at the sticker-and-stamp station.

After a collaborative team decision on the assessment technique and tasks for the performance-based assessment, the team next asks, "How will we gather the students' information?" They chose to create an observation tool, like the one in figure 5.7 (page 130) and committed to using it while observing students engaging at the three

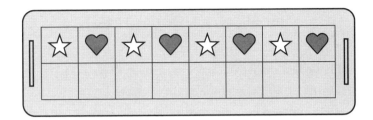

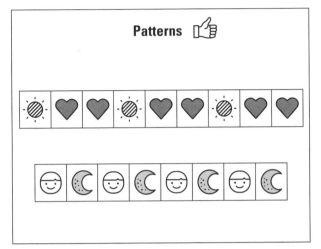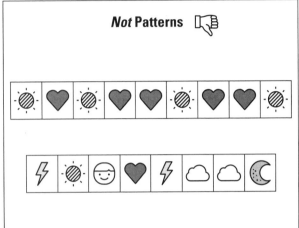

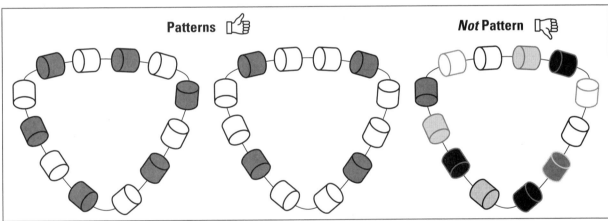

Figure 5.6: Materials students use in three pattern stations during a teacher-observation assessment.

learning stations over the course of three days. Notice how there are blank lines in the Observation Notes boxes labled *Other*. Here, teachers have a place to describe specific observations that may be useful and important relative to other mathematics essential standards (ones the team is not currently measuring) or in other cross-curricular areas (such as SEL or communication). However, these observations do not directly relate to the learning of the mathematics essential standards the team is currently assessing.

Patterns Assessment Center Time		
Prerequisite skill: The student will sort objects by one attribute.		
Grade-level essential skill: The student will identify and copy simple AB patterns.		
Extension skills: The student will extend patterns and create non-AB patterns.		
Center description: Ice cube station Fill ice cube trays with pattern on top row, and students use materials to copy pattern to bottom row. **Scaffolds and supports:** Provide students with sorting-circles container or paper placeholders where they can sort the materials needed, before copying the pattern. **Materials:** Ice cube trays, buttons, stickers, colored counters, sorting containers or circles, and so on	**Center description:** Sticker station Make assorted pattern cards with stickers (AB, ABB, ABC, and so on) and some nonpattern cards. Students distinguish pattern cards from nonpattern cards and copy patterns on the blank cards using stickers. **Scaffolds and supports:** Pattern and nonpattern sorting circles **Materials:** Sticker pattern and nonpattern cards and sorting circles, blank pattern cards, stickers, and so on	**Center description:** Bracelet station Make assorted bracelet cards with patterns (AB, ABB, ABC, and so on) and some nonpatterns. Students distinguish a pattern card from nonpattern cards and copy the pattern using the pipe cleaner and beads at the station. **Scaffolds and supports:** Pattern and non-pattern sorting circles **Extension:** Students create their own patterns using the beads. **Materials:** Pattern-bracelet picture cards and nonpattern cards, pipe cleaners, assorted beads (varied colors and shapes), and so on
Academic language lookfors: Repeat, extend, copy, identify		
Content language lookfors: Pattern		
Social language lookfors: Parallel play versus cooperative play and engagement with reciprocal conversations and socially appropriate actions (helping, sharing, and so on)		
Observation Notes		
Name: _____	Name: _____	Name: _____	Name: _____
☐ Sort by one attribute ☐ **Identify pattern** ☐ **Copy pattern** ☐ Extend patterns ☐ Create patterns Other: _____ Other: _____	☐ Sort by one attribute ☐ **Identify pattern** ☐ **Copy pattern** ☐ Extend patterns ☐ Create patterns Other: _____ Other: _____	☐ Sort by one attribute ☐ **Identify pattern** ☐ **Copy pattern** ☐ Extend patterns ☐ Create patterns Other: _____ Other: _____	☐ Sort by one attribute ☐ **Identify pattern** ☐ **Copy pattern** ☐ Extend patterns ☐ Create patterns Other: _____ Other: _____
Next steps:	Next steps:	Next steps:	Next steps:

Figure 5.7: Student-observation tool—Patterns.

*Visit **go.SolutionTree.com/PLCbooks** for a free reproducible version of this figure.*

The team is now ideally situated to bring the data to their next team meeting and use the assessment results to improve student learning and teacher practice by sharing strategies that helped those students who showed proficiency. The assessment technique, task, and data-collection tool also enable the teachers to set goals and clearly share the data with students and families. Figure 5.8 illustrates the assessment method progression the team engaged in for this scenario.

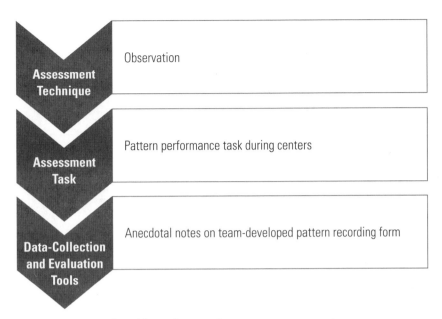

Figure 5.8: Preschool learning and assessment scenario.

Second-Grade Scenario

In this scenario, a second-grade team developed a mathematics common formative assessment using the grade-level essential standards for measurement. They decided the primary assessment technique would be student independent response but also discussed ways to incorporate observation and some interview questioning with select students. The assessment task would primarily be multiple choice and free response questions, but there was one learning target the team would assess using a performance-based task item. The assessment occurred over multiple days in small teacher-guided groups while other students worked independently or collaboratively at self-initiated learning stations. During the small group work, the teachers recorded observations on sticky notes, which they attached to students' assessment when they were finished. This way, teachers had two data-collection tools together. After the assessment, the team used another data-collection and evaluation tool for students to self-assess.

In chapter 4 (page 75), we talked about the importance of students taking ownership of their learning through student goal setting and being part of the process of monitoring their own growth. For students to self-monitor learning, as they acquire the metacognitive skills and language required, it can be useful for them to go back and discover what they know and what they still need to learn. Teams can accomplish this through the use of an *exam wrapper* (Lovett, 2013), which, for our purpose, we will think of as an *assessment wrapper*. Figure 5.9 (page 132) depicts the tool the team used to have students reflect on the assessment they took, determine what they need to learn next, and make a plan for learning it.

Student name: _____

Measurement Assessment Wrapper

Directions: Review your assessment and shade the questions green that you answered correctly. Shade the questions red that you answered incorrectly.

Measuring the Length of Objects

I can accurately use a measurement tool to measure the length of an object.	**Question 1**	**Question 2**	**Question 3**

I can estimate the length of objects (units of inches, feet, centimeters, and meters).	**Question 4**	**Question 5**

I can measure to figure out how much longer one object is than another.	**Question 6**	**Question 7**

What have you learned so far?

_____

_____

What do you still need to learn?

_____

_____

What is your new learning plan?

_____

_____

Telling Time

I can tell and write time from analog and digital clocks to the nearest five minutes, using a.m. and p.m.	Question 8	Question 9	Question 10

What have you learned so far?

_____

_____

What do you still need to learn?

_____

_____

What is your new learning plan?

_____

_____

Problem Solving

I can use addition and subtraction to solve word problems involving lengths.	Question 11	Question 12	Question 13

I can solve word problems involving dollar bills, quarters, dimes, nickels, and pennies and correctly use $ and ¢ symbols.	Question 14	Question 15	Question 16

What have you learned so far?

_____

_____

Figure 5.9: Assessment wrapper data-collection and evaluation tool—
Measurement assessment.

continued →

What do you still need to learn?

_____

_____

What is your new learning plan?

_____

_____

Here, the second-grade team's decision-making process was the same as preschool team's in the previous scenario. However, you can see how different the assessment experiences between them are as the teams tailored their assessments to their students' needs (see figure 5.10). Both teams developed developmentally appropriate assessments and can now use the data they collect to discuss students' progress and design differentiated plans to reteach and extend learning. You will learn more about these in the next chapter.

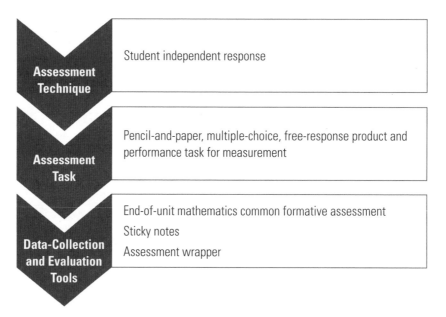

Assessment Technique

Student independent response

Assessment Task

Pencil-and-paper, multiple-choice, free-response product and performance task for measurement

Data-Collection and Evaluation Tools

End-of-unit mathematics common formative assessment
Sticky notes
Assessment wrapper

Figure 5.10: Second-grade learning and assessment scenario.

Guiding Questions

Use the following guiding questions to learn together and build shared knowledge.

- Do all team members understand why common formative assessments are critical to not only student achievement but also to teachers' growth? If not, how will you build the common understanding and common knowledge to answer the second critical question of a PLC?

- What systems, practices, or protocols might you need to establish for your team to do the collaborative creation of assessments, rubrics, learning progressions, data collection, and so on?

- How will the school leadership team and team members help reduce the anxiety teachers may develop about openly sharing instructional strategies and student data?

- Is there a need for schoolwide or team-specific professional development on the various early childhood assessment techniques or assessment tools? If so, who can provide the professional development, and what resources do participants need? Is there a teacher on the team or in the school who already uses one or more of these techniques or tools that others can observe?

Discussing Data and Monitoring Progress

How Do We Respond When Some Students Do or Do Not Learn?

After teams administer common formative assessments, it is the job of all team members to collectively analyze students' data, use the data to drive instruction, and make specific plans for supporting and extending students' learning. Figure 6.1 (page 138) illustrates these phases in the work of early childhood teams in a school that functions as a PLC. The team must clarify its response to the third and fourth critical questions of a PLC: How will we respond when some students do not learn it? and How will we extend learning for students who have demonstrated proficiency? (DuFour et al., 2016). Teams answer these questions by establishing a data protocol to assist in data discussions and then use the information to set goals and monitor student progress.

There are many demands on a team's collaborative time, but staying focused on answering the four critical questions of a PLC helps to ensure that time leads to higher levels of student learning. In this chapter, we begin with a vignette that reflects a first-grade team's approach to using collaborative meeting time to have discussions around student data. Next, we take deeper dives into both conducting data discussions and monitoring students' progress as follows.

- **Data discussions and data-analysis protocols:** We offer explanations of key concepts in the collaborative data-analysis process that form the basis for a team's common understandings when discussing students

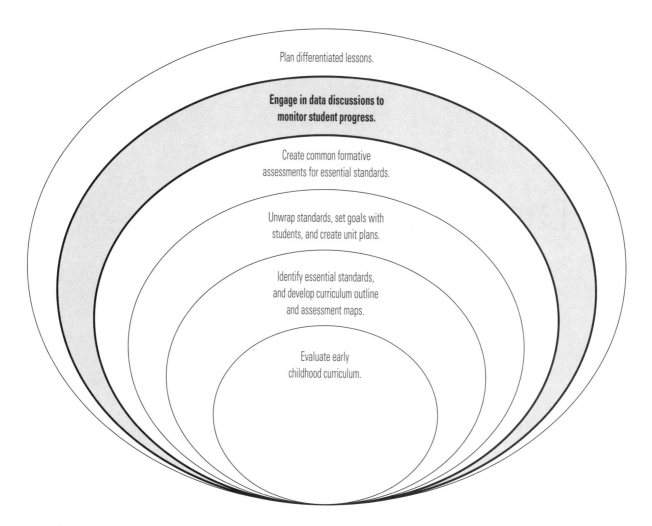

Figure 6.1: The work of early childhood teams in a PLC—Data discussions and monitoring student progress.

and their current skill levels. We also share a data-analysis protocol tool teams can use to ensure their data discussions lead to an action plan that includes setting goals to achieve high levels of learning for *all* students. We then thoroughly explore using the data-analysis protocol to make data discussions an important part of the recursive process of instruction and assessment (and reteaching and reassessment).

- **Student monitoring:** How do you know if the action plan created as a result of the data discussion led to higher levels of student learning? Collecting, organizing, and analyzing data throughout the school year is important work. However, every data point is about a student, and teams must constantly determine if each student is making expected progress, adjusting the plan for any students who are not. To help teams with this important part of their work, we provide comprehensive details on how to monitor students' progress toward goals. You will also learn about methods and tools teams can use to closely monitor the learning of the whole child when intensive interventions are required in early childhood. We close with a discussion about using students' data to enhance a team's professional development.

Let's begin.

Vignette: *A First-Grade Team Takes a Whole Child Approach to Monitoring Progress*

As the middle of the school year approaches, a first-grade team gathers for a progress-monitoring meeting after collecting midyear reading data. The team gave the Developmental Reading Assessment (DRA; 2019) and had a data discussion about how to group students for instruction and refine their practices. As a result, the team members decide to take a closer look at the reading progress of those students who, during the year, needed additional time and support in reading or who participated in reading interventions. This includes the following.

- Students with a diagnosed learning disability

- Students early in their English language acquisition

- Students on the team's radar since preschool for having difficulties with early reading behaviors

- Students who recently hit a bump in the road on their path to becoming literate and who will be the focus of team discussion for the first time

There are also several students the team will discuss not because the teachers have concerns about them not mastering the essential standards but because they are so proficient on those standards they would benefit from extension (or are working on skills beyond their grade level).

As a result of this meeting, the team intends to put in place a specific plan and individual reading-growth goals for any student who needs additional time and support, regardless of whether they are identified for special services. The team will then monitor these students over the next six weeks, until the next progress-monitoring meeting. Because the team wants to consider the whole child (not just his or her reading score), the team includes many other school staff members. While the guidance counselor, speech teacher, and art, music, and physical education teachers may be unable to be present for the entire meeting, the team asks them to give insights about specific students who they have connected with in order to consider the strengths, interests, and what motivates and engages each student outside the classroom. This knowledge will help the students' primary teachers provide more effective reading instruction in the future.

The following discussion shows how teachers come together to consider each student's specific needs. In this case, the team has already reflected on several students, but now needs to focus on one particular struggling student. Using positive language and focusing on what they can do, the team collaborates to put a plan in place to ensure the student learns at high levels. While the student in this vignette is fictional, the scenario is typical of collaboration and coordination necessary in a PLC culture where teachers take collective responsibility for the learning of all students and consider the needs of the whole child, even when focusing on a specific content area.

Marie (first-grade teacher in role of timekeeper for this meeting): This next student, Stephen, is going to take longer than most to discuss since we have so many things in place to support him that could influence his reading growth. Let's share what's working first.

Leslie (guidance counselor): I am meeting him at the bus each morning and bringing him to my office to practice his calming strategies and go over his schedule for the day, so he knows what to expect. I think removing him from the classroom during that ten minutes, while all the students are moving around and unpacking, has eliminated one of the times that was challenging for him to control his body. This way, he's starting his day without being overstimulated, and he's able to participate in the morning reading activities that he used to miss because he was frequently in the office.

Pat (first-grade homeroom teacher): That has been huge! Transitions remain hard for him, so while he has been able to participate in our whole-group lessons, he often refuses to come to the table for his small-group guided-reading time. Because I have to teach the other four students in his group, I can't spend the time convincing him to join us. I think that's a primary cause of his lack of reading progress.

Marie: If it is the transition to small-group work that is hard, can we eliminate that one transition, since access to reading instruction is essential for him? Could you rearrange your small-group schedule so his group is the first one you see after your whole-group lesson on the carpet ends? That way, you can just have him and his group remain on the carpet with you instead of moving to the table where you usually do guided reading?

Pat: Ugh. I guess so, but I have a lot of supplies at the table that I use for guided reading.

Beth (English language teacher): I can help you with that. Since I work in so many different classrooms throughout the day, I've got extra magnetic letters, dry-erase boards, and a tabletop easel we can set up for you to use on the carpet.

Pat: OK. I guess let's try that strategy. After all, we make decisions based on what's best for students, not what's most comfortable for us. I just hope he stays on the carpet with us and benefits from guided-reading instruction if we're going to all this hassle.

Malik (music teacher): I'm wondering if he would also benefit from using a wobble chair on the carpet. I just started using a wobble chair with him this week in music class, and it seems to be helping him release extra energy and define his space so he can better control his focus and attention. If you want to try it a few times on the carpet to see if it helps, there is an extra one in the upstairs closet with the self-regulation tools.

Pat: That's interesting! I'll try it out this week and see if that can help him as well.

Tom (physical education teacher): He also really enjoys the time he spends in the gym with me running laps before lunch. I know we started that because he had trouble controlling his body in the unstructured setting of the cafeteria, but since he enjoys it so much, could we use it as an incentive for him participating in reading groups? If he completes two consecutive days of guided reading, he could bring a friend with him to the gym, and I'll let them race. I think that would motivate him and maybe help with friendships in the classroom.

Marie: That's a great idea! I feel like this puts some things in place to help with the primary reason for his lack of reading achievement, his self-regulation difficulties, and his lack of participation in guided reading. So, if we anticipate him now spending more time accessing the reading instruction, how are we going to target that instruction? What do his current reading data indicate about the goals we should set for him?

Pat: He reads at a level 4 with 92 percent accuracy, but he rushed through and was not able to retell events in sequence using character names or details after reading. Most of his decoding errors were on sight words. He has good phonics skills and can blend sounds in sequence, but on words that are not decodable, he just guesses based on the first letter. As a result, he confuses sight words like *what*, *where*, and *were* and does not go back to self-correct when what he reads doesn't make sense.

Marie: I've got a group working on sight words during our second rotation of reader's workshop stations on Tuesdays and Thursdays. He could join that group for intervention.

Pat: That's a good fit; but remember, he doesn't do well with transitions. For now, I think we need to keep him with me for instruction and not go to a different teacher.

Marie: What if we switch, and you take the sight-word group, and I'll take one of your groups?

Pat: That'd be great! I'd like to keep the retelling group because he could fit well with them also. How about if you take my fluency group?

Marie: OK, so he'll get guided-reading and sight-word support from you. How often will each of those groups meet, and how many students are in them?

Pat: We kept his guided-reading group small, so there's only four in that group. The sight-word group he is joining has six students in it. I think that might be too many peers working in a group for him.

Beth: I have some students we haven't talked about yet who need sight-word support, so let's take two students out of that group, and they can join my sight-word group.

Marie: Sounds good. So, what's his goal for the next six weeks until our next progress-monitoring meeting?

Pat: This week, he read correctly eleven of the first twenty-five sight words. I really think he's a fast learner, but his self-regulation and social-emotional needs have been getting in the way of his academic growth. Since we've got a good plan to address those things, let's set an ambitious goal. How about we target that in six weeks, he will read all twenty-five sight words and apply them in context to read a level 8 text with at least 90 percent accuracy?

Beth: Great! Let's go for it. What about his retelling? You said he just rushed through the reading and couldn't retell afterward. Should we set a specific goal for retelling too?

Pat: You're right. Let's add to it that he will retell at least five events in sequence.

Marie: What assessments will we need to bring next time to determine if he's met that goal?

Pat: I'll redo the assessment of the first twenty-five sight words that we just gave him, do a running record on a level 8 text, and take anecdotal notes while he retells to monitor the number of events he includes in order. Do we need to collect any data on how the self-regulation accommodations are working?

Tom: I could make a sheet to keep in the gym to record how many laps he runs on the days he gets to bring a friend to race. Since bringing a friend is positive reinforcement for using his calm-down strategies and staying focused enough to participate in a full guided-reading group, would that help?

Marie: Excellent! I've been filling out his progress-monitoring chart as we talked. Let's look at it together so you can help me capture anything we're missing.

At this point, the team reviews the document in figure 6.2 (page 144).

Team Common Understandings

As you reflect on the first-grade team's progress-monitoring discussion in this chapter's vignette, you might be asking yourself, "How are teachers able to monitor the developmental needs of every student to this degree?" The answer is, they're not. There are not enough hours in the day to apply this level of collaboration to every student. However, teams can and should answer the third and fourth critical questions by monitoring the learning of essential standards for those select students who need additional time and support, as well as those who need extension. In this section, we begin explaining how teams do this.

Teams label *skills*, not *students*.

As a team, say it out loud: "*We label skills, not students.*"

When you catch yourself or a colleague saying or even thinking something about "my low babies," "that high group," "the bubble kids," or "the lowest readers" in a class—even when it is said with love in your heart or out of a desperate desire to help—try to stop and repeat this message: "*We label skills, not students.*"

The words teachers use frame their thinking, and when teachers call a student *low*, *high*, or any derivative thereof, they categorize them as people. Teachers may call a skill *low* or *high* to describe a *current* condition or data point that is malleable and changeable over time. When teachers think of a student as low (such as Stephen from this chapter's vignette)—*low reader, in the low comprehension group*, and so on—they subconsciously lower their expectations and absolve themselves of the responsibility to find ways to improve the student's specific skills. How would it impact teaching if every educator eliminated the term *low* and replaced it with student-first language that focuses on skills, such as "Students decoding below grade level," "Students with low fluency," or, "My comprehension group"?

If the goal is to label the skill and not the student so a group of educators can collaborate to improve those skills, then teams need to have a common understanding

Student: Stephen
Team: First grade

Strengths, Passions, or Interests: Pokemon, running, martial arts, and nonfiction topics: music, art, physical education, and library

Developmental Area	Date and Concern Baseline Data	Cause	Skill Level (extension, grade level, prerequisite, or foundational)	Intervention Action Steps	Frequency and Length of Instructional Focus	Duration and Ratio	Data Collection and Assessment	Person Responsible	Goal met?
Social-Emotional Development Self-awareness Self-management Social awareness Relationship skills Responsible decision making	January 20 Beginning to participate in whole-group lessons but has difficulty with regulating behavior during transitions and less-structured time, such as arrival and lunch	Needs explicit support in self-management skills (impulse control, self-discipline, and self-motivation)	Grade level	Greet him at the bus and escort to counselor's office for self-regulation strategy practice, review schedule for day, and support his safe transition into classroom morning routine.	Five times per week for fifteen minutes	May scale back if no longer necessary after three weeks One teacher to one student	Student self-assessment of using calm-down strategies	Leslie (counselor)	
		Needs frequent physical movement breaks as he works on body awareness, impulse control, and self-motivation	Grade level	Bring a friend to gym to race laps with him before lunch after two consecutive days of guided-reading participation. Provide flexible seating options during guided-reading instruction, such as a wobble chair.	When earned for five minutes	Six weeks, one teacher to one or two students	Chart laps in gymnasium and the number of days he participates in guided reading	Tom (physical education teacher)	
Physical Development Gross motor Fine motor Other	January 20 Strong gross-motor skills but difficulty maintaining a safe body (being addressed with social-emotional development)								

Language Speech articulation Listening Speaking (English language development)	Does not require support.							
Cognitive Development: Literacy Speech articulation Reading Writing	January 20 DRA 4 with 92 percent accuracy Did not pass retelling comprehension Was eleven of twenty-five with sight words	Struggles with self-regulation, resulting in inconsistent access to guided-reading instruction	Grade level	Guided reading on carpet with flexible seating option	Four times per week for twenty minutes	Six weeks	Running record	Pat (first-grade homeroom teacher)
		Rushes through reading, so confuses visually similar sight words and does not remember events in order to retell in sequence	Prerequisite	Sight-word group	Twice per week for twenty minutes	One teacher to four students	Anecdotal notes on retelling Sight-word assessment	
Cognitive Development Mathematics Other content areas (social studies, science, and so on) Learning skills (executive functions and so on)	Does not require support							

Source: Adapted from Buffum, Mattos, Weber, & Hierck, 2015; Source for SEL competencies: CASEL, n.d

Figure 6.2: Early childhood student progress-monitoring chart.

*Visit **go.SolutionTree.com/PLCbooks** for a free reproducible version of this figure.*

and clarity about the terms they use to label skills. Part of *common understanding* means understanding how your team refers to the skills students need at the start of the school year and those skills students acquire during the school year. Buffum et al. (2018) refer to *foundational prerequisite skills* as the content that comes from previous grade levels, whereas *immediate prerequisite skills* relates to content covered from prior months or units during the current grade level. For the purposes of this book, we define four categories of skill levels: (1) foundational skills, (2) prerequisite skills, (3) grade-level skills, and (4) extension skills. Figure 6.3 lists these skills with their corresponding definitions and examples. The examples focus on one of the skills Stephen struggled with, retelling (which requires comprehension), and shows what it looks like across the skill continuum. Figure 6.3 also includes a note in the Prerequisite Skills column to indicate where Stephen was with this skill at the time of the vignette.

Foundational Skills	Prerequisite Skills	Grade-Level Skills	Extension Skills
The skills taught in multiple prior grade levels	The skills taught in the current grade level's previous units or in the immediate prior grade level	Grade-level skills taught in the current unit of study	Grade-level skills taught in future units of study or skills taught at the next grade level
Comprehension Example	**Comprehension Example**	**Comprehension Example**	**Comprehension Example**
Reads for meaning and can retell some information from the book and answer questions when the teacher prompts	Retells events in sequence from the beginning, middle, and end of the book Notes from Stephen's progress-monitoring page place his instructional level here: "Rushes through reading, so does not remember events in order to retell in sequence"	Retells important events and details in sequence with specific vocabulary from text	Summarizes the important events in a text

Figure 6.3: Defining skill-levels with a student example.

Consider what the vignette's first-grade team understood about Stephen and how figure 6.3 clarifies his ability to comprehend text. From this information, you can derive that Stephen understands that a book tells a story and can tell teachers about what he reads, so he is past the foundational-skill level for comprehension (as the team defines it). However, he is not yet consistently retelling events in sequence. So, when the team discusses his comprehension, members are talking about the needed prerequisite skills for readers at his grade level. As the team focuses on developing that skill, Stephen may begin to not only tell events in sequence but also do so with specific vocabulary from the text. The power of the language teachers apply to students and skills is that, rather than the first-grade team deeming Stephen a *low reader*, they used specific and targeted instruction to move him from working on a prerequisite skill to working on a grade-level skill. By understanding that any deficit language should be about the skills, not the student, the team in this example understood it was Stephen's comprehension that needed to improve, not Stephen.

Notice how Stephen's information on the progress-monitoring chart in figure 6.2 (page 144) provides information on his current baseline data (DRA, 2019). The DRA (2019) assesses several reading skills, such as fluency, self-correcting, and making connections. Yet, that information is not included on Stephen's progress-monitoring chart because the team is only putting a plan in place to target the specific skills they need to monitor, and Stephen did not need additional time and support with those skills. The team also could not assume he requires intensive instruction in all content areas. In fact, notice how the mathematics section in figure 6.2 is blank. Before the progress-monitoring meeting, Stephen took a mathematics common formative assessment and demonstrated full understanding of grade-level skills and concepts related to numeracy. As a result, the blank section of the chart tells the team that he does not need support in mathematics or any other cognitive area. He only needed additional time and support with self-management skills and specific areas of literacy.

While compiling information about student learning in this way for data discussions and progress monitoring may initially seem like a big task for teams who have not yet tackled this work, you can see from our example with Stephen that it actually simplifies and puts a laser-like focus on the task ahead because teams develop common understanding of exactly what needs to be done for each student instead of feeling overwhelmed with so many students with so many needs.

Data Discussions and Team SMART Goals

Now that you understand the importance of having common understanding and what it looks like to monitor the progress of one student, you might be asking, "What happens if the data from my teams' common formative assessment shows that a significant percentage of my students did not meet grade-level benchmarks? What are my next steps?" Well, you need the power of your team.

The next layer of work for the team after creating common formative assessments is to collect and organize students' data to use during team data discussions. This ultimately involves team implementation of a data protocol (see Data-Analysis Protocols, page 154), which results in your team clarifying its response to the third and fourth critical questions of a PLC and enabling it to monitor the learning of all students. At the start of the school year, teams develop SMART goals. The importance of these goals is that they provide clarity for the team about what it wants to achieve. About SMART goals, DuFour et al. (2016) write, "While district and school goals tend to be broad goal statements, the SMART goal acronym (Conzemius & O'Neill, 2014) provides much-needed clarity for the kinds of goals teams pursue" (p. 89). As we introduced in A Results Orientation (page 26), goals are SMART when they are:

- Strategic and specific (aligned with the organization's goals)

- Measurable

- Attainable

- Results oriented

- Time bound (specifying when the goal will be achieved; Conzemius & O'Neill, 2014)

SMART goals always start with teams identifying a current reality and then setting a strategic, measurable, attainable, results-oriented, and time-bound goal to mark progress. The following is an example of a year-long SMART goal to be measured with end-of-year assessments. Teams can write goals, such as this one, for a number of areas, including essential standards, specific topics, district benchmarks, and common end-of-unit assessments.

> **Our reality:** *Last year, 76 percent of our students met the proficiency standard on our end-of-year reading assessment.*

> **Our goal:** *This year, we will increase the percentage of students meeting the proficiency standard on the end-of-year reading assessment to 83 percent or higher.*

In "Goal Statements and Goal-Directed Behavior," O'Hora and Maglieri (2006) reinforce the importance of goal setting by stating, "Goal setting is one of the simplest and most effective organizational interventions that can be used to increase employee performance" (p. 132).

In the following set of sections, we examine how teams gather data, plan a data discussion, and create SMART goals.

Organize Data

In chapter 5 (page 109), we talked about a team of preschool teachers who created a mathematics common formative assessment to determine if students were able to identify, copy, and extend simple AB patterns. To effectively analyze and manipulate the resulting data, the team used an electronic spreadsheet to create a data chart for all the students in the grade level. During this process of collating student data across classes, members worked together to determine the criteria they would use to determine students' current skill levels. The preschool team decided to use colors in the spreadsheet as a way to highlight the skills for which students may need extra support or extension. The team applied the following criteria.

- They highlighted in green students they observed demonstrating not only grade-level skills but also extension skills.

- They highlighted in yellow students who demonstrated learning of all grade-level concepts.

- They highlighted in red students who were unable to demonstrate the grade-level skills. For these students, the team conducted further analysis to determine which students could sort objects by at least one attribute (the prerequisite skill level, light red) and which students could not sort by one attribute (the foundational skill level, darker red).

Figure 6.4 (page 150) illustrates this collating process. For simplicity, it reflects only dark-grey shading (red) for those student skills the team identified as needing additional support and light gray (green) for students who are ready for extension. Notice how students are not labeled, nor are student names highlighted; instead, the team only highlights data when classifying current skill levels.

In this scenario, the team collectively developed the electronic tool, but each team member entered and organized his or her own data. This allowed the team to do the work before the data-discussion team meeting, giving teachers ample time in their team meeting to look collectively at trends across the grade level. Notice in figure 6.4 how the column for teacher names is next to each student. This allowed the team to sort the data by class for input and then change to sorting by skill so the team could see all the students who need additional support across the grade level for a given skill. Having this kind of flexibility enables teams to implement a better plan.

Plan for a Data Discussion

In a school where teachers work in isolation, each teacher might take his or her own data and go back to his or her classroom to devise a learning plan for students solo. However, in a school that functions as a PLC, teachers have an opportunity to learn from one another and develop new skills to support students' learning. Remember, all students are *your* students.

Time is always a factor, but when teams make time to collaborate about the right work, it makes a difference for students. Purposeful planning requires the use of targeted focused agendas, which assist teams in doing the right work promptly while also enhancing their professional growth. In *Learning by Doing*, DuFour et al. (2016) emphasize the importance of protocols:

> When teacher teams use protocols and tools to help structure their conversations about student learning, they sharpen their pedagogy and deepen their content knowledge. According to the National Turning Points Center (NTPC, 2001), teachers who use protocols have a more complete and comprehensive understanding of what students know and are able to do. The regular use of protocols also helps teachers develop a shared language for assessing student work and promotes the creation of a common understanding of what quality student work looks like. (p. 157)

Student Name	Teacher Name	Foundational Skill: Observe similarity and difference of objects	Foundational Skill: Match objects	Prerequisite Skill: Sort by one attribute	Grade-Level Skill: Identify pattern	Grade-Level Skill: Copy pattern	Extension Skill: Extend pattern	Extension Skill: Create Pattern other than AB	Current Skill Level
Nate	Tiana	NA	NA	NA	Yes	Yes	Yes	Yes (ABC, ABB)	Extension
Meg	Ayaan	NA	NA	NA	Yes	Yes	Yes	Yes (ABCD)	Extension
Jario	Ayaan	NA	NA	NA	Yes	Yes	Yes	No (can create AB)	Grade level
Ben	Janice	Yes	Yes	Yes	No	Yes	No	NA	Prerequisite
Jenn	Tiana	Yes	No	No	No (needs prompts)	No	No	NA	Foundational

Figure 6.4: Team data chart from a common formative assessment on patterns.

The first step in making team meetings meaningful and efficient is a well-designed team-meeting agenda and data protocol. We address the data protocol in the Data-Analysis Protocols section (see page 153). For now, let's focus on the agenda for data-discussion meetings. Figure 6.5 shows an example of an agenda for this meeting.

Date: January 13

Time: Sixty minutes

Team members present: Janice (grade-level teacher); Ayaan (grade-level teacher); Hana (grade-level teacher); Tiana (grade-level teacher); Jayla (English language teacher); Christina (special education teacher); Janine (principal)

Time	Topic	Guiding Questions	Tasks to complete prior to the team meeting
Five minutes	**Celebrations**	How can we celebrate our team's creation or use of assessment tools or positive data outcomes? Is there something new we learned from the assessment process?	None
Twenty-five minutes	**Data discussion** using data-analysis protocol	What trends do we see in our assessment data for patterns? (Evaluate the team's mathematics SMART goal in relation to the current data.) Who needs extra time and support to meet grade-level benchmarks? Who should have their learning extended?	Look at the data for trends. Complete the highlighted questions on the data-protocol form and record your students' names on the form.
Ten minutes	**Group students** based on specific needs	How will we group students to support or extend their learning? What workshop models can we put into practice to support guided instruction?	None
Twenty minutes	**Make instructional plan** to support students' needs	How can we create an instructional plan and implement specific strategies and best practices that allow for reteaching, spiraling, and extending learning?	Bring instructional resources you used with your students to successfully support their learning to share with your teammates.

Figure 6.5: Data-discussion meeting agenda focusing on patterns.

*Visit **go.SolutionTree.com/PLCbooks** for a free reproducible version of this figure.*

To open the team's data-discussion meetings, ask members to share a quick celebration. Common formative assessments and celebrations go hand in hand. Celebrations are a quick way to set a positive tone for the meeting and remind team members it is not about the numbers but about learning. Celebrations also provide a chance to share and tell the team's story. Celebrations can be anything: a student's or colleague's success, something new students learned, someone taking a risk, data results, and so on. You'll learn more about celebrations in the epilogue of this book (page 203).

After celebrating comes reflecting. It's important to give team members time to reflect on their individual data as well as trends across the team and grade level. Using a structure, like turn and talk to a partner, can help teachers process data, and sharing with just one person first may make teachers feel safer before opening up to the whole group. It is important for all team members to look at their data and those of their teammates in a transparent way. As the team goes through the process of analyzing the data, they start to form ideas about instructional plans to support all students' needs. They may find great value in sharing ideas about the various learning formats that the team can use to support students' needs. This could involve the process of forming small student groups or specific student partnerships within and across the grade level.

Although student data are used to make specific instructional decisions about learning, teams also use them to monitor the overall growth of the team and progress toward their SMART goals.

Determine Team SMART Goals

As teams begin to collectively own the data, they break down barriers and begin to operate as one. Determining a team goal helps drive the team's work. All goals should align with the team's SMART goals, which should align to the schoolwide goals and focus on improvement from the previous level of performance (Conzemius & O'Neill, 2014). Figure 6.6 illustrates a preschool team's document to create a mathematics SMART goal at the beginning of a school year. It shows how, for the previous year, 80 percent of the students met the grade-level benchmark on three out of six of the fundamental mathematics assessments. The team's SMART goal for the new year states that 85 percent of students will achieve the grade-level benchmark on *all six* fundamental mathematics assessments by the end of the school year (May 14.) In the Progress Toward Student Learning and Team Goals section (page 163), we discuss how teams use assessment data gathered throughout the year to monitor the team's SMART goal.

The next necessary step after teams set an agenda and SMART goal is to establish a data-analysis protocol to help structure conversations about students' learning.

Current Reality and Team SMART Goal	Strategies and Action Steps	Who is Responsible	Target Date or Time	Evidence of Effectiveness
Last year, 80 percent of students met the grade-level benchmark on **three of the six** mathematics fundamental assessments (counting, sorting, patterns, geometry, measurement, and composing and decomposing). **Team SMART Goal:** This year, 85 percent of the students will meet the grade-level benchmark **on all six** mathematics fundamental assessments by May 14.	1. Each team member will observe other team members implementing best practices in small-group targeted instruction. 2. Each team member will look at the data from each mathematics-fundamental assessment and determine best practices of teammates who yield high pass rates on each skill and share ideas and strategies. 3. Team members will reteach concepts and develop specific strategies to target instruction and continuously administer each of the six mathematics fundamental assessments throughout the year until we meet our team goal of 85 percent on all six assessments.	All team members are responsible for achieving the SMART goal.	All team members will administer each original mathematics-fundamental assessment on a designated day in the yearly mathematics assessment calendar. Following the data discussion for each mathematics-fundamental assessment, team members will reteach and re-administer the assessment after three to four weeks of instruction.	Student performance on all six of the mathematics-fundamental assessments meets the grade-level benchmarks

Figure 6.6: Team SMART goal for mathematics.

*Visit **go.SolutionTree.com/PLCbooks** for a free reproducible version of this figure.*

Tips for **Administrators**	*Tips for* **Coaches**	*Tips for* **Teachers**
Support culture by attending team data-discussion meetings when possible and engaging in the learning along with the teachers. Support teams in understanding the why of creating and maintaining SMART goals as well as learning about and fostering clarity regarding the SMART goal acronym.	Help teacher teams in building common understanding and using common language. Assist teams in planning focused and meaningful data discussion agendas. Think about ways to help the team collectively own the data as one.	Look for opportunities to celebrate your students and your teammates when looking at students' data. Be mindful of your own thoughts and language when evaluating student data. Promote the idea of labeling the skill, not the student.

Data-Analysis Protocols

If common formative assessments are the linchpin of the PLC process, then a good data-analysis protocol is the linchpin of the work of teams. To keep analyzing data together from becoming a blame game, a competition, or a venting session about "those kids," teams use a data protocol to have rich discussions about data and to make important instructional decisions for students and their collective and individual practices. Figure 6.7 shows an example of this protocol. It begins with an overview of student results on a team-administered assessment. It then provides a template for teams to answer seven questions about the data they collect. Within each section, teams provide individual statements or team-collaborated answers, depending on which context is most appropriate.

The following analysis is based on our team's common assessment of mathematics patterns.

Assessment date: December 15

Teacher	Pass Rate
Overall Team Pass Rate	70 percent
Janice	70 percent
Hana	80 percent
Ayaan	62 percent
Tiana	70 percent

Based on data obtained from the team's common formative assessment, answer the following questions.

1. **Which students need additional time and support to achieve at or above proficiency?**

   Janice (teacher): Anthony, Ben, Ann, Javier, Ishaan, Terrell, Ian

   Hana (teacher): Nick, Braden, Layla

   Ayaan (teacher): Jack, Kelly, Tim, John, Nancy, Han, Stephanie, Jamal, Kyan

   Tiana (teacher): Jodi, Mike, Jenn, Matt, Aaliyah, Ally

2. **Which students need time to extend their learning?**

   Janice (teacher): Ethan, Jake, T.J.

   Hana (teacher): Darnell

   Ayaan (teacher): Meg, Zach

   Tiana (teacher): Nate, Mateo, Ahmed

What is our plan to extend learning for students who are highly proficient?

For ten minutes, once a week over two weeks, the teacher will meet with these students in a small group about transferring patterns (a kindergarten grade-level skill), so they can apply new knowledge learned while engaging at the pattern learning stations.

During the next unit of study, keep two patterns stations (for making beaded bracelets and using stickers and stamps). Include non-AB patterns in both stations (ABC, ABBA, and so on) for all students to access; encourage students to create their own patterns; and give them opportunities to extend the patterns. Provide time for these students to work together at stations and verbally explain to one another the different patterns they create.

3. **What is an area where students in my classroom struggled?**

Janice (teacher): Some students identified patterns that are not true patterns (see query).

- *Anthony, Javier, and Ishaan*—Identify some obvious patterns but not when one shape placement changes to make it a non-pattern; unable to copy patterns

- *Ben, Terrell, Ian*—Can copy AB patterns and identify some obvious patterns but not when one shape placement changes to make it a non-pattern

- *Ann*—Can't identify or copy patterns

More obvious nonpattern

Less obvious nonpattern

Hana (teacher):

- *Nick*—Can't identify or copy patterns, but can sort by one attribute (shape or color)

- *Braden, Layla*—Can only identify patterns

Many students at grade level were only able to create AB patterns, so they were not able to meet the extension skill level. Also, when asked to extend the pattern, students had misconceptions.

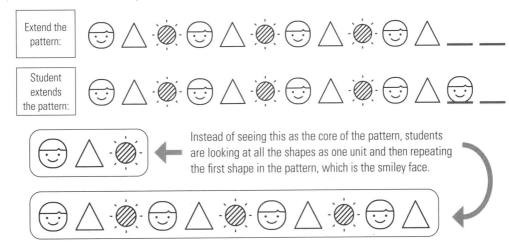

Ayaan (teacher):

- *Jack, Kelly, Tim, John Nancy, Han, Stephanie, Jamal, Kyan*—Can all identify patterns but can't copy patterns (they can all sort by one attribute: shape, color, or size)

Tiana (teacher):

- *Jodi, Mike*—Were able to identify a pattern, but when asked to copy a pattern, the students used the same shapes without actually copying the pattern, nor did the shapes they used repeat to form a pattern

- *Jenn, Aaliyah, Matt, Ally*—Not able to identify or copy patterns, but can sort by one attribute (color and shape)

Figure 6.7: Data-analysis protocol.

continued →

*Visit **go.SolutionTree.com/PLCbooks** for a free reproducible version of this figure.*

4. **What strategies did the team member use when students performed well?**

Ayaan: In all my morning meetings for the past two weeks, I used pattern quick images. I flashed a pattern card up quickly for a few seconds, put it down, and asked the students if it was a pattern or nonpattern. I have them explain their thinking of why they think it is or is not a pattern. I then put the card back up, and we have a class discussion about it. If it is a nonpattern, we talk about how we can change it to make it a true repeating pattern. During this activity, I have tools out on the carpet to help me model and explain to students how to think about patterns. This was a very successful activity, and after doing it several times, many of my students started to make meaningful connections to the learning.

Tiana: During my transition from snack time to center time, I played the *Banana Banana Meatball* song by GoNoodle (https://gonoodle.com), and we made up gestures to go along with the song.

Hana: I used a lot of movement patterns with my transitions throughout my day with students. I also had them do a lot of pattern sorting at stations (pattern or nonpattern), and we looked for patterns on students' clothing during our morning meetings.

Janice: During play, I would interact with students and create patterns with the foods in the play-kitchen area. I noticed when I was not there, students began doing it on their own with other play objects. I also noticed two students who were struggling to copy patterns at the learning stations. I decided to print those students' photographs and mine. I then used my photograph with theirs as tools to create and copy patterns with these two students.

5. **What is an area where our entire team's students struggled?**

When we modeled patterns, we mostly used AB patterns, so we did not use a lot of other types of patterns. As a result, many students were unable to access the extension skills in the assessment because they were not exposed to a lot of other types of patterns, like ABC, ABBA, and so on.

Many students were only able to identify nonpatterns when they were very obvious.

6. **What do we believe is the cause of students' struggles?**

We spent too much time and attention modeling examples of AB patterns. We also didn't show enough examples and nonexamples of patterns and emphasize how to fix or adjust nonpatterns into patterns.

7. **What is our plan for improving students' results?**

For students who need extra support to learn grade-level skills:

- Provide small-group instruction to focus on specific skills (identifying and copying patterns). Ensure a three-to-one student-to-teacher ratio. Meet with students for ten minutes during center time three times a week for three weeks.

- Engage students in similarity-and-difference activities. Have students copy teacher- or peer-made patterns and, when students make errors, have them look for similarities and differences and fix their errors to accurately copy the pattern.

- Print students' photographs, and use their photographs and the teacher's photograph (or those of other adults in the school building, parents, or siblings) to create AB patterns. Have students copy the patterns.

- Reassess students working at the support level during the first week of February. (Give students grade-level prompts and possibly extension prompts, if they are ready.)

Continued learning for all students:

- Continue to have students use movement patterns during transitions throughout the day (include a variety of repeating patterns beyond just AB patterns; for example, ABC; ABBA, and so on).
- Two to three times a week during morning meetings, have students engage with pattern quick images. (If needed, see Ayaan for a tutorial.)
- Use more GoNoodle videos and songs connected to patterns during snack time.
- Email specialist teachers and ask them to incorporate patterning into lesson plans when appropriate.
- Work with students during play (joining them in centers and using questioning during play). Focus on AB patterns and other non-AB patterns.
- Keep the stamps-and-stickers and beaded-necklace pattern stations going during center time for an additional one to two weeks.
- Incorporate pattern ideas into the new unit about community helpers.
- Reassess students' progress during the first week of February. (Students who did not meet the grade-level benchmarks will access the grade-level prompts, and students who met all grade-level benchmarks will access the extension prompts.)

In the following sections, we elaborate on the process of answering each question on the data-analysis protocol. This involves answering seven questions.

1. Which students need additional time and support to achieve at or above proficiency?

2. Which students need time to extend their learning?

3. What is an area where students in my classroom struggled?

4. What strategies did the team member use when students performed well?

5. What is an area where our entire team's students struggled?

6. What do we believe is the cause of students' struggles?

7. What is our plan for improving students' results?

As you review the following sections, return to this example and reflect on how you would envision how your team discussion might take place as your team uses this tool in alignment with the team assessments.

Which Students Need Additional Time and Support to Achieve at or Above Proficiency?

Using formative common assessment data, teachers determine which students have not yet reached proficiency and need reteaching. In this example, teachers looked at the data highlighted in dark grey (red) in figure 6.4 (page 150) to identify any student unable to identify or copy patterns. Each teacher examines his or her respective classroom data to determine who needs extra time and support for learning foundational or prerequisite skills and records their names to answer the first question in the data-analysis protocol (see figure 6.7, page 154).

Which Students Need Time to Extend Their Learning?

Teachers look at their individual classroom data to see if any students need their learning extended. In this example, teachers include any students highlighted in light grey (green) in figure 6.4 (page 150). These are the students who could identify, copy, extend, and create patterns. Each team member records these students' names to answer the second question in the data-analysis protocol (see figure 6.7, page 154).

This leads to a follow-up question for teams to address: What is our plan to extend the learning of students who are highly proficient? When teams do not use a protocol for this, they often focus only on the students needing reteaching and run out of time before addressing the needs of the students who need extension. Because in a PLC culture *all* means *all*, teams must expect every student to learn at high levels. This means teachers expect even those students coming into a unit with strong skills in that area to achieve growth. In this example, the team decides each teacher will work with a small group of students once per week for ten minutes for the next two weeks. This leaves the majority of teacher time in the classroom available to address the needs of other students while still ensuring dedicated time and a solid plan to extend learning. Just as teams consider the needs of the whole child when designing interventions, teachers also partner with students to consider learning extensions by encouraging these students to verbally explain to one another their extended learning. In addition to learning additional skills, this positions these students to extend their social and communication skills.

What Is an Area Where Students in My Classroom Struggled?

For the third question in the data-analysis protocol (see figure 6.7, page 154), each team member provides information about assessment areas in which students in his or her classroom struggled. As each member of the team shares what his or her students struggled with, it is important to be as specific as possible. It is often useful for teachers to bring artifacts to support their conclusions, rather than just looking at the scores in the spreadsheet. Teachers often find themselves feeling vulnerable when sharing how students did not make expected progress knowing that teammates' students may not have had the same struggle. When there is an area for growth in a teacher's data, focusing on artifacts of student work helps teachers remember this is about how to help the students improve their learning and not a blame game. These artifacts can include the actual student assessment recording forms, anecdotal notes the teachers took, and tools they used during the assessment. Keep these artifacts available at the meeting, so all team members can analyze what may have been at the root of students' misconceptions.

What Strategies Did the Team Member Use When Students Performed Well?

In addition to analyzing students' areas of struggle, it is important to think about what strategies worked for those students who performed well. This allows teachers to gather new ideas from their peers, ask clarifying questions, and celebrate learning. This process also opens the door to examine differences between classrooms, where perhaps in one classroom, students showed a higher level of success than others. Although teams plan lessons together, the language each teacher uses in his or her classroom may have been different, and assessment results can reflect this. For example, discussion of these differences may reveal that some teachers may have added strategies or scaffolds to meet the needs of students in the moment. Other teachers may have added more activities beyond the lesson, possibly at the beginning or end of the day. Use the answer to the fourth question in the data-analysis protocol (see figure 6.7, page 154) to collaborate on ways for teachers whose students experienced success with an assessment to support teachers whose students did not. (We are big fans of peer observation, which not only allows us to learn together while teaching but models for students how we all learn together).

What Is an Area Where Our Entire Team's Students Struggled?

When students struggle more broadly—that is, struggles are not isolated to small groups or a specific classroom—teams must analyze why. By definition, a PLC is "an ongoing process in which educators work collaboratively in recurring cycles of collective inquiry and action research to achieve better results for the students they serve" (DuFour et al., 2016, p. 10). Using a data-analysis protocol is a form of collective inquiry because it requires teams to identify areas where students across the grade level struggled. Through this analysis, team members reflect on how they planned the unit and what they might improve during reteaching. If there is a trend across the grade level that many students in different classes struggled in a common area, then the team may need to adjust its lesson plans and make time to reteach the whole class rather than small groups of students. In answering the fifth question of our example data-analysis protocol (see figure 6.7, page 154), the preschool team noticed that, in general, most students were only able to identify and create AB patterns.

What Do We Believe is the Cause of Students' Struggles?

It is sometimes challenging to determine the cause of a struggle; however, team members benefit from this reflection because they will be teaching this unit again next year. Therefore, this examination ensures team members are also using the data to refine their practices so the next year's students have the opportunity to go even further. In this scenario, the team determined the data showed many students only created AB patterns at the learning stations. The teachers concluded that too many of their lessons focus on AB patterns, and they should have given students more exposure to a variety of patterns, such as ABBA, ABC, and so on. This conclusion provides an action item for the team to execute during reteaching and for instruction the next year.

What Is Our Plan for Improving Students' Results?

With an understanding of all the factors that led to students' struggles, whether in isolated cases or across the team, it is the team's job to come up with a plan for ensuring that any learners who have not met grade-level standards have the opportunity to get there. Approaches to this step will vary depending on the reasons teams determined for why some students didn't learn. Teams may need to engage in whole-group reteaching for all students on certain skills. In many cases, teams must determine how teachers will support and extend the needs of learners in smaller groups. To affect this, teams should use the answer to the seventh question in figure 6.7 (page 154) to consider sharing students across classrooms to carve out common intervention and extension time. This can make it easier to group students with peers working at the same skill level. Consider the following examples.

- If there are just a few students who need extension, one teacher might choose to work with all students at this level once or twice per week at the same time.

- If teachers on the team each have a few students needing skill A and a few who need skill B, they could decide one teacher will take the students needing skill A while the other takes the students needing skill B. In this way, they each teach one group (usually no more than six students) instead of two smaller groups. This frees up an additional time slot for each teacher.

- In the case of students who need more substantial support, a teacher who supports the grade level such an English language or special education teacher might build in time to incorporate the reteaching of content skills concurrent with existing instruction to those students who need it (even if they do not have an individualized education plan or English learner designation).

Teams should be creative in using the information they've acquired to make adjustments based on the specific course content and what the data communicate. The preschool team members who put together the data-analysis protocol in figure 6.7 decided they would each support the learners in their own classrooms to meet grade-level benchmarks. They decided on a plan to work with these students in small groups three times per week for ten to fifteen minutes on specific learning tasks the team talked about during the data discussion. Members also decided on the following next steps.

- Because Janice had a great deal of success with students' use of photographs of themselves and their peers as a tool for creating and copying patterns, the whole team decided to use this as a strategy for supporting students in relearning grade-level skills and concepts.

- In Ayaan's class, all students were able to identify patterns, which he attributed to his use of quick images. So, the team agreed each teacher would try that activity during the morning meeting with students a few times a week for a couple more weeks.

- All team members said they would incorporate movement patterns into their transitions and play the silly pattern song and videos during snack time.

- Although the team will move on to start a new unit of study, members also decided to keep a few key patterns at the mathematics centers, while making sure to add in a variety of patterns and not just AB patterns. At times, the team will intentionally form heterogeneous student partnerships or groups based on student skill levels.

- One team member volunteered to email the physical education teacher, who works with the preschool students, to let her know the specific pattern learning targets students are working on, so she can incorporate them into her physical education lessons.

After three weeks of reteaching and executing these decisions, the team determined it would reassess students using the same assessment tool. This included not only students who needed extra support to meet grade-level benchmarks but also students who met those benchmarks but who did not have access to the extension skills. The team's goal with this assessment was to gauge if their reteaching strategies worked.

Throughout the seven steps of the data-analysis protocol (see figure 6.7, page 154), it is important that teams both record the information and save it to a central location where every team member can access it. If the team has a rich discussion using the data-analysis protocol but does not record the information discussed, it is likely that each team member will walk away with a slightly different understanding of the results and, therefore, any action plans that derive from the results. This doesn't mean team members can't leave the meeting having learned something new, resulting in an effective shift in practice. They could! But for team members to hold one another accountable, maintain a collective understanding of what they find in data, and perform the actions they agree to, it requires a written record.

Ensuring this record is easily accessible to everyone also conveys that it is everyone's responsibility to follow the plan set in place and support one another through the process. While immersed in the work, if a teacher discovers a new powerful strategy that is working for his or her students, it becomes that teacher's responsibility to share that useful strategy (tool, idea, game, and so on) with all team members. Teachers can share this information quickly in the hallway before students arrive, at a team debrief at the end of the school day, through an email or texting a picture of what worked, or by putting a copy of the activity (along with a quick description) in everyone's mailbox. When high-functioning teams reach this level of collaboration and collective responsibility, the data-analysis protocol goes from being a template for a single meeting to a plan with maximum impact. The following list provides a useful summary for the steps teams follow to maximize the value of their data discussions.

1. Set a date for the data discussion to ensure it happens in a timely manner. Input and compile the assessment data in preparation for the meeting.

2. Use the data-analysis protocol to guide the data discussion and record the reflections and analysis the team shared in response to each question.

3. Store the recorded discussion in a central location for all team members to access, reflect on, and use on an ongoing basis.

4. Implement the action plans the team decided on to improve student learning.

5. Continually communicate as a team after the data-discussion meeting and add to the plans.

Tips for **Administrators**	*Tips for* **Coaches**	*Tips for* **Teachers**
Understand that having teams analyze data together is non-discretionary, a tight aspect of the school's culture. Hold teams accountable for doing this important work. Hold yourselves accountable for providing the necessary time, training, tools and support for teachers to engage in this work.	Find current or new research regarding best practices, strategies, and tools that might be useful to the team when thinking about how to make instructional plans for supporting student needs.	Use electronic tools to help organize and analyze data. When analyzing data, look for trends.
Ensure teams utilize a data-analysis protocol. This is critical because the true essence of collaboration "represents a systematic process in which teachers work together interdependently in order to *impact* their classroom practice in ways that will lead to better results for their students, for their team, and for their school"(DuFour et al., 2016 p.12).	Determine what coaching moves and techniques you can use to promote a psychologically safe environment, where team members are willing to be transparent and share ideas.	Bring assessment tools students used (student assessments, mathematics manipulatives, and so on) to the data-discussion meeting to help you explain specific details about what students may have struggled with or who demonstrated beyond the grade-level skills
		Be willing to think outside of the box when making instructional plans. Are there opportunities to have students work with a particular teacher or student (or students) in another classroom sometime during the day or the week?

Progress Toward Student Learning and Team Goals

Data discussions using the data-analysis protocol in figure 6.7 (page 154) allow teams to develop a plan for interventions or extensions, but team members still need to determine if their plans led to additional learning via reassessing and comparing the resulting data to team goals.

The preschool team example we use in this chapter wrote a team SMART goal in the area of mathematics at the beginning of the school year (see figure 6.6, page 153). The team goal said they expected 85 percent of the preschool students to meet grade-level benchmarks on all six mathematics fundamental assessments by the end of the year (May 14). The preschool team administered one of the six mathematics fundamental assessments (related to patterns) in December. After the first assessment, 70 percent of the students had met grade-level benchmarks. During the team's data-dialogue meeting, they determined that to reach their end-of-year SMART goal, they would reteach concepts and skills relating to patterns to those students who did not make the grade-level benchmark over the next three weeks. At the end of that time, teachers would readminister the patterns assessment to students who had not yet met the grade-level benchmark. The team used the SMART goal monitoring document pictured in figure 6.8 to record their goal of getting 80 percent of the students to meet the grade-level benchmark by January 12.

Year-Long Team SMART Goal: This year, 85 percent of the students will meet the grade-level benchmark on all six mathematics fundamental assessments by May 14.				
Team SMART Goals **Our current reality:** Only 70 percent of the students met the grade-level benchmark on the end-of-unit patterns common formative assessment. **Our goal:** 80 percent of students will meet the grade-level benchmark on the end-of-unit patterns common formative assessment on January 12.	**Strategies and Action Steps** We will use small, focused groups with targeted instruction to reteach pattern concepts for students still working on meeting the grade-level benchmark (pattern quick images, copying and creating patterns with student and teacher picture cards, and so on).	**Who is Responsible** All team members are responsible for meeting this goal.	**Target Date or Time** We will reassess students who did not meet the grade-level benchmark on the original assessment on January 12.	**Evidence of Effectiveness** Student performance on the patterns common formative assessment will show if students have met the grade-level benchmark.

Figure 6.8: Monitoring team SMART goals throughout the year.

With this monitoring plan in place, the preschool team got to work. Table 6.1 (page 164) shows how the team continued to see growth in student learning over time as they retaught and reassessed students throughout the year.

Table 6.1: Preschool Patterns Assessment Pass Rates Over Time

Teacher	December	January	February	March
Janice	70 percent	83 percent	92 percent	100 percent
Hana	80 percent	92 percent	100 percent	100 percent
Ayaan	62 percent	75 percent	83 percent	92 percent
Tiana	70 percent	83 percent	92 percent	100 percent
Overall Pass Rate	70 percent	83 percent	92 percent	98 percent

Notice how the team exceeded their January SMART goal by three percentage points and were two points away from reaching their end-of-year goal of 85 percent of students reaching proficiency. While the team made significant strides, the members did not accept *close* as a valid outcome. Even as they continued with the curriculum, members briefly discussed new strategies to put into place to support the 17 percent of students who had not achieved proficiency with the grade-level benchmarks and continued to work with those students. The team reassessed these students yet again in February (after continued reteaching in small groups), and exceeded its original end-of-year goal with 92 percent proficiency. This was not enough for the team, as many members felt the remaining 8 percent of students were very close to proficiency on their learning goals. Because this goal represented part of an essential need-to-know standard, the team carved out time to continue reteaching just those few students who still needed it, and, in March, 98 percent of students knew how to identify and copy AB patterns.

Think for a moment about the consequences for students had the team stopped in December and accepted 30 percent of their students *not* meeting the grade-level benchmark. What would the result be for both those students and the kindergarten teachers they would have next year? Not only would the kindergarten teachers have to teach to their own grade-level standards, but they would also have to spend additional time on interventions just to bring more students to preschool-level proficiency.

Now consider what happens if the kindergarten teachers do not successfully bring these students to grade level. Without collective responsibility and schoolwide systematic interventions in place for every student every year, the gap widens year after year. Take a moment to think about if your own child was part of the 30 percent who didn't meet the grade-level benchmark. We believe it is a teacher's moral obligation to ensure all students are learning at high levels, and the PLC process provides the most effective culture to ensure that learning in the early childhood years occurs. To that end, in the following sections, we examine how teams use effective monitoring techniques to increase rigor from the beginning of the school year to the end and to ensure that this monitoring reflects the whole child, not just his or her academics.

Increasing Rigor From Beginning of the Year to the End of the Year

The work teams put into ensuring all students learn also comes with a standards mandate that the learning have sufficient rigor. It is unacceptable for students to just retain information; rather, teams need to push students to understand and communicate their thinking about essential standards. Society needs students to be critical and creative thinkers, skillful mathematicians, and prolific readers, which requires teachers to evolve their instructional practices and shift their mindsets. Teachers must be cognizant of the level of rigor they expect even in early childhood education so there is a foundation to prepare students to access all opportunities for higher-level classes in later grades. The best way to achieve this kind of rigor is to maximize the number of students receiving extension (Buffum et al., 2018). Neither teams nor students should see extensions as busy work or just more of the same work. When Brian's daughter was in elementary school, she was regularly pulled from class because she showed mastery in some concepts in mathematics. She came home one day and said that she didn't want to be pulled out anymore because instead of getting ten problems, she was getting twenty of the same problems. She felt she was being punished for being successful. Extension is not merely more work. It's about providing students with "opportunities to pursue their interest, extend their understanding, and broaden their learning experiences" (Guskey, 2010, p.56).

Consider the preschool team data in table 6.2.

Table 6.2: Extension Access Rates on Preschool Pattern Assessment

Teacher	December	February
Janice	25 percent	58 percent
Hana	8 percent	33 percent
Ayaan	17 percent	50 percent
Tiana	25 percent	58 percent
Overall Pass Rate	19 percent	50 percent

This table shows how only 19 percent of students access extension standards in December. Recall the team concluded this low number of students showing above-grade-level proficiency was the result of members focusing too much time on AB patterns during their direct instruction without exposing students to creating and extending a variety of pattern types. We'll address the February reassessment, but first, take the time to think about why it might be important for teachers to allow all students to learn about a variety of patterns and create their own patterns. Exposure is not mastery. In this case, the team does not expect all students to create and extend a variety of patterns, but ask yourself and your team the following questions.

- "Is the act of exposing students to this learning beneficial?"

- "Is the act of creating a variety of patterns engaging for preK learners?"

- "Is it powerful to have learners communicate with one another about the work they create?"

These questions do not reflect pressure to perform but rather the benefits of elevating rigor by exposing students to these skills in a safe environment with teachers providing scaffolds and supports. This preschool team was starting a new unit of study and didn't have a great deal of time to devote to extending these concepts, but members decided to fit extra instruction into other parts of the day outside the main focus lesson, such as at the start of the day; during transitions and snack time; as part of physical education, playtime, and center time; and by incorporating these ideas into the next unit. As table 6.2 (page 165) shows, when the team reassessed students in February, 50 percent of the students at grade level met the above-grade-level benchmarks. This included a few students who had started at the support level in December and then jumped beyond grade-level expectations. There was no telling in December which students needing support would make that jump, but think about the compounding positive effects for those young learners when teachers take the approach of maximizing the number of students receiving extension. Even for students who did not exceed grade-level standards, the exposure to an increased level of rigor may have set them up to be more successful when they encounter that standard in the next grade level, thus helping to close the opportunity gap.

Monitoring the Learning of the Whole Child Throughout the Year

The use of a data-analysis protocol can anchor the team and keep it focused on the right work, as members engage in a data discussion during which they share practices and make a plan for reteaching and extending after an end-of-unit assessment. However, those assessments also give teams information about individual students that let teachers monitor the learning of each student over time. In a school that functions as a PLC, teams monitor students' learning throughout the school year to ensure all students are getting what they need cognitively, socially, emotionally, physically, and linguistically. However, teams need collective understanding about how to do this work. Each student is unique, with various gifts, talents, and developmental needs that teams must monitor to support each student's learning at high levels. While teachers constantly monitor student progress, teams must schedule more formal progress monitoring, and doing that in conjunction with a data discussion works well. While data discussions happen after each end-of-unit assessment, progress-monitoring meetings can be less frequent, perhaps every six to eight weeks or quarterly. The purpose of the progress-monitoring meeting is to bring together multiple data points about individual students who require close monitoring because they regularly access interventions or extensions beyond the core instruction.

So, how does your team get to the place where it is looking at the needs of the whole child and monitoring student progress? Let's first begin with the *why* then get to the *how*. To answer why it is important to monitor students' progress, RTI experts Austin Buffum, Mike Mattos, and Chris Weber (2012) say because students' instructional needs vary, and students don't all learn at the same rate, teachers must meet the individual needs of each student. To realistically meet all the individual needs of each student in a classroom, many schools use RTI at Work (Buffum et al., 2018), a systematic process to ensure every student receives the necessary additional time and support, so *all* students learn at high levels. The inverted pyramid in figure 6.9 represents the RTI at Work process.

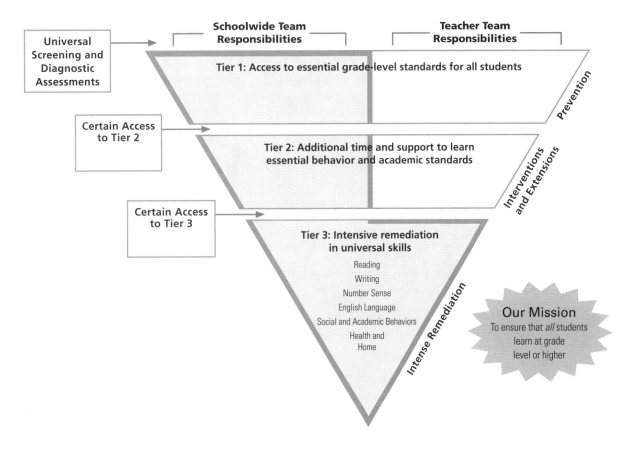

Source: Buffum et al., 2018, p. 18.

Figure 6.9: The RTI at Work inverted pyramid.

Of this pyramid, Buffum et al. (2018) write:

> The traditional pyramid seems to focus a school's intervention system toward one point: special education. Subsequently, schools then view each tier as a required step that they must try to document prior to placing students into traditional special education services. Tragically, this approach tends to become a self-fulfilling prophecy because the organization starts interventions with protocols designed to screen and document students for this potential outcome.

> To challenge this detrimental view of the traditional pyramid, we intentionally inverted the RTI at Work pyramid, visually focusing a school's interventions on a single point—the individual student. (pp. 18-19)

In essence, RTI at Work establishes that Tier 1 instruction begins with a broad base of quality instruction (at the top). By ensuring all students have access to grade-level essential standards in core instruction (Tier 1), teams decrease the degree to which they must reteach skills and concepts to students. No student is denied grade-level learning. But, even with access to high-quality core instruction, some students may need additional time and support based on their individual needs.

At Tier 2, teachers may need to intervene and provide students with timely supplemental support for them to become proficient with current grade-level essential curriculum. This Tier 2 support is timely and flexible (often with teachers sharing students across classes) so that students can move fluidly and flexibly out of Tier 2 supports as they master grade-level essential standards. Teacher teams use common formative assessments to consistently monitor students' achievement and growth throughout the year and to help both teachers and students determine what students already know and still need to learn. These common formative assessments help teachers determine their next instructional steps and make plans to provide differentiated instruction. They also alert teams to which students may require discussion at the next progress-monitoring meeting. It is erroneous to only closely monitor the progress of the small percentage of students receiving Tier 3 supports.

Tier 3 support is for students who are working on foundational skills more than a year below grade level. It is the most intense level of support, delivered in small groups or even individually over an extended period. Classroom teachers can provide Tier 3 support, but it is common for this support to come from a resource teacher or specialist at a designated time (when the student won't be missing new instruction on essential standards). While students are filling in the holes in their foundational skills in Tier 3, they may concurrently be getting support at another time in the day to receive Tier 2 supports to work on current grade-level skills. It is important to document all the interventions a student receives (as the team did for Stephen in this chapter's vignette, page 139) to see what is working and change course when expected progress is not being made.

It's critical for teams to be judicious in monitoring students' progress. What does each student's data communicate about his or her needs? Instead of waiting to intervene when students are failing, teams have an opportunity to respond to each student's individual needs faster, minimizing the chances of a student falling behind and narrowing the learning gap. Therefore, teams must also monitor those students accessing Tier 2 supports. That might mean providing additional time and support for students who need their learning supported or extended in multiple areas, and considering putting a specific plan in place to meet these students' individual academic needs. When teams have an RTI system in place, they become more proactive versus reactive.

When monitoring the progress of an individual student throughout the year, teams must consider the whole child's development, look at multiple data sources, and have many voices at the table who know the student in different contexts. This ensures the teams are meeting the individual student's social-emotional, physical, linguistic, and cognitive needs (see figure 6.10). Think back to the vignette at the beginning of the chapter and consider what would happen if the team only highlighted Stephen's lack of reading achievement and addressed this need with more reading instruction, instead of focusing on the social-emotional supports he needed before he could even access the literacy domain.

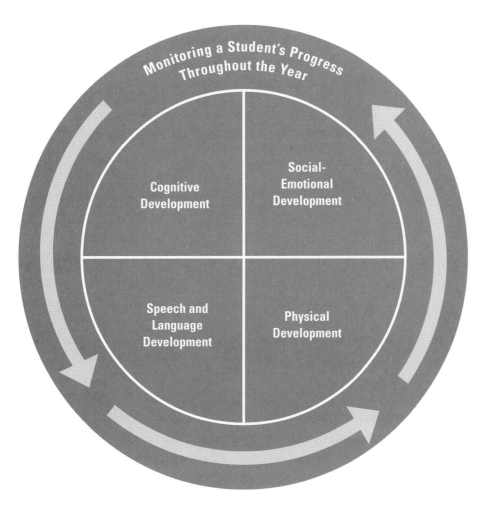

Figure 6.10: Considering the needs of the whole student.

Progress-monitoring meetings should occur several times throughout the year to monitor early childhood student development in four areas: (1) cognitive, (2) social-emotional, (3) physical, and (4) speech and language. Research shows the importance of early intervention (Karoly, Kilbrun, & Cannon, 2005). It is critical for schools to have a system in place for teams to communicate data from one grade level to the next so students who need high levels of support can access that support from the beginning of the school year. This prevents teacher teams in subsequent grade levels from losing time, waiting until a progress monitoring meeting towards the end of the first quarter to put a plan in place. RAND Corporation (https://rand.org) researchers Lynn A. Karoly, M. Rebecca Kilburn, and Jill S. Cannon (2005) state:

> There is increasing recognition that the first few years of a child's life are a particularly sensitive period in the process of development, laying a foundation in childhood and beyond for cognitive functioning; behavioral, social, and self-regulatory capacities; and physical health. Yet many children face various stressors during these years that can impair their healthy development. Early childhood intervention programs are designed to mitigate the factors that place children at risk of poor outcomes.
>
> Early childhood intervention programs have been shown to yield benefits in academic achievement, behavior, educational progression and attainment, delinquency and crime, and labor market success, among other domains. (p. 1)

The sooner teams intervene on behalf of students the better, and a document such as the one the first grade team used to support Stephen helps track individual student interventions over time, even across grade levels, to ensure all teams follow through on everything the student needs. This work aligns with how teams determine when to make interventions more intense over time for students who are not meeting their goals. Buffum et al. (2018) recommend five ways teams can intensify instruction.

1. Increase time.

2. Increase frequency.

3. Increase duration.

4. Decrease student-teacher ratio.

5. Consider the expertise of the person providing the intervention.

Note that the columns in figure 6.2 (page 144) allow teachers to consider these factors when determining and reflecting on their approach to intervention with a specific student. (Visit **go.SolutionTree.com/PLCbooks** for a free reproducible version of the figure.)

Tips for **Administrators**	*Tips for* **Coaches**	*Tips for* **Teachers**
Build your common understanding of the RTI process. Consider consulting the book *Taking Action* (Buffum et al., 2018) and reading chapter 1, which gives a detailed explanation of the Tiers as well as defining key terms like intervention, extension, and remediation.	Guide teams in structuring a system for monitoring their SMART goal throughout the year.	Work as a team to monitor the growth and learning of the whole child and use comprehensive tools that focus on all domain areas.

Ensure that the leadership team or guiding coalition in your school creates a master schedule that allows for students to have access to all Tiers of support, as needed. It's important to remember that for students to close the gap, the RTI Tiers are not seen as an *either* or *or* but an *and*. Students who need it receive Tier 1, Tier 2, and Tier 3 supports but should never be taken out of current essential grade-level instruction to receive interventions (Tier 2) or remediation (Tier 3).

Support the team in defining and building a common understanding of rigor. Think about how you can help the team incorporate rigor into the learning of all students.

Think about and implement ways to communicate students' learning and growth with parents or caregivers.

Using Student Data as Professional Development to Improve Practices

By this point, teams have addressed all four critical questions of a PLC. While there is still one more chapter to go that focuses on lesson planning, you can already see how the processes in this book can enhance, enrich, and target instruction. The incredible job-embedded professional development that occurs when teacher teams work together to improve their practice and then deliver results for students ensures this. As lifelong learners working as part of a PLC, teachers value job-embedded professional development. It is time to shift educators' focus from thinking all professional development occurs in a sit-and-get model and embrace the learning that occurs throughout this process.

All the team tasks we discuss throughout chapters 2–6 are job-embedded and qualify as professional development that empowers teachers to know the answer is in the room, among team members. Teams do not need to wait to have someone come in to do professional development *to* them. After participating in workshops, conferences, in-services, and staff development meetings across the span of our careers, we realize one reason the knowing-doing gap exists in education is because many professional development initiatives may increase teacher knowledge, but do not inspire lasting changes in teacher practices. This is in contrast with the PLC process, which leads to sustained changes in both individual and collective practices.

Learning Policy Institute researchers and authors Linda Darling-Hammond, Maria E. Hyler, and Madelyn Gardner (2017) reviewed thirty-five studies to identify the features of effective *professional development*, which they define as "structured professional learning that results in changes in teacher practices and improvements in student learning outcomes." Hammond et al. (2017) find that effective professional development includes the following.

- Ensuring beginning content is focused, collaborative, and reflective
- Using active learning and effective practice models
- Providing sustained expert support over the long term

In the following sections, we consider how early childhood educators using the PLC process to answer the four critical questions also meet the requirements of effective professional development.

What Do We Want Our Students to Learn?

In chapter 3 (page 47), we note how teams should work collaboratively to identify grade-level essential learning standards and have vertical conversations with other grade-level teams about the essential standards the teams chose in the previous and subsequent grade levels. Think about the learning the adults acquire as they accomplish these team tasks.

In chapter 4 (page 75), teachers work together to unwrap essential learning standards. They then use the essential standards chart to have rich discussions about student learning that comes before and after the grade-level essential standards. Teams also determine what level of rigor a standard expects and what assessment techniques and tasks (observation during play, performance task, student independent response, and so on) offer the best approach to assessing the standards. During this process, teachers build common understanding about what students need to learn, helping them form a deep-rooted knowledge base of the content.

How Will We Know If Each Student Has Learned It?

When teams create common formative assessments, teachers have an opportunity to learn from their peers as they engage in the process of evaluating assessment items. Teacher learning happens as team members work together to determine if test items match the standards or when they determine the level of cognitive demand (low or high) of each test item. As teams evaluate assessment items, think about how this action has the power to inform the practice of individual teachers and the collective team, as well as promote equity for all students. Sit back and take a moment to picture a team learning and doing this work together as they ask one another questions; evaluate, create, and modify assessment items; and model how students should use tools to answer assessment items.

In chapter 4, we also discuss the value of student goal setting. Student goal setting becomes an opportunity for teachers to think about the learning progression of standards and concepts. Think about how this one action—building a learning progression—can deepen a teachers' understanding of concepts and help them develop scaffold supports and extensions to support differentiation.

How Will We Respond When Some Students Do Not Learn It and How Will We Extend Learning for Students Who Have Demonstrated Proficiency?

For this section, we'll examine critical questions three and four together because teachers consistently gain knowledge from their teaching experiences and learn from both their successes and failures. When teachers engage in data discussions, they have opportunities to learn from one another and build a repertoire of best practices. During progress-monitoring meetings, teachers come together to discuss effective learning strategies and generate ideas to help support the students' needs. When an English language teacher shares specific strategies about how students learn language, the whole team has an opportunity to learn. Or, when a special education teacher shares specific details about how to support a student who struggles with executive-functioning skills, again, each teacher is learning and banking this knowledge in his or her teaching toolkit.

Please note, we are not saying traditional professional development models are ineffective or don't serve a purpose (when teachers use them appropriately); we are saying, teachers learning together is more valuable than one teacher learning a new idea in isolation. Think about the power of learning together during the school day versus learning after the school day (a very traditional professional development model). For example, let's look back at the preschool team in the vignette in chapter 2 (page 31).

In that vignette, there was a schoolwide literacy initiative for teachers to learn about interactive read-alouds and how teachers can use them to support student learning of essential literacy skills and concepts. This team learned together and alongside the school's literacy specialist. First, the literacy specialist built teachers' background knowledge on the concept of using interactive read-alouds. Then, teachers observed the literacy specialist modeling an interactive read-aloud with students. Finally, the team had an opportunity to debrief together and ask questions, share observations, and make plans for trying interactive read-alouds in their own classrooms.

What if the literacy specialist had done a one-and-done after-school training for these same teachers on using interactive read-alouds with students? Would teachers have learned? Probably, but would the professional development have been as meaningful and led to sustained changes in teachers' instructional practices the way it did after teachers *observed it in action with their actual students?* We argue the answer is, *no.* If teachers only meet after school for professional development, the students have already gone home, so learning on the job and navigating real-life problems with students is not an option.

One thing teacher teams can do during planning time is have data discussions using the data-analysis protocol form (see figure 6.7, page 154). When teachers transparently look at one another's data, reflect, and ask questions about what was working well in other classrooms, another opportunity for job-embedded professional development emerges.

This method of teachers learning from one another through structured observation is an effective practice. When teachers open their classrooms for vertical observation from peers at lower or higher grade levels, a world of possibilities await. Teacher learning from these observations include the following.

1. Classroom management

2. Assessments methods

3. Intervening and extending techniques

4. Relationship and engagement activities

We recommend the following protocol for peer observations.

1. **During observation:** The observer looks for evidence of student learning and effective practices. This person is an observer, not an evaluator.

2. **Post-observation reflection:** Observers take a few minutes to reflect on their observations and record questions.

3. **Post-observation discussion:** If the person being observed is present, he or she should always have the opportunity to share his or her thoughts on the lesson experience first. Next, the participants share their observations, possibly using sentence frames, like the following, that the team posts in the room to organize thinking and keep the discussion focused.

   • Student learning was happening when . . . .

   • The effective practice I observed was . . . .

4. **Post-observation questions:** After the teachers have an opportunity to share their observations, they can ask questions.

Figure 6.11 and figure 6.12 (page 177) show examples of peer observation and reflection forms teams can use during and after peer observations.

Date: _____

Evidence of an Effective Early Childhood Classroom Environment	
Physical environment:	**Cultural environment:**
☐ Visual daily schedule	☐ Socially and emotionally positive climate
☐ Safe spaces for large and small group activities; privacy for independent practice or rest	☐ Teacher and student strong relationships
	☐ Well-defined procedures, routines, and expectations
☐ Classroom material (books; mathematics manipulatives; technology tools; music, art supplies, play materials, and dramatic props; fine and gross motor material; and so on)	☐ Well-planned timing and transitions
	☐ Teacher facilitates student learning
☐ Materials well-organized and easily accessible to all students	☐ Students feel safe to ask questions, take risks, and give wrong answers
☐ Materials to challenge, engage, and promote exploration and experimentation	☐ Student choice (student-initiated activities)
	☐ Focus on community building and students' family values, beliefs, cultures, and language)

Observation notes:

Evidence of Effective Early Childhood Assessment Practices
☐ Student self-assessment and goal setting
☐ Authentic performance-based assessment tasks
☐ Portfolios
☐ Project assessment tasks
☐ Teacher observations
☐ Student interviews or conferences
☐ Independent student response (pencil-and-paper assessment tasks—free response and multiple-choice items)
☐ Computer-based assessment items and tasks

Observation Notes:

Figure 6.11: Early childhood teacher–observation tool.

continued ↓

Evidence of Effective Early Childhood Instruction

☐ Rich and engaging learning experiences

☐ Inquiry-based and problem-solving learning experiences

☐ Project-based learning experiences

☐ Play-based learning experiences (teacher and student guided)

☐ Large-group teacher-directed guided instruction

☐ Small-group teacher-directed guided instruction

☐ Small-group stations and learning centers (student centered with teacher- and student-choice activities)

☐ Learning through technology use (computers, tablets, and so on)

Observation Notes:

Evidence of Effective Early Childhood Teaching Practices

☐ Differentiation offers scaffolds, supports, and appropriately challenging and engaging tasks and activities

☐ Integrated learning within and across various content areas

☐ Use of specific feedback

☐ Modeling and demonstrating

☐ Use of high-level questions and prompts

☐ Use of visuals aids and other nonlinguistic representations

☐ Use of vocabulary support

☐ Emphasizing effort

Observation Notes:

Source: Adapted from Marzano, 2005; NAEYC, 2009.

Visit **go.SolutionTree.com/PLCbooks** *for a free reproducible version of this figure.*

Protocol
During observation: You are an observer, not an evaluator. Look for evidence of student learning and effective practices, and record your observations on the teacher-observation tool (see figure 6.11, page 175).
Observation reflection: Take a few minutes to reflect on what you observed and record any questions you may have for the teacher (or teachers) observed in the Observation Reflection section of this tool.
Observation discussion: Focus your discussion using sentence frames when sharing what you and others observed: • Student learning was happening when . . . . • The effective practice I observed was . . . .
Follow-up questions: Ask clarifying questions to understand the teacher's thinking behind the instructional decisions made that led to the observed outcomes.

Observation Reflection	
Evidence of an Effective Early Childhood Classroom Environment	**Evidence of Effective Early Childhood Instruction**
Evidence of Effective Early Childhood Assessment Practices	**Evidence of Effective Early Childhood Teaching Practices**

Figure 6.12: Teacher peer observation–discussion tool.

Visit go.SolutionTree.com/PLCbooks for a free reproducible version of this figure.

A great deal of learning can happen when teams collaboratively observe other teachers in action, instead of a lone teacher in another teacher's classroom trying to pick up on whatever he or she can. For example, a team of first-grade teachers wants to learn more about setting up a workshop model for students to work independently or with partners, allowing time for teachers to work with smaller groups of students on particular concepts and skills. The team heard the kindergarten and second-grade teachers had recently started using a mathematics workshop model. After advocating for themselves to get the administrators to cover their classes for a short time (ninety minutes), the team went into a few of the kindergarten and second-grade classrooms together, while the administrators creatively secured substitute coverage. The team used the early childhood teacher–observation tool (figure 6.11) to record the effective teaching practices they saw during the observations and then met with representatives from the kindergarten and second-grade teams to reflect using the peer observation–discussion tool (figure 6.12, page 177) and ask follow-up questions. At the next first-grade team meeting, the teachers spent time brainstorming ideas for how they could start incorporating a mathematics workshop model into their daily instruction.

For those of you thinking, "We don't have the manpower to cover four classrooms for thirty minutes at the same time," keep in mind teachers make decisions based on what's best for students, not what is most comfortable for adults. Teachers are in a profession that undoubtedly requires hard work, collaboration, creativity, and ingenuity, especially when there is a lack of resources. In a school that functions as a true PLC, the entire staff takes collective responsibility for the learning of *all* students, making all students *our* students. Find ways to ensure teachers have time to improve their practices through collaborative job-embedded professional development that fulfills the mission of high levels of learning for all.

Guiding Questions

Use the following guiding questions to learn together and build shared knowledge.

- Do all teams systematically use the data protocol to improve individual teacher effectiveness *and* the entire team's effectiveness, based on the data? If not, what steps will you take to help teams make this a priority?

- Does your team have a norm to ensure that its assessments occur by the team's agreed-on date and that the data is entered and available for the data discussion? If not, how do you hold each other accountable for this process and being prepared for the meeting?

- How will your school build common understanding about the RTI process?

- How will you ensure that students have access to Tier 1, Tier 2, and Tier 3 supports?

- Do you have a multi-faceted approach to job-embedded professional development? If so, what does it look like? If not, how could you ensure that teams have the time to answer the four critical questions of a PLC and receive opportunities to observe each other as well as other opportunities to share expertise schoolwide?

Planning Instruction

How Do We Respond When Some Students Do or Do Not Learn?

Recall the three big ideas of a school that operates as a PLC: (1) a focus on learning, (2) a collaborative culture and collective responsibility, and (3) a results orientation (DuFour et al., 2016). That first big idea of a focus on *learning*, rather than *teaching*, is not just a matter of semantics. Many schools fail to make sustainable gains in student learning because teachers' collaborative time focuses on planning what they will teach rather than on what students will learn. Notice, as figure 7.1 (page 180) illustrates, only after discussing how teams determine what students must learn, how they will know if they've learned it, and how they monitor student progress is it appropriate to discuss what collaborative planning looks like in a PLC. This remains true in the early childhood years.

For preK–2 teams in a PLC, it is essential to start with the end in mind. Because the end goal is high levels of student learning, rather than *start* team meetings with questions like, "What are we going to teach this week?" and "What are we going to have the students do?" teams *end* team meetings by answering these questions. Teams do this because the answers become clear during the earlier conversations about student learning. That's why planning is a way to answer the third and fourth critical questions: How will we respond when some students do not learn it? and How will we extend learning for students who have demonstrated proficiency?" (DuFour et al., 2016).

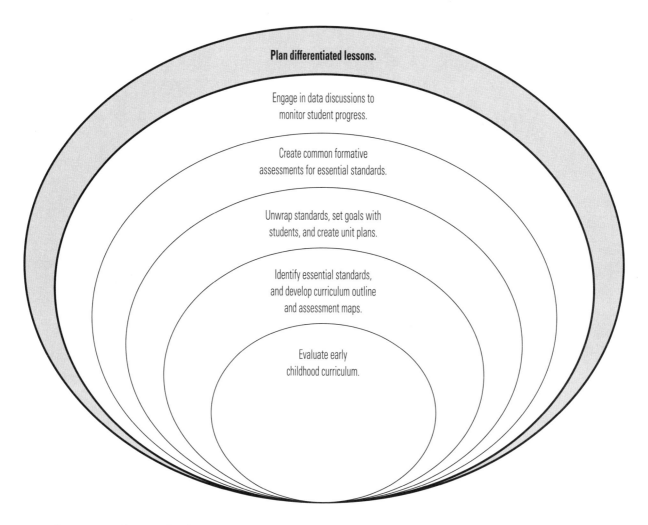

Plan differentiated lessons.

Engage in data discussions to
monitor student progress.

Create common formative
assessments for essential standards.

Unwrap standards, set goals with
students, and create unit plans.

Identify essential standards,
and develop curriculum outline
and assessment maps.

Evaluate early
childhood curriculum.

Figure 7.1: The work of preK–2 teams in a PLC—Planning.

Lesson planning should be a living, breathing entity that is constantly evolving during and after each lesson as teams respond to the actual student learning that occurred (or didn't occur) during a lesson. Collaborative lesson-planning time becomes a chance to reflect on the lessons each teacher set out to teach and then adapt upcoming lessons through the lens of how to reteach and extend learning. A team's goal is to design engaging lessons within Tier 1 instruction that ensure high levels of learning for all, including those students who require additional time and support as well as those who should access extensions.

In chapter 6 (page 137), we write about how data discussions lead teams to monitor the progress of students who require Tier 2 or Tier 3 interventions and extensions, but when teams meet weekly to make plans for upcoming Tier 1 instruction, they must additionally think about how data can and should influence students' needs with new content. In other words, teams must consider how teachers will differentiate their initial core instruction to best serve each student.

When teams plan differentiated lessons, members essentially reflect on the third and fourth critical questions of a PLC and specifically include instructional plans from the outset that do not just teach toward the middle third of the class but enable teachers to proactively support and extend the learning within unit lesson planning. That means sharing plans with team members becomes more about sharing best practices to ensure student learning, and that's some powerful job-embedded professional development!

You might be asking yourself, "What are the benefits of planning lessons as a team? Does everyone have to teach the same lesson each day? What if a teacher wants to try something new and it was not discussed at the planning meeting? Are there specific lesson-planning tools teachers can use during this process?" In this chapter, we culminate all work in this book by discussing the process of planning differentiated lessons and creating systems for common planning and shared resources. We also give examples of specific early childhood learning structures, models, and best practices for various content areas. To begin, the following vignette is about a first-grade team meeting that will help you envision how the conversation could shift at your own team meetings so it is frontloaded with student learning objectives and leads to planning for how to achieve those objectives.

Vignette:
A First-Grade Team's Collaborative Approach to Lesson Planning

At the start of the school year, a first-grade team consisting of three classroom teachers and the English language teacher who supports first grade had already met to identify essential standards connected to geometry, listed in figure 7.2 (page 182). The team routinely meets for one hour each week for mathematics planning. At last week's meeting, with those essential standards for geometry in mind, the team worked together to answer the questions on the essential standards chart graphic organizer to determine students' proficiency with prerequisite and extension skills for their upcoming unit. Now, they are ready to use that information to help them develop an end-of-unit common assessment for geometry and think through how to differentiate lessons to ensure students learn the grade-level essential standards in the geometry unit. Notice how the planning of the common assessment and planning of instruction are not two distinct tasks but are intricately integrated so as not to separate learning from assessing for either the teachers or the students.

As the team reflected on the essential standards shown in figure 7.2 (page 182), the following discussion ensued.

Monika (team facilitator): We've already done a lot of work to prepare for this unit, but today, we need to develop the end-of-unit common formative assessment we'll use and think about lesson planning. For the last unit, we spent a majority of our planning

| **Grade:** First |
| **Subject:** Unit 6—Geometry |
| **Duration:** Weeks 27–32 |
| **Time Frame:** March–April (28 days) |

Skill: Reason with shapes and their attributes.*

 1.G.A.1: Distinguish between defining attributes (e.g., triangles are closed and three-sided) versus non-defining attributes (e.g., color, orientation, overall size); build and draw shapes to possess defining attributes.

! **1.G.A.2: Compose two-dimensional shapes (rectangles, squares, trapezoids, triangles, half-circles, and quarter-circles) or three-dimensional shapes (cubes, right rectangular prisms, right circular cones, and right circular cylinders) to create a composite shape, and compose new shapes from the composite shape.**

1.G.A.3: Partition circles and rectangles into two and four equal shares, describe the shares using the words *halves*, *fourths*, and *quarters*, and use the phrases *half of*, *fourth of*, and *quarter of*. Describe the whole as two of, or four of the shares. Understand for these examples that decomposing into more equal shares creates smaller shares.

*All essential grade-level standards (bold type); need-to-know essential standards (★); important-to-know essential standards (**!**); nice-to-know grade-level standards (not bold).

Source for standards: NGA & CCSSO, 2010b.

Figure 7.2: Team-developed first-grade essential standards in geometry.

time on developing focus lessons and student-learning stations with independent and partner practice. Do we want to approach this unit in the same way?

Geoffrey (first-grade teacher): I was thinking, these geometry standards may really lend themselves to student learning by means of a project.

Paulene (first-grade teacher): I love this idea! I've used projects as a vehicle for student learning in the past, and my students have found projects to be very engaging.

Jillian (English language teacher): I like the idea, but I want to make sure students are actually learning the content and not just having fun. I'd be up for doing this, but I think we need to ensure student learning is occurring.

Monika: I agree, maybe we need to think about backward design principles and think first about how we are going to capture students' learning through some kind of common end-of-unit assessment.

Geoffrey: We've been using a combination of student interview questions and performance-based tasks as our main common assessment tool in mathematics this year. What if we still conduct a student interview, but we instead focus our questions on students' projects?

Jillian: OK, but before we do that, let's decide on a project based on the essential standards and then generate assessment questions we can ask students in an interview or conference.

Geoffrey: What if students had an opportunity to create a city using 2-D and 3-D shapes? I'm looking at our essential standards chart, and it says that students have to, "Compose two-dimensional shapes (rectangles, squares, trapezoids, triangles, half-circles, and quarter-circles) or three-dimensional shapes (cubes, right rectangular prisms, right circular cones, and right circular cylinders) to create a composite shape, and compose new shapes from the composite shape."

Jillian: Maybe we should make it something they have more background knowledge about and can really relate to, like a playground?

Monika: We could introduce the project by posing a question or problem to the students, like, "A new school is being built, and they need a new playground. Can you design a playground using shapes?"

Geoffrey: I like it, but let's be more specific and say, "Can you design a playground by creating and using 2-D and 3-D shapes?" since the standards says they have to build and draw shapes with defining attributes and compose those shapes to form composite shapes.

Monika: Good. So, the end product is that students will create a design of a playground using 2-D and 3-D shapes. What tools will we give students to create their playgrounds?

Geoffrey: What if we ask students to bring in 3-D recyclable objects from home? Also, we can ask teachers throughout the school to donate specific 3-D recyclable objects that match the shapes in our standards, like paper towel and toilet paper rolls, tissue boxes, cereal boxes, and so on. We can also tie it in with our science standards that relate to conservation and recycling.

Jillian: Great, I'll type up the parent letter to go home and send an email to faculty in the school.

Geoffrey: We also have playdough and popsicle sticks in our classrooms. Students can create shapes for their playgrounds using these items as well.

Paulene: Are we thinking they'll work in teams or individually?

Monika: I like the idea of collaborating in teams. That way, we could also incorporate some oral language and social-emotional skills into the project.

Geoffrey: So, let me see if I understand what we are doing. Students will work in teams, and after they create the playground from composing 2-D and 3-D shapes to form composite shapes, we are going to confer with each student individually about the project and ask him or her specific questions that connect to the geometry standards? Can we start generating these assessment questions?

Next, the team creates a list of assessment interview questions and a teacher checklist based on the criteria in the geometry standards. The team added a column for science and drafted an interview question related to the science essential standard. It then added two more columns to the checklist for communication and social skills. The team decided it would specifically assess these two standards through observation during student group work. Just before the meeting ends, the team generates a rough draft of a rubric for the project. One team member agrees to take all the team-generated ideas and put them into an electronic document all members can access. The discussion continues.

Monika: I'll type up the rubric and save it on our team drive. Everyone, please make sure to check it out before our meeting next week, and we'll tweak it if we need to. For now, we have ten minutes left, so let's map out a timeline for the project and minilessons we need to teach to support student learning. I'll start a calendar, and we can put our daily lesson ideas on it. Our curriculum outline shows we have twenty-eight days to teach and assess these geometry concepts. We also want to include the teaching of the science standards as well, but we will do that during our science block. I'm thinking the student conferencing and interview assessment will take about three days. How much time are we going to give students to create their 2-D and 3-D playgrounds?

Paulene: Maybe a week and a half? That would be three days of assessment after eight days for collaborating on the project, plus maybe two days for students to share their projects with the class. That is a total of thirteen days, so that gives us fifteen days to use minilessons and student-learning stations to build students' background knowledge of these geometry and science concepts.

Geoffrey: Let's take students on a shape hunt throughout the school and onto the playground for one of the first lessons. Maybe they could take pictures with our class iPads or sketch pictures of our school playground with the shapes they see and label each shape.

Jillian: I love this idea, but I'd like to frontload students with vocabulary first so they know what they are looking for when they go on the shape hunt. Last year, students learned about 2-D and

3-D shapes, so they should have some background knowledge about them. The standard says they have to, "Distinguish between defining attributes (e.g., triangles are closed and three-sided) versus non-defining attributes (e.g., color, orientation, overall size); build and draw shapes to possess defining attributes." Before the shape hunt, we could talk about the defining attributes of shapes, such as rectangles, squares, trapezoids, triangles, half circles and quarter circles, cubes, and so on.

Monika: Our school library has some great books about shapes. What if we read a few books about shapes and, together with the students, we can generate an anchor chart of all the 2-D and 3-D shapes and label the attributes and names of each? Students could use the pattern blocks we have in our classrooms to create shape pictures, like robots and butterflies. I also have some pattern-block shape puzzles. This would involve the act of using smaller shapes to compose larger shapes, which is one of our essential standards. We can rotate the shape puzzles between classrooms and share with the whole team.

Jillian: After students have a lot of practice with the puzzles, what if we put away the big pieces? That will force students to use smaller shapes to compose larger shapes. Also, tangram puzzles are great because students must compose the different triangles together to form larger triangles, squares, and rectangles.

Geoffrey: OK, so together with the students, we will read a few geometry literature books and create an anchor chart using relevant vocabulary. In our learning stations, students will use pattern blocks to create their own shape pictures and use the pattern-shape puzzles and tangram puzzles. Then, we go on the shape hunt throughout the school and playground. I think we should give students something with the names of the shapes and their attributes as a scaffold to help them during the shape hunt.

Jillian: I can make a graphic organizer they can use during the shape hunt. It can have the shape with its name and a box next to it so students can sketch the playground items that match the shape. I'll also provide a space where they can free sketch the playground features so they can begin to gather some ideas for their own playground. After the shape hunt, we can have a whole-class conversation about the shapes they saw on the playground and describe their attributes. We can help facilitate the discussion and record students' thinking and ideas on our anchor chart.

Paulene: I was thinking many of our students have only been to our school playground and might need to get ideas from other parks to help them with designing their playground.

Jillian: What if, we show students pictures of famous parks with playgrounds throughout the world and have them identify and label the 2-D and 3-D shapes and their attributes? Or, to make it more interactive, we could print out and put the various playground pictures on different tables in our classrooms. Students could move from table to table and have discussions with their peers about the shapes they see, their attributes, and so on. What if we each find a picture of one playground in a famous park and print out a copy for each team member to use during the lesson?

Monika: Sounds like we've got a great week of introductory lessons, that are focused on both essential geometry standards.

A System for Common Planning and Sharing Resources

As you reflect on this chapter's vignette, consider the thoroughness of this collaboration. The team has left its meeting having crafted a common end-of-unit assessment and generated a week of lessons. At the next week's planning session, they finalize the common assessment tools and generate lessons for the following week. The team framed many ideas around an assessment and lessons. It is important that these ideas are not just said aloud but also recorded so they can be shared and built on throughout the unit. Designating common planning time is important, but having systems in place so that these team meetings are useful and meaningful is just as important.

As your team progresses through all the layers of this work to get to the point of planning lessons, each teacher must put in a lot of time with their collaborative team. This often leads to questions like, "Where do we save all our work this year so we don't have to reinvent the wheel each year?" and "What happens if some staff leave and they happened to be the ones with the curriculum outline for a given unit saved on their computers?"

To ensure teams have systems for working smarter rather than harder, members must capture and post the products of their collaborative work in a place accessible to everyone. The chart in table 7.1 shows the answers to some frequently asked questions we've seen come up when teams try to collaborate on the right work and want to be as productive as possible from week to week and year to year. Just as team members must take collective responsibility for student learning, they must also take collective responsibility for this work. It doesn't matter who has which title or which team member's computer an artifact or tool was created on; all team members must commit to ensuring students learn and take responsibility for preparing and sharing the resources necessary for that learning to happen.

Table 7.1: Questions and Answers Related to Team Lesson Planning

Common Questions	Answers to Common Questions
Who is at the early childhood lesson–planning table?	The team should include all classroom teachers for one grade level plus those who support the daily learning for students in that grade level, including specialists, English language teachers, special education teachers, instructional coaches, and so on. If specialists are not able to be at the table, there is an expectation that they communicate with team members and access the documents and resources created during the collaborative planning time.
How can early childhood teams remain productive and efficient during their designated collaborative team planning time?	To support productivity and efficiency, team members collaboratively decide who will fulfill certain roles for the team and for what duration (some teams rotate roles monthly or quarterly), such as the following. • **Facilitator:** Creates an agenda with topics and times, supports the team in sticking to team-designated agenda items, and poses important questions to the team to ensure current work leads to fulfilling long-term goals • **Timekeeper:** Helps keep the team on track by monitoring the designated time the team allots to each agenda item • **Recorder:** Captures important ideas, notes, and dates and ensures all team members have centralized access to the information discussed and recorded during the meeting; may also be the communicator of these ideas with administration, vertical teams, and specialists, as needed • **Best-practice seeker:** Poses questions to the team and looks for opportunities for the team to embed specific discipline-related best practices into lessons
Who facilitates the early childhood collaborative team planning meetings?	Team members can take turns facilitating meetings. Just because your school doesn't have a designated facilitator, instructional coach, or content specialist to lead the meetings does not mean they won't be every bit as effective as long as the person serving as facilitator keeps the team focused on the right work of answering the four critical questions of a PLC. The following reflects this decision based on the participant's primary role. **Teachers:** All teachers can take turns facilitating meetings. Teams decide if this role will rotate monthly, by unit of study, or so on. Once a team clearly defines the expectations and duties of the facilitator, then teachers know which aspects of the role are tight and may facilitate differently based on individual styles. Being the facilitator does not mean being the rule maker or the only person who can speak. The facilitator is like a point guard in basketball or a conductor of a music ensemble. They make sure all participants are involved. **Content specialists:** A reading or mathematics specialist or instructional coach can support facilitation of meetings (if your school has one). In some instances, when schools are just beginning their learning journey of becoming a school that functions as a PLC, an administrator may facilitate meetings as a model for the teams. **Cofacilitation:** A content specialist and grade-level classroom teacher could meet briefly to set the agenda, each drawing on his or her background knowledge and strengths and then sharing the role of cofacilitator at the meeting. Teams can also share this collaborative effort between a grade-level classroom teacher and a special education or English language teacher, or so on.
Who creates the early childhood team-meeting agendas for lesson planning?	The team can decide on topics for the next week's agenda at the end of every weekly team-planning meeting; or, the person facilitating the meeting can initially create a draft agenda, send it out in advance of the meeting, and ask the team members to add other agenda items or give feedback before the meeting.

continued →

Common Questions	Answers to Common Questions
How can the early childhood team capture and save shared ideas for lesson plans and instructional resources discussed in the team meeting?	It is extremely important to the collaborative process that resources created for use across the team are not housed on any one person's device but stored in a common drive or folder. As teams take collective responsibility for planning, it does not matter who actually creates a document or resource; rather, it needs to be saved electronically in a way that everyone has immediate and ongoing access to it without having to track down the person who made it, asking them to email it to them or print it out. There are several electronic tools available so teachers can have a common place to house lesson plans and instructional resources (assessments, learning tasks, student activities and games, pacing guides, and so on). Electronic tools that provide access for all teachers to edit and view the documents simultaneously is important. Educators all process information differently, so some team members may need time to go back and look at the ideas and tools discussed during the meeting. If a teacher is unable to attend a team meeting, it's also important for him or her to review what the team discussed and what lessons and resources the team will use with students for the week. While many teachers choose to use lesson-plan books or even sticky notes for their personal planning, weekly team planning (including agendas, notes, and resources that connect to the planning) should all be digital so team members can build on the ideas working for students year to year. Teams can also make electronic folders available to all other grade-level teams and specialists, so any teacher can view and use the instructional learning resources to either support or extend the students he or she is working with.

Visit **go.SolutionTree.com/PLCbooks** *for a free reproducible version of this table.*

Establishing an electronic system to store and share the work of your collaborative team will help it make continual forward progress instead of going back each year to redo the work of identifying essential standards, mapping the curriculum, unwrapping the standards for a unit, and developing common formative and end-of-unit assessments for those standards. This will make your collaborative team planning much more targeted and efficient because the tools members need to ensure lesson plans focus on the essential standards will be readily available. This is not to say your team won't add more resources to the folder or revisit and collectively have deep conversations each year about the standards, but keeping an electronic file ensures your starting point will be further along each year.

The other necessary component to ensure teams develop quality lesson plans is to always start with an agenda for planning meetings, so your team can be as productive as the team in the vignette at the beginning of this chapter. In *The Big Book of Tools for Collaborative Teams in a PLC at Work*, Bill Ferriter (2020) writes, "Working together doesn't improve teaching and learning, DuFour liked to say; *doing the right work together* improves teaching and learning—and specific work products can help teams spend more of their collaborative time doing the right work" (p. 6). An agenda that focuses the team on the right work may include the school mission, team norms, the four critical questions of a PLC, or other prompts that help teams stay focused on the right work. In figure 7.3, you'll see one possible agenda template (with sample data) teams can use to ensure their collaborative time is meaningful and efficient. The sample data shown here derives from a first-grade team at Spradling Elementary, a Model PLC at Work school in Fort Smith, Arkansas.

Spradling's Mission: Every child, every day. Whatever it takes to achieve a better future!	
Team Meeting Agenda	
Team: First Grade	**Date:** March 26
Team members present:	**Norms:**
Ms. B. (assistant principal)	Start on time, end on time.
Ms. C. (first-grade teacher)	Come prepared.
Ms. L. (first-grade teacher)	Balance the conversation between members.
Ms. B. (instructional facilitator)	Stay on topic.
Ms. D. (interventionist)	Share responsibilities.
C. R. (practicum student)	
Roles	
Facilitator:	**Timekeeper:**
Ms. L.	Ms. C.
Recorder:	**Other:**
Ms. B	
Possible purposes for meeting:	**Purpose or goal for *this* meeting:**
☐ Unwrap essential standards for a unit.	Analyze data from the common formative assessment given on March 22.
☐ Create learning progressions.	
☐ Build a unit plan.	Determine which students are still struggling and discuss instructional strategies to help improve students' understanding.
☐ Create common assessments.	
☑ Analyze student work.	
☑ Design an explicit lesson or set of lessons.	
☑ Share strategies for interventions and extensions.	

Discussion or decision summary:

Looked at students' writing common formative assessments.

Sorted student writing based on learning progression skills they needed to continue to work on.

Created a plan for small-group supports and discussed instructional strategies to target those specific skills.

We continued a conversation with our literacy coach regarding the need for all teachers to understand the learning targets and how to communicate with the interventionists if they miss a team meeting.

Interventionist would like to see the students' actual work from the common formative assessment and the end-of-unit assessment so they know the misconceptions of the students.

Review of sight words with groups is needed during intervention time.

What follow-up is needed based on the information shared at this meeting?

Figure 7.3: Example of a collaborative team meeting agenda template.   continued →

Action steps and person responsible:	Data to collect and bring to the next meeting:
All team members will start a new small-group schedule or plan on Monday.	Small-group observations
Ms. L will debrief interventionists when a meeting is missed.	
Classroom teachers will place completed common formative and end-of-unit asssessments in interventionists' boxes so they can see the student work.	
Ms. B. will put data in the online team folder for the assessment.	
Next meeting: April 5	
Agenda:	**Reflection of norms:**
Classroom teachers and interventionists will attend.	Come prepared norm—addressed issues of what happens when someone has to miss the meeting.
Instructional facilitators will be available to assist with strategies for small groups. All teachers should put small-group observations in the team folder before the meeting.	Share responsibility norm—we really appreciate how well the team is doing this.

Source: Adapted from Spradling Elementary, Fort Smith, Arkansas.

*Visit **go.SolutionTree.com/PLCbooks** for a free reproducible version of this figure.*

You'll notice there is a box in figure 7.3 that provides space to specify the purpose of each team meeting and another box preceding it with possible purposes to choose from. These choices serve as a reminder to teams of what the *right work* is for a team meeting. Each collaborative team meeting will look a little different depending on where your team is in the unit for a given content area. This agenda is not only useful for lesson planning but also for all meeting purposes. For example, the meeting may involve team members unpacking an essential standard or designing a common formative or end-of-unit assessment at the beginning of a unit, while the team's focus may shift to lesson planning or data discussions toward the end of a unit.

In chapter 4 (page 75) we explained the process a team might go through to plan an entire unit of study. This team unit-planning tool can help support the team in staying focused and on pace, as well as help team members decide how to craft their weekly agenda. Teams need to act responsively to what is happening in real time, so teams usually craft the following week's agendas at the end of the weekly team meeting or through electronic communication tools (such as with emails or in a shared online space). Figure 7.4 shows how the work of a team might evolve over the course of a five-week writing unit given a sixty-minute weekly common planning–meeting time. Think how the agenda and use of time each week would be different depending on the purpose of the meeting. For example, the agenda in Figure 7.3 aligns to the work of the team in week four of their unit, as they examined a common assessment. However, the following week their work would look different. What remains constant is, taken as a whole, the six weeks' worth of meetings document the team answering the four critical questions of a PLC.

Meeting	Agenda Goals
Meeting one Date: 2/5 (Before the unit begins)	Identify essential standards for persuasive writing unit (or if already done, review and tweak), and unwrap writing standards using the graphic organizer. (Thirty minutes) Begin to build the unit plan and decide on end-of-the unit common assessment and data-collection tools. (Thirty minutes)
Meeting two Date: 2/12 (Week 1 of instruction)	Finish the unit plan, create learning progressions, and come to a consensus on student anchor papers that represent each level on the learning progression. (Twenty-five minutes) Use unit webbing to determine necessary supports and scaffolds for English learners. (Ten minutes) Use mentor texts to dig deeper into the unit content and build common understanding, then plan unit introduction and week 1 lessons. (Twenty-five minutes)
Meeting three Date: 2/19 (Week 2 of instruction)	Share celebrations and reflections from unit introduction and week 1 lessons. (Ten minutes) Plan week 2 and 3 lessons including differentiated daily learning tasks and a common formative assessment in week 2. (Fifty minutes)
Meeting four Date: 2/26 (Week 3 of instruction)	Share celebrations and reflections from week 2 of instruction. (Ten minutes) Collaboratively score a few pieces of student writing from each class on the week 2 common formative assessment to ensure team members have common understanding of the learning progression. (Thirty minutes) Determine small groups for reteaching based on common formative assessment results. (Twenty minutes)
Meeting five Date: 3/5 (Week 4 of instruction)	Share strategies that worked in small-group reteaching. (Ten minutes) Plan week 4 and 5 lessons, including differentiated daily learning tasks and an end-of-unit common assessment. (Forty minutes) Clarify teacher prompts for end-of-unit assessment, and plan end-of-unit writer's celebration. (Ten minutes)
Meeting six Date: 3/12 (Week 5 of instruction)	Bring student writing samples, and share celebrations and reflections from end-of-unit. Reflect on unit, and put notes in unit plan for next year. (Fifteen minutes) Create a shared document to capture end-of-unit data, set date for next week's data discussion, and clarify what data need to be input in preparation. (Ten minutes) Identify essential standards for the next unit and unpack standards (if not already done). Build or tweak the end-of-unit common assessment for the next unit. (Thirty minutes)

Figure 7.4: First-grade collaborative planning cycle throughout a writing unit.

Notice how this schedule lists two or three agenda items for each meeting. As your team works to answer the four critical questions of a PLC, one team task logically flows into the next step, as seen in figure 7.1 (page 180) and the parallel images leading off previous chapters. Sometimes a team needs to go deeper into a particular step before moving forward. For example, at meeting two in figure 7.4, the team had already unwrapped the essential standards and had discussed the essential standards chart to clarify the standards it's teaching. However, it needed to dig deeper into the content by studying mentor texts while thinking through specific supports and scaffolds to use with English learners. The team could also have used the time after studying mentor texts to generate ideas for extending students since it is sometimes more challenging to decide what to do with writers who are already proficient than it is to think about how to help those at the beginning stages of the learning progression.

You'll notice in figure 7.4 (page 191), after the team planned and executed the first weeks' lessons, the third, fourth, fifth, and sixth meetings all began with celebrations and reflections on lessons or assessments from the previous week. This is important. A culture of celebration is crucial to being *positive by design* rather than *negative by default*. In a school that functions as a PLC, data drives teams, but that does not mean it is all about the numbers. The important thing for teams is to use data to intervene and extend for students, inform instruction, and improve individual and collective practice, which increases the learning of the students the teams serve. If your team is doing these things, there is always something to celebrate—even when the data may not look promising on paper. By constantly reflecting on collaborative teaching, teams build capacity and collective teacher efficacy.

To be positive by design, some teams may need an explicit reminder to share celebrations. In chapter 6 (figure 6.5, page 151), we offered a different agenda template that the example team used to hold a data discussion. The agenda begins with celebrations and then uses guiding questions to allow for a more specific agenda to support a data-discussion meeting. The structure and design of your weekly team meeting agenda is entirely up to the preference of the team and its members. So long as the agenda includes elements that keep the team focused on the right work and overall needs of all team members, any of the templates we offer in this book or that your team might create can serve to focus your collaborative discussion and work.

So far, we have taken time to share several ideas about how teams can structure their weekly meeting time to collaborate around the right work. In the next section, we share ideas and tools that teacher teams can use when that right work focuses on planning out rich, engaging, and meaningful lessons.

Tips for **Administrators**	*Tips for* **Coaches**	*Tips for* **Teachers**
Continue to monitor the products around the four critical questions of a PLC that come from the work of the team. Because team folders are electronic and accessible to all, this should be easy to do.	Think about your role at weekly team meetings. How can you use coaching techniques to support the strengths and personalities of the team and its members?	Review team meeting agendas ahead of time and come prepared to share ideas and resources. Remember, this is about your instructional strengths and how team members can use them to support each other (such as use of technology, scaffolding instruction, and so on).
Although we don't advocate for administrators having to be at all team meetings, we do encourage administrators to drop in and be learners from and with the teams. Being vulnerable and sharing with the team that you want to learn from them builds trust and shows teachers they are leaders as well.	If your primary role is facilitation, ask how can you assure all team members have a voice so that teams make decisions collectively.

If your role is not the facilitator, think about specific coaching moves and techniques you can use during these meeting times. | Use electronic tools to help organize and share your lesson plans, assessments, and instructional resources. |

Early Childhood Lesson-Planning Best Practices

When teams apply the backward design concept (beginning with the end in mind) by unwrapping essential standards into learning targets and creating end-of-unit assessments for those targets *before* teaching the unit, they've done a great deal of work that strengthened the team's knowledge around the essential standards. While this approach greatly increases your chance of helping students reach their learning goals, it won't happen unless teams pair that knowledge about the standard with effective early childhood instructional practices.

There is a great deal of thought that goes into planning an effective lesson. If the team is using a district unit-planning guide—or if team members created one themselves using a template, like the one we provide in figure 4.18 (page 103)—they might find it helpful to have each member choose one section based on his or her interest, experience or expertise to prepare for and lead the team's discussion. If the team chooses to divide the work in this way, then each team member should review their section of the planning guide before the meeting and be prepared to share ideas for that week's lessons. Not only will this help build each teacher's background knowledge and pedagogy, but it can also strengthen the overall team discussion as it considers all the sections in the unit-planning guide. This supports the team in choosing the most effective lesson resources to use with students.

As the team begins to share and select ideas and make instructional decisions about the resources, materials, and strategies they'll use when teaching specific lessons, designating someone to review each section of the planning guide beforehand makes the collaborative discussion during the planning meeting more valuable. It means that you will hear various teammates probe and push the team ahead with questions, such as the following.

- "In what specific order are we introducing the learning targets and teaching the standard, and are we teaching multiple standards from the same unit simultaneously during our lessons?"

- "What instructional tools, strategies, or resources can we use to support the learning?"

- "How can we make the lessons engaging?"

- "How can we integrate standards from other content areas?"

- "How are we differentiating learning?"

- "How are students communicating their ideas with one another?"

- "What technology tools can we use to share ideas?"

- "How can we ensure equity for students but allow for teacher autonomy?"

The question, "How are we differentiating learning?" is one that sometimes seems overwhelming for teams. It is important to understand that differentiation can easily be a product of team conversations. As teams gain a deeper understanding of the different needs of their students and learning together, it makes choosing the appropriate materials, questioning, and products that allow students access to the learning less complicated. Sometimes differentiation is as simple as changing out the materials during play or at a learning station.

The last question "How can we ensure equity for students, but allow for teacher autonomy?" strikes at the heart of the loose-tight nature of a school that functions as a PLC (see A Guaranteed and Viable Curriculum or the Educational Lottery, page 42). Do not shy away from answering this question collectively or from answering any of these questions under the false assumptions that all classrooms must look exactly the same, with teachers losing their individuality. The curriculum must be guaranteed and viable, but there is a great deal of teaching that goes on beyond the essential standards. The reason teams use planning time to go into this depth of collaboration about the essential standards is because it builds equity in curriculum and instruction. The team should agree on *what* is in the lesson, but *how* each teacher goes about teaching the content can vary. Collaborative planning time helps teams find the balance between equity, giving all students access to grade-level essential standards, and teacher autonomy—the freedom for each teacher to use her or his own style.

When grappling with this idea, teachers often ask if all team members need to make common use of learning tasks, extensions, scaffolds, and so on. In high-functioning teams, the level of collaboration is such that one team member shares an idea and someone else adds on it to make it even better, making the whole greater than the sum of the parts. In this way, all teachers walk out of planning meetings with resources of higher quality than any one of them could have developed by themselves. Teachers always have the option to include other resources and practices as they implement collaboratively designed lessons in their individual classrooms. Most often, the best practices are those that come from the rich discussions in collaborative planning meetings. PLC cultures recognize teachers are different. They have different styles and personalities, and their approaches to instruction can vary. We expect teachers to embrace those differences, yet we also expect them to share back with the team how their different approaches impacted student learning so that team members can learn from each other and collectively improve. Additionally, classrooms full of students introduce their own variables, as teachers embrace those unexpected teachable moments that occur daily, practice responsive instruction, and adapt lessons in the moment to meet the needs of each unique student. Through these day-to-day interactions and adjustments, each teacher will experience different autonomous successes. That is why teams begin collaborative planning meetings with celebrations; as team members embrace their autonomy in their own way and then come back and share those teaching successes, everyone grows instead of developing silos of excellence behind certain classroom doors.

This approach to celebrating successes also has the effect of helping team members support one another as they discover how differences in their respective approaches can lead to different levels of student success. Figure 7.5 shows how two different classroom teachers conducted a preschool science lesson based on the team-identified essential standard for their sink-or-float unit. As you review the scenarios, consider the following questions.

- Are the learning targets the same in each lesson?

- Did each teacher follow the agreed-on plan from the team lesson-planning meeting?

- Do you think the students in each classroom are getting an equitable experience?

- Which teacher is using best practices, and how might the other teacher benefit from including reflections and celebrations as part of the weekly team agenda?

Classroom A	Classroom B
Standard: The student will make observations, separate objects into groups based on similar properties, use simple investigation tools, develop questions based upon observations using the five senses, and conduct simple scientific investigations.	
Teacher A sits on the carpet in a circle with her students. She has a tub filled with water and a set of objects next to it. She holds up an object and students raise their hands to say if they think it will sink or if it will float. After the class makes the prediction, the teacher puts the object into one of two circles on the floor labeled *Sink* and *Float*. After testing all the objects, the teacher creates a picture graph on an anchor chart and has students come up and tape on the preprinted objects tested during the experiment. When the picture graph is complete, the teacher asks the following questions. • "How many objects floated?" • "How many objects sank?" • "Why do you think some floated and some sank?"	Teacher B sits on the carpet in a circle with her students. She has a tub filled with water and a set of objects next to it. She asks the students to turn to a shoulder partner and decide which objects they think will sink and which ones will float. As student pairs talk about this, the teacher passes out sets of small baggies with the objects for the pairs to touch, feel, and hold. Student pairs explore and discuss the objects and then circle the ones they think will float on a recording sheet. The teacher facilitates a whole-class discussion and students share their predictions, explain their thinking, and ask one another questions. The teacher models how to carefully place an object on the surface of the water in her tub, and the class finds out if their first prediction was correct. Next, she tells the students to take their baggie of objects back to their tables. Each table has a tub of water so students can see if they get the same result, and then conduct the remaining experiments. After they test each item, student pairs sort the objects into containers labeled with the words *Sink* and *Float*, in addition to a picture of an object on or below the water. After the experiment, the teacher calls the students back to the carpet and asks them to study their predictions with their partner and discuss if their predictions match the results of their experiment. The teacher poses the following question, "Why do you think some objects floated and some sank?" Students use a variety of sensory and comparative vocabulary to describe the size, shape, weight, feel, and sound of objects from their experience placing objects in the water The teacher records the students' ideas on an anchor chart, saying she wants to share what they discovered in their experiment with the principal. She asks students for ideas on how they could record their discoveries on chart paper. To support their ideas, the teacher adds writing paper and graph paper to the writing center so students can continue to learn and share about objects sinking and floating.

Source for standard: Virginia Department of Education, 2013.

Figure 7.5: Implementation of a team-developed science lesson.

Both teachers left their collaborative planning time with the same sink-and-float lesson plan. While teacher A executed the plan without any major problems, her students obviously would have learned at higher levels had they been a part of teacher B's classroom. When teacher A reflects on this lesson, will she likely have a celebration to share at the next team meeting? Probably. Would she also learn and grow as she listens to teacher B's reflection and celebration of her very different lesson implementation? Definitely. Teacher A had the autonomy to implement the lesson the way that worked for her, but the job-embedded professional development indicative of a school that functions as a PLC means she now has ideas from her teammates that could improve similar lessons in the future. Further, when the results of the common assessments are analyzed across the grade level, there will be evidence demonstrating if there is a need for her to change and improve her practices.

Teams functioning at a higher level of collaboration can more effectively identify and eliminate these kinds of gaps in instruction. Taking time to collaborate about effective lesson structures and share best instructional practices for the essential standards during lesson planning is one of a team's most powerful school-improvement tactics—and it doesn't cost a thing! Teacher B would not have lost anything by sharing her ideas at the planning meeting, yet think of what teacher A (and all her future students) would gain if they collaborate. Think of how exposing all students to the richer lesson ensures there are not just pockets of excellence in education, but equity for all learners. All of the students on this team belong to every teacher. They are all our students; teacher A's students are teacher B's students and vice versa. This is how a culture of collective responsibility plays out at all times in schools that embrace the PLC process.

Further, as teams plan specific lessons, it is important for team members to decide on the structures or designs of students learning that will happen during the unit. Consider the following questions.

- Will the teacher and students be engaging in a workshop model where students are learning independently, collaboratively, or with the teacher in small-group guided instruction?

- Will students utilize learning stations?

- Will the team use a project as a vehicle for students' learning?

- Will students engage in self-initiated play during certain aspects of the lesson?

While individual teachers have the autonomy to make instructional decisions, if members of a team have very different answers to these questions, chances are those teachers are functioning as a *group* rather than a *team* with a common goal and simply have not collaborated about best practices. Because of this, the teacher used to a whole-group learning model for the majority of instruction will continue to do so not because it is what is best for young students but because it is what is comfortable and familiar for the adult. To ensure high levels of learning for the students, teams must first ensure high levels of learning for the adults. Some of the best professional learning can come from the teacher a few feet down the hall who walked away from a team planning meeting with the same weekly lesson plan as her colleague but made instructional decisions in the implementation of that lesson plan that led to better results.

Tips for **Administrators**	*Tips for* **Coaches**	*Tips for* **Teachers**
Be a creative problem solver to find coverage for teachers to observe one another teaching the lessons they plan together to improve their collective practices.	Use time spent coaching, modeling, and observing peers to create opportunities for teachers to learn about various effective learning models.	Think about the learning models you are most comfortable using and if they match the needs of your students.
Engage in lesson-planning meetings (when possible) not by taking a leadership role, but by becoming an active listener. Model productive, positive dialogue as an active team member.	Support teachers in designing engaging lessons, and share current research and best practices during team meetings.	Decide if your current learning environment best supports the learning models you are using on a daily basis, and think about any modifications to your learning environment that may be needed to support students' needs.

Early Childhood Lesson-Planning Structures and Designs

Teachers make hundreds and possibly thousands of decisions a day, and many aspects of the school day challenge teachers to think on their feet, responding in the moment. However, and as you have seen throughout this book, other aspects of the day teachers carefully design and plan out. Teams can help ensure a guaranteed and viable curriculum by carefully planning lessons that teach the essential standards using best practices. Many lesson-planning formats focus on teaching rather than learning, but because the first big idea of a PLC is a focus on learning (DuFour et al., 2016), it helps to use a lesson-plan template that ensures student learning is the focus of team discussions while lesson planning. When designing a lesson, the team should consider the standard being taught within the lesson, and its timing, pacing, transitions, structures, and instructional best practices.

According to instructional effectiveness consultant and Utah State University Professor Emeritus M. David Merrill (2002), teachers promote learning when they do the following.

- Engage learners in solving real-world *problems*.
- *Activate* existing knowledge as a foundation for new knowledge (use prior experience from relevant past experience as a foundation for the new skills and knowledge or *scaffolding*).

- *Demonstrate* new knowledge for the learners (show them, rather than just tell them).

- Require the learners to *apply* the new knowledge, so they use the new knowledge or skill to solve problems.

- *Integrate* the new knowledge into the learners' world, so they can demonstrate improvement in their newly acquired skills, and modify the new knowledge for use in their daily work. (One way to achieve this is reflecting on the learning experience.)

In figure 7.6, we provide a lesson-design template based on many of Merrill's (2002) principles (modified to support learning in early childhood). The template contains five sections with suggested time allotments and learning structures. What sets this lesson-planning template apart is the focus on learning structure in the middle column. This is so important for teachers of young students to consider. Planning does involve focusing on the materials, resources, differentiation, and language that teachers can use, but it also means planning out the conditions that optimize student learning. Think back to teachers A and B who each did the sink-and-float lesson with very different learning structures in place. Had that team been using this template, the discoveries the teachers made after the lesson would have been addressed in the planning of the lesson, resulting in a more equitable experience with best practices in place in both classrooms.

Figure 7.7 (page 200) illustrates how a team might use the lesson-design template to plan best practices for a language arts lesson; we intentionally bold text of the instructional best practices teachers embed into the lesson. In this example, look for specific best practices related to language arts and consider how your team might approach planning lessons that enhance a unit.

As you reflect on this example, note that although we introduce it because it helps teams focus on the first big idea of a PLC (a focus on learning), the process of planning lessens together in this way also deepens the second big idea (a collaborative culture and collective responsibility). Together, this results in stronger lesson plans than any one teacher could have developed individually, improving the third big idea (a results orientation).

Early Childhood Lesson-Design		
Team: _____	**Unit:** _____	**Lesson:** _____
Lesson standard: What standards are teachers teaching within the lesson? **Lesson time:** How much total time will teachers allot to teaching the lesson? **Integrating within the lesson:** What other content area or standard can teachers integrate into the lesson? **Integrating beyond the lesson:** After the lesson, how will teachers integrate the concept or skill into other aspects of the day, such as transitions, morning meeting, stations, play, independent practice? **Assessment:** What formal or informal assessments will teachers use with students for learning?		
Component	**Learning Structure**	**Guiding Questions**
Connecting prior knowledge to new concepts and skills (five minutes)	**Teacher led:** • Whole-group learning • Partner learning • Independent practice	How will we stimulate students' prior knowledge and help them make connections to new concepts and skills? Is there vocabulary teachers need to explicitly introduce to students for them to understand the new learning?
Guiding learners to new concepts and skills (ten to fifteen minutes)	**Teacher led:** • Whole-group learning with the teacher modeling, questioning, and providing visuals	How will we introduce the new concepts and skills to learners? How will we differentiate learning (questions, strategies, tasks, tools, and so on) to meet the needs of all learners?
Applying new concepts and skills to solve problems (thirty to forty minutes)	**Active learning through play:** • Teacher-guided play-based learning • Self-initiated play with teacher observation **Workshop model:** • Teacher-led small-group learning • Learning stations in groups, pairs or individually	How will we allow learners to explore, practice, and apply their new learning of concepts and skills (such as problem solving, real-life tasks, projects, self-initiated play, and so on)? How will we differentiate learning (questions, strategies, tasks, tools, and so on) to meet the needs of all learners?
Reflecting on new concepts and skills (five minutes)	**Teacher led:** • Whole-group learning • Partner learning	How will we help learners reflect on newly learned concepts and skills (such as with a peer partner or teacher at the end of the lesson by sharing new knowledge and skills, engaging in a quick reflective assessment task, and so on)?

Figure 7.6: Early childhood lesson-design template.

*Visit **go.SolutionTree.com/PLCbooks** for a free reproducible version of this figure.*

Early Childhood Lesson-Design		
Team: First grade	**Unit:** Narrative unit	**Lesson:** Week 3, November 16

Lesson standard: Retell stories, including key details, and demonstrate understanding of their central message or lesson. (RL.1.2)

Lesson time: One hour

Integrating within the lesson: Communication (such as active listening and turn and talk) and relationship skills (such as social engagement and whole-class conversation)

Integrating beyond the lesson: Offer activities for play (act out a skit that conveys a central message), transition (play a song and ask what the central message is), and writing (draw a picture and describe the central message).

Assessment: The teacher transcribes whole-class conversation (to analyze for comprehension information as well as conversation skill needs), anecdotal notes during small-group reading, and exit-ticket sticky notes.

Component	Learning Structure	Lesson Plan Details
Connecting prior knowledge to new concepts and skills (five minutes)	Teacher-led whole group	Review how to: (1) determine what a character learns in a story, and (2) restate that specific lesson as a more global central message. For the second component, refer to an **anchor chart** with pictures of five book covers you have already read aloud to students. Show cover of a book new to students, and have them **make predictions** of what the character might learn based on the title and illustration.
Guiding the learner to new concepts and skills (ten to fifteen minutes)	Teacher-led whole-group and partner learning	Conduct an interactive read-aloud, stopping four times to ask **thinking questions** that draw students' attention to the book's deeper meaning; have **partners turn and talk** to share their thoughts. Conduct a **whole-class conversation** about what a character learned and how students could restate that learning as a bigger idea or central message. Add a picture of the cover of the new book to the anchor chart, and write the central message together as **shared writing**.
Applying new concepts and skills to solve problems (thirty to forty minutes)	Small-group, partner, and independent learning	Challenge students to determine the central message of a book they read independently or with a partner or listened to on the computer during reading workshop. Invite them to add a sticky note with their name to the central-message anchor chart if they find a message to **share** by the end of reading that day. Meet with a **reading group** for twenty minutes and **confer** with four students individually for the next fifteen minutes, while the rest of the students do two of the following. • Read independently. • Read with a partner. • Listen to reading on the computer. • Write a response to their reading focusing on the central message.
Reflecting on new concepts and skills (five minutes)	Whole-group learning	Allow students who put sticky notes on the anchor chart to share what they discovered about the central message, and encourage someone from the teacher's reading group to **share the group's discussion**.

Source for standard: NG & CCSSO, 2010a.

Figure 7.7: Sample language arts lesson-design plan.

*Visit **go.SolutionTree.com/PLCbooks** for a free reproducible version of this figure.*

Guiding Questions

Use the following guiding questions to learn together and build shared knowledge.

- How do you set agendas for collaborative planning time to ensure the time is well spent doing work that answers the four critical questions of a PLC?

- Do your agendas across a unit vary to incorporate time to take a wide look at long-term planning with unit webbing, as well as include short-term deeper dives into specific lesson planning for essential standards?

- Are you focusing on sharing best practices during collaborative planning time, or are you dividing and conquering by splitting up the work into individual tasks that get the job done, but does not provide professional development and improve students' learning? How can you ensure that sharing best practices becomes a part of your culture?

- How can you more purposefully incorporate developmentally appropriate learning structures and integrate processes to build lifelong habits (such as problem solving, questioning, and communicating) into lesson plans across content areas?

- What is your system for housing team-developed unit plans and resources for specific lessons so everyone has common and easy access? Are all instructional staff (including paraprofessionals, interventionists, specialist teachers, and so on) aware of these resources, and do they know how to access them?

Epilogue: Putting It All Together in Early Childhood

· ·

Throughout this book, we attempt to provide early childhood educators with a clear understanding of not only what a PLC *is* and *is not* but also establish why the PLC culture provides an ideal process to support the work of early childhood teams and set up students for success as they progress in their schooling. At this point, you can define and clarify the key elements that must be in place for all early childhood teams to achieve deep implementation of the PLC process. You should have clarity regarding the work your team and school must do to establish its mission, vision, values, and goals, as well as answer the four critical questions of a PLC. The vignettes, examples, tips, tools, artifacts, and guiding questions we provide throughout the book are meant to bring this process to life for everyone from administrators, teachers, and instructional assistants (paraprofessionals) to any educator who works with early childhood teams and students. In this epilogue, we end with a discussion of two additional tools teams should not overlook: (1) celebrations and (2) storytelling. We then close with a final reflection on the importance of *Why?*

Celebrations

One of the most powerful tools for retaining teachers and providing momentum for the PLC process is purposeful, frequent celebrations. Working in the field of early childhood education is difficult. Teachers work tirelessly on behalf of their students. Celebrations lift spirits and make the entire community feel good about the work being done. Celebrations create an environment that makes the school a place everyone wants to be a part of, including students. For this reason, schools need a system of celebrations, and teams must embed celebrations into their work. These celebrations communicate to the school community that the school is making progress, and what the school celebrates communicates the school's values.

DuFour et al. (2016) explain why celebrations are important to the PLC process, citing leadership experts James M. Kouzes and Barry Z. Posner (2003): "Study after study of what workers want in their jobs offer the same conclusion: they want to feel appreciated" (p. 225). Similarly, authors and consultants Robert Kegan and Lisa L. Lahey (2001) conclude, "nearly early every organization or work team we've spent time with astonishingly under communicates the genuinely positive, appreciative, and admiring experiences of its members" (p. 92).

As teams develop and see the successes of their collaboration in student achievement and in their own learning, they want to share those experiences with the world and forge ahead into the process of continuous improvement. Mathematics leader, author, and consultant Timothy D. Kanold (2017) quotes Heritage Middle School (Liberty, Missouri) Principal Scott Carr, who reflects on the power of teams and celebrations:

> They become very proud of who they are as a team and what they hope to become. They begin to add a future to their current story by contemplating where they are heading next and what it will take to get there. Once they start sharing, there's no stopping them! Stories and celebration drive the culture in our school. (p. 144)

Teams celebrate in many ways, both privately and publicly. Private celebrations are notes or emails to individual teachers from someone who observes something wonderful happening throughout the school. For example, when we walk into a preschool classroom and observe students actively engaged in a mathematics game and practicing how to take turns, we often take a picture and send it to the adults working in the classroom (teachers and instructional assistants) with a short message saying what a joy it was to see the students learning both a mathematics essential standard and the social skill of taking turns. We also share such photos and explanations with school staff that highlight the value of the collaborative process. In Mason Crest's weekly staff newsletter, there is a section for celebrations that we encourage all staff members to contribute to. Our staff often include pictures or short messages to shine a light on all the wonderful things happening in the school. Mason Crest staff members also share how much they look forward to the weekly spotlights and often seek out others to ask questions and learn from one another. Our teams also incorporate celebrations as agenda items into their weekly meetings (see an example in figure 7.4, page 191).

The possibilities for early childhood teams' celebrations are infinite. Celebrate an English learner speaking her first word after a month of school, a student reaching his goal of learning fifteen uppercase letters, and a student reaching a specific social-emotional skill goal. Team meeting celebrations could also include celebrations of one another, bolstering the efficacy of the collaborative team. Table E.1 lists some examples of public and private celebrations.

Table E.1: Examples of Celebrations

Public (All Staff and Teams)	Private (Individual Teachers or Teams)
• Sending a newsletter • Sending photos or videos to share the work of teams collaborating on the four critical questions of a PLC • Sharing improved student-achievement data linking to the team's goal • Using social media to celebrate the work of teams and the school • Asking all staff to share and celebrate throughout the year evidence of collaborative efforts aligning to the school's mission of high levels of learning	• Emailing a picture from a class drop-in with a positive comment linking engagement and student learning • Sending photos or videos to share the work of teams collaborating on the four critical questions of a PLC. • Meeting with individuals and teams to celebrate student-achievement goal data linked to their team goals • Asking all staff to share and celebrate throughout the year evidence of their collaborative efforts or those of their colleagues aligning to the school's mission of high levels of learning for both students and adults

Storytelling

In their book, *Starting a Movement*, coauthors and consultants Kenneth C. Williams and Tom Hierck (2015) write about how telling stories about your school has the power to reshape its culture and how this important approach is underutilized: "if we wanted the story of our school to change, then we had to take responsibility to change it" (p. 146). We couldn't agree more! For too long, many educators looked at early childhood education as an afterthought, something not worthy of the collective spotlight. If early childhood educators want to begin to have more say and credibility, and answer the question, What about us? then they must shout to the world what they do every day. Tell your story. If not you, then who? Also, consider that if it's not you, the *who* telling your story may not tell it accurately or without getting close to doing justice to the amazing learning taking place on a minute by minute, hourly, daily, weekly, monthly, and yearly basis in your team's classrooms. Williams and Hierck (2015) identify five reasons why compelling stories create a culture of collective responsibility:

1. Stories make a point.
2. Stories make the point memorable.
3. Stories make the point meaningful.
4. Stories create and reveal emotions.
5. Stories build connections. (pp. 150–151)

With these reasons in mind, we would like to end this book with a story of a second grader and an early childhood team that felt an urgency to save and change the trajectory of his life. To better understand this moral imperative and the imperative of a culture of collective responsibility, we think this story aligns perfectly with Williams and Hierck's (2015) five reasons for compelling storytelling. We omitted the student's name to protect the student's identity, as well as some other information to ensure anonymity, but the collective actions of the adults are real. Although the following does not go into great detail about the specific plan, because it was tailored to the needs of this specific student, it is important to note how the team collaborated to ensure members addressed the student's needs. As you read the story, consider how it aligns with the mission of ensuring high levels of learning for both students and adults and with the idea of a culture of collaboration and collective responsibility.

This second-grade student was not born in the United States. Although he had not been in the United States long, this was the second U.S. school he had attended. He came to the second school with a special education label, *specific learning disability*, and was reading at the kindergarten level. His parents told the early childhood team they were very concerned about his last school, as from their perception, the kindergarten and first-grade teachers just wanted to get him out of their class. In his file, the previous school had noted he had extreme behavior challenges and was very impulsive and quick to anger.

During his first two days, teachers gave the student some quick mathematics and reading assessments to target his strengths and areas of need. Within the first week of his arrival, the early childhood team met to discuss the student. This team included the second-grade team, a special education teacher, a counselor, an English language teacher, a reading specialist, a mathematics specialist, a social worker, a psychologist, and administrators. The team created an initial plan to support and accelerate his achievement in all areas (academic, social, emotional, and behavioral) based on the information from the previous school and the current teachers' assessments.

In coordination with the special education and classroom teachers, the reading specialist and English language teacher agreed to support the student every day with specific foundational skills he had not acquired in prior years. This coordination was critical; the team understood the student had to have access to grade-level essential learning outcomes and get support with foundational skills. As Buffum et al. (2018) say, "If a student receives below-grade-level instruction all day, where will he or she end up at the end of the year? Below grade level, of course" (p. 7). In order for this student to catch up, the team knew he needed access to *both* grade-level essential learning outcomes and intense remediation on foundational skills.

During the team's initial conversation regarding the student, the mathematics specialist noted the student seemed to have very solid mathematics skills. The specialist even noted on some mathematics strands, he was at or above grade level and suggested he needed (when appropriate and with support) access to advanced mathematics content, depending on the unit and his readiness. The special education teacher realized through this conversation, many of the student's academic goals were being addressed, but observed that the number of his behavior goals seemed fairly lengthy. The counselor and social worker led a discussion with the team and came up with a plan to support those behavior goals inside and outside class. In essence, the entire team (not an isolated special education teacher) was re-creating the student's Individual Education Plan. At this school, the special education teacher acted as the case manager for students with these plans but was not solely responsible for the delivery of instruction, if at all. The team decided who could best meet the needs of each student, label or not.

The team put the plan into place with the understanding that, at any time, it could adjust it. Team members agreed to revisit the plan in three weeks. There was one problem the team did not entirely anticipate: the student's behavior was so severe he disrupted every aspect of his day, his class, and to an extent, the entire school. He was in crisis. To address this, the team asked all staff who worked with him at any time during the school day to attend a team meeting. The meeting was set for 8:00 a.m., before the start of the next school day. When the administrators walked into the library to attend the meeting, they *could* believe their eyes (because of the culture of this school), but still were in awe. Twenty-five staff members were there, ready to brainstorm and plan to support this young student, "their student," to ensure they gave him the best "chance to have a life filled with endless opportunities and possibilities" (Mattos, 2019).

The staff needed a coordinated schoolwide approach to proactively support some of the disruptive behaviors the student was demonstrating, which included turning over desks, destroying the classroom, running from the classroom, and being verbally and physically aggressive toward students and staff. In this instance, the music teacher became critically important because the student loved her and had a passion for music. That relationship was key to his eventual successes. As a result of this meeting, the English language teacher also built a strong relationship with the student and his family. The counselor agreed to check in each morning and work with him on a plan for dealing with challenging situations and then check in with him again in the afternoon. The physical education teacher would bring him in before the day started to have him do activities in the gym to help with his energy and focus. Meanwhile, the reading teacher continued with his intense reading instruction on foundational skills, and the mathematics teacher continued to ensure the grade-level team was providing him access to above grade-level material with scaffolding or supports. The administrators agreed to make it a point to call his parents when things were going well and say a positive word directly to him each day. His classroom teacher and grade-level team were excellent at sharing strategies to support him and the other grade-level team members. This team purposefully included instructional assistants to ensure those educators knew how to support him in class, in the lunchroom, and at recess.

After three months of intense support and constant monitoring and tweaking of the plan, the student made dramatic improvements both behaviorally and academically. He still needed support and by no means were things perfect, but he had made such progress that, by the end of January, the student was exited from special education entirely because he was reading on grade level, and his behavior had improved dramatically.

This did not all happen because of one heroic individual teacher (that would have been impossible), and it didn't solely happen because of the grade-level team's support. It happened because the entire school said, "Not on our watch. We will work to ensure our student will not be unsuccessful because of what we fail to do." It was the moral imperative and culture of collective responsibility that drove this focus on ensuring this student acquired the essential academic, social, and behavior skills he needs to be successful in the subsequent years and throughout his life. This school staff created a sum that was greater than its parts.

Although this may seem to be an extreme case—and it was—it continues to be an example of the kind of collective responsibility that is just the fabric of this school. Although we did not use the child's name or the school's name, the events in the story are true. This story and stories like it occur every day in PLC schools around the world. In fact, one of the coauthors of this book (Jacqueline Heller) wrote a blog with Rebecca DuFour titled "What a Gift!" which is an example of a culture of collective responsibility (DuFour & Heller, 2015). It depicts the story of a kindergarten team and other staff at Mason Crest who said, "We've got this," in reference to their communication and collaboration on behalf of a student who needed intense support upon entering the school.

The Importance of Why

Comedian and children's author Michael Jr. is known for performing comedy that inspires. He says, "When you know your why, your what has more impact, because you are walking in and toward your purpose" (Michael Jr., 2017).

Why did we end this book with a story about a culture of collective responsibility? First, as this quote states, if you know the *why* (and your *why* as an early childhood educator is to ensure *all students learn at high levels*), then the work of educating *all* students takes on even more significance knowing if you fail them, a life of poverty, prison, ill health, and early death awaits (Mattos, 2017).

In this context, learning at high levels means all students learn the essential academic, social, emotional, and behavioral skills they need to be successful at the next grade level and, ultimately, in life (the first big idea of a PLC; DuFour et al., 2016). There is an urgency to your collective work as early childhood educators. Your primary responsibility is to every student who steps through your doors every day. The comfort level of the adults should never take precedence over any student. Early childhood educators can no longer allow themselves to ignore or disregard the most promising practices at the expense of student learning. One of the most promising practices is creating a culture of collaboration in which members of the early childhood teams take collective responsibility for every student (the second big idea). And, finally, use evidence of learning to monitor student progress to frequently assess if those collaborative efforts are working (the third big idea).

We shared the story in this epilogue to highlight what it will take to help some of the most *at-promise* (*at-risk* is too stigmatizing) students succeed, and it took all the school's educators' collective wisdom to give a single student a fighting chance. Can you imagine continually putting that challenge on the back of one isolated teacher? Given the research about collective teacher efficacy from Hattie's (2016) work and its incredible effect size of 1.57, to allow a teacher to work in isolation is akin to educational malpractice. You are better than that! You are the professional that allows every other professional to exist. Individuals who heed the call to enter early childhood education are as noble, hardworking, deeply caring, and committed to students and their futures as any other professional.

The four of us have been humbled and honored to work with teams, schools, and districts from Minnesota in the United States and Manitoba in Canada to Melbourne in Australia and numerous places in between, and we are pleased to call ourselves educators in this profession. We have experienced the power of what high-performing early childhood teams look like, and we know there are scores more schools and districts around the world where early childhood educators are engaged in life-saving work on behalf of students. Many of these educators continue to say, "What about us?" but we, the authors of this book, don't. We no longer need to because, through the work of our PLC, we make it our job and our responsibility to control the narrative about early childhood education and educators.

Tell our story. Tell your story! If early childhood educators continue to learn together and develop their skills collectively to benefit every student, the question, *What about us?* becomes a statement. Through this work, the PLC process is alive and well because it's *all about the students* in early childhood!

References and Resources

Ackerman, D. J., & Coley, R. J. (2012). *State pre-K assessment policies: Issues and status* [Policy Information Report]. Accessed at https://eric.ed.gov/?id=ED529449 on February 27, 2020.

Ainsworth, L. (2015, March 15). *Unwrapping the standards: A simple way to deconstruct learning outcomes* [Blog post]. Accessed at https://blogs.edweek.org/edweek/finding_common_ground/2015/03/unwrapping_the_standards_a_simple_way_to_deconstruct_learning_outcomes.html on January 7, 2020.

AllThingsPLC. (n.d.). *Apply to be a model PLC.* Accessed at www.allthingsplc.info/evidence-submission-online on March 18, 2020.

Angelo, T. A., & Cross, K. P. (1993). *Classroom assessment techniques: A handbook for college teachers* (2nd ed.). San Francisco: Jossey-Bass.

Annie E. Casey Foundation. (2010, January 1). *Early warning! Why reading by the end of third grade matters: A KIDS COUNT special report on the importance of reading by 3rd grade.* Accessed at https://www.aecf.org/resources/early-warning-why-reading-by-the-end-of-third-grade-matters on January 7, 2020.

Bakken, L., Brown, N., & Downing, B. (2017). Early childhood education: The long-term benefits. *Journal of Research in Childhood Education, 31*(2), 255–269.

Bandura, A. (1997). *Self efficacy: The exercise of control.* New York: W. H. Freeman and Company.

Berman, S., Chaffee, S., & Sarmiento, J. (2018). *The practice base for how we learn: Supporting students' social, emotional, and academic development.* The Aspen Institute National Commission on Social, Emotional, and Academic Development. Accessed at www.aspeninstitute.org/publications/practice-base-learn-supporting-students-social-emotional-academic-development on May 10, 2020.

Bohart, H., & Procopio, R. (2018). *Spotlight on young children: observation and assessment.* Washington DC: National Association for the Education of Young Children.

Brenneman, K. (2014, March 7). *Teacher-led? Child-guided? Find the balance in preschool classrooms* [Blog post]. Accessed at https://nieer.wordpress.com/2014/03/07/teacher-led-child-guided-find-the-balance-in-preschool-classrooms on January 7, 2020.

Brookhart, S. M., (2013) *How to create and use rubrics for formative assessment and grading.* Alexandria, VA: Association for Supervision and Curriculum Development.

Brown, T. T., & Jernigan, T. L. (2012). Brain development during the preschool years. *Neuropsychology Review, 22*(4), 313–333. Accessed at www.ncbi.nlm.nih.gov/pmc /articles/PMC3511633 on January 7, 2020.

Buffum, A. (2019, April 30). *Concentrated instruction.* Presentation at the RTI at Work™ Institute, Pasadena, CA.

Buffum, A., & Mattos, M. (Eds.). (2015). *It's about time: Planning interventions and extensions in elementary school.* Bloomington, IN: Solution Tree Press.

Buffum, A., Mattos, M., & Malone, J. (2018). *Taking action: A handbook for RTI at Work.* Bloomington, IN: Solution Tree Press.

Buffum, A., Mattos, M., & Weber, C. (2012). *Simplifying response to intervention: Four essential guiding principles.* Bloomington, IN: Solution Tree Press.

Buffum, A., Mattos, M., Weber, C., & Hierck, T. (2015). *Uniting academic and behavior interventions: Solving the skill or will dilemma.* Bloomington, IN: Solution Tree Press.

Butler, B. K. (2019, July 9). *What about us? The PLC at Work Process in Early Childhood.* Presentation at the Professional Learning Communities at Work® Institute, Atlanta, GA.

Calkins, L.(n.d.) *Units, tools, and methods for teaching reading, writing, and phonics: A workshop curriculum—grades K–8.* Portsmouth, NH: Heinemann. Accessed at https://samplers.heinemann.com/uos/overview_download on May 13, 2020.

Carle, E. (1987). *The very hungry caterpillar.* New York: Philomel.

CASEL. (n.d.). *Core SEL competencies.* Accessed at https://casel.org/core-competencies on April 16, 2020.

Chappuis, J., Stiggins, R., Chappuis, S., & Arter, J. (2012). *Classroom assessment* for *student learning: Doing it right—using it well* (2nd ed.). Upper Saddle River, NJ: Pearson.

Clements, D. H. (2015, April 15). *What is developmentally appropriate math?* [Blog post]. Accessed at http://nieer.org/2015/04/15/what-is-developmentally-appropriate-math on January 7, 2020.

Conzemius, A. E., & O'Neill, J. (2014). *The handbook for SMART school teams: Revitalizing best practices for collaboration* (2nd ed.). Bloomington, IN: Solution Tree Press.

Crews, D. (2010). *Ten black dots.* New York: Greenwillow.

Cruz, L. F. (2019, April 2). *Redefining effective leadership in schools: Influence, productivity, and support through a collective lens.* Presentation at Leadership NOW, Las Vegas, NV.

Darling-Hammond, L., Hyler, M. E., & Gardner, M. (2017, June 5). Effective teacher professional development. *Learning Policy Institute.* Accessed at https:// learningpolicyinstitute.org/product/effective-teacher-professional-development-report on January 6, 2020.

Developmental Reading Assessment. (2019). *Reading opens up a world of possibilities* (3rd ed.). Accessed at www.pearsonassessments.com/content/dam/school /global/clinical/us/assets/dra3/dra3-information-sheet.pdf on March 2, 2020.

Dodge, D. T., Heroman, C., Charles, J., & Maiorca, J. (2004). Beyond outcomes: How ongoing assessment supports children's learning and leads to meaningful curriculum.

Young Children, 59(1), 20–28. Accessed at http://jstor.org/stable/42729034 on January 7, 2020.

Drake, S. M. (2012). *Creating standards-based integrated curriculum: The Common Core State Standards Edition* (3rd ed.). Thousand Oaks, CA: Corwin.

DuFour, R. (2015a, June 10). *First things first: Building the solid foundation of a Professional Learning Community at Work.* Presentation at the Professional Learning Communities at Work Institute, Las Vegas, NV.

DuFour, R. (2015b). *In praise of American educators: And how they can become even better.* Bloomington, IN: Solution Tree Press.

DuFour, R. (2016a, August 17). *Building the solid foundation of a Professional Learning Community at Work.* Presentation at the Professional Learning Communities at Work Institute, Milwaukee, WI.

DuFour, R. (2016b, October 18). *A focus on learning and the four essential questions of a PLC* [Video]. Accessed at www.youtube.com/watch?v=UjrLOQr9k64 on May 15, 2020.

DuFour, R. & DuFour, R. (2012). *The school leader's guide to Professional Learning Communities at Work™.* Bloomington, IN: Solution Tree Press.

DuFour, R., DuFour, R., Eaker, R., Many, T. W., & Mattos, M. (2016). *Learning by doing: A handbook for Professional Learning Communities at Work®* (3rd ed.). Bloomington, IN: Solution Tree Press.

DuFour, R., & Heller, J. (2015, February 11). *What a gift!* [Blog post.] Accessed at www.allthingsplc.info/blog/view/285/what-a-gift on March 16, 2020.

DuFour, R., & Marzano, R. J. (2011). *Leaders of learning: How district, school, and classroom leaders improve student achievement.* Bloomington, IN: Solution Tree Press.

DuFour, R., & Reeves, D. (2016). The futility of PLC lite. *Phi Delta Kappan, 97*(6), 69–71.

Durlak, J. A., Weissberg, R. P., Dymnicki, A. B., Taylor, R. D., & Schellinger, K. B. (2011). The impact of enhancing students' social and emotional learning: A meta-analysis of school-based universal interventions. *Child Development, 82*(1), 405–432.

Dweck, C. S. (2006). *Mindset: The new psychology of success.* New York: Ballantine Books.

Eaker, R., & Marzano, R. J. (Eds.). (2020). *Professional Learning Communities at Work and High Reliability Schools: Cultures of continuous learning.* Bloomington, IN: Solution Tree Press.

Epstein, A. S., Schweinhart, L. J., DeBruin-Parecki, A., & Robin, K. B. (2004, July). Preschool assessment: A guide to developing a balanced approach. *National Institute for Early Education Research, 7,* 1–11. Accessed at http://nieer.org/wp-content/uploads/2016/08/7-1.pdf on January 7, 2020.

Evans, M. (2018). When Texas schools don't make the grade. *KERA Education News.* Accessed at http://stories.kera.org/saving-schools/2018/04/16/when-texas-schools-dont-make-the-grade on February 17, 2020.

Farran, D. C., Aydogan, C., Kang, S. J., & Lipsey, M. W. (2006). Preschool classroom environments and the quantity and quality of children's literacy and language behaviors. In D. K. Dickinson & S. B. Neuman (Eds.), *Handbook of early literacy research* (Vol. 2, pp. 257–268). New York: Guilford Press.

Ferguson, H. B., Bovaird, S., & Mueller, M. P. (2007, October). The impact of poverty on educational outcomes for children. *Pediatric Child Health, 12*(8), 701–706. Accessed at www.ncbi.nlm.nih.gov/pmc/articles/PMC2528798 on May 14, 2020.

Ferriter, W. (2020). *The big book of tools for collaborative teams in a PLC at Work®.* Bloomington, IN: Solution Tree Press.

Francis, E. (2017, May 9). *What is depth of knowledge?* [Blog post]. Accessed at https://inservice.ascd.org/what-exactly-is-depth-of-knowledge-hint-its-not-a-wheel on May 4, 2020.

Giganti Jr., P. (1988). *How many snails? A counting book.* New York: Greenwillow.

Guskey, T. R. (2010). Lessons of mastery learning. *Educational Leadership, 68*(2), 52–57

Hammond, Z. (2017, May 4). *Zaretta Hammond: Culturally responsive teaching and the brain webinar* [Video file]. Accessed at https://youtube.com/watch?v=O2kzbH7ZWGg on January 7, 2020.

Hattie, J. (2009). *Visible learning: A synthesis of over 800 meta-analyses relating to achievement.* New York: Routledge.

Hattie, J. (2012). *Visible learning for teachers: Maximizing impact on learning.* New York: Routledge.

Hattie, J. (2013, November 22). *Why are so many of our teachers and schools so successful? John Hattie at TEDxNorrkoping* [Video]. Accessed at www.youtube.com/watch?v=rzwJXUieD0U on May 26, 2020.

Hattie, J. (2016). *Collective teacher efficacy (CTE) according to John Hattie.* Accessed at https://visible-learning.org/2018/03/collective-teacher-efficacy-hattie on May 26, 2020.

Hattie, J. (n.d.). *Hattie ranking: 252 influences and effect sizes related to student achievment.* Accessed at https://visible-learning.org/hattie-ranking-influences-effect-sizes-learning-achievement on March 26, 2020.

Heckman, J. J., & Masterov, D. V. (2007, April). *The productivity argument for investing in young children* [IZA Discussion Paper No. 2725]. Accessed at https://ssrn.com/abstract=982117 on February 2017, 2020.

Hulen, T., Heller, J., Kerr, D., & Butler, B. (2019, Spring). What about us? The PLC at Work® process in preschool. *AllThingsPLC Magazine,* 18–25.

Illinois Early Learning Project. (2013). *2013 Illinois early learning and development standards (IELDS): List of goals, standards, and benchmarks.* Accessed at https://illinoisearlylearning.org/ields/ields-benchmarks on February 26, 2020.

International Reading Association & National Association for the Education of Young Children. (1998). Learning to read and write: Developmentally appropriate practices for young children: A joint position statement of the International Reading Association (IRA) and the National Association for the Education of Young Children (NAEYC) Adopted 1998. *Young Children, 53*(4), 30–46. Accessed at www.jstor.org/stable/42728456 on January 7, 2020.

Jones, D. E., Greenberg, M., & Crowley, M. (2015). Early social-emotional functioning and public health: The relationship between kindergarten social competence and future wellness. *American Journal of Public Health, 105*(11): 2283–2290.

Jones, S. M., & Kahn, J. (2017). *The evidence base for how we learn: Supporting students' social, emotional, and academic development.* The Aspen Institute National Commission on Social, Emotional, and Academic Development. Accessed at www .aspeninstitute.org/publications/evidence-base-learn on May 10, 2020.

Kanold, T. D. (2017). *HEART! Fully forming your professional life as a teacher and leader.* Bloomington, IN: Solution Tree Press.

Karoly, L. A., Kilburn, M. R., & Cannon, J. S. (2005). *Proven benefits of early childhood interventions* [Research brief]. Accessed at https://rand.org/pubs/research_briefs/ RB9145.html on January 7, 2020.

Kegan, R., & Lahey, L. L. (2001). *How the way we talk can change the way we work: Seven languages for transformation.* San Francisco: Jossey-Bass.

Kouzes. J. M., & Posner, B. Z. (2003). *Encouraging the heart: A leader's guide to rewarding and recognizing others.* San Francisco: Jossey-Bass.

Kramer, S. V., & Schuhl, S. (2017). *School improvement for all: A how-to guide for doing the right work.* Bloomington, IN: Solution Tree Press.

Leong, D. J., & Bodrova, E. (2012). Assessing and scaffolding: Make-believe play. *Young Children, 67*(1), 28–34. Accessed at www.researchgate.net/publication/292513144 _Assessing_and_scaffolding_make-believe_play on January 7, 2020.

Lovett, M. C. (2013). Make exams worth more than grades: Using exam wrappers to promote metacognition. In M. Kaplan, N. Silver, D. Lavaque-Manty, & D. Meizlish (Eds.), *Using reflection and metacognition to improve student learning: Across the disciplines, across the academy* (pp. 18–52). Sterling, VA: Stylus.

Many, T. (2016, June). Is it R.E.A.L. or not? *AllThingsPLC Magazine,* 34–35.

Many, T. W., Maffoni, M. J., Sparks, S. K., & Thomas, T. F. (2018). *Amplify your impact: Coaching collaborative teams in PLCs at Work.* Bloomington, IN: Solution Tree Press.

Martin Jr., B., & Sampson, M. (2004). *Chicka chicka 1, 2, 3.* New York: Simon & Schuster.

Marzano, R. J. (2003). *What works in schools: Translating research into action.* Alexandria, VA: Association for Supervision and Curriculum Development.

Marzano, R. J. (2010). The art and science of teaching/When students track their progress. *Health and Learning, 67*(4), 86–87. Accessed at www.ascd.org/publications /educational-leadership/dec09/vol67/num04/When-Students-Track-Their-Progress. aspx on January 7, 2020.

Marzano, R. J., Heflebower, T., Hoegh, J. K., Warrick, P. B., & Grift, G. (2016). *Collaborative teams that transform schools: The next step in PLCs.* Bloomington, IN: Marzano Resources.

Marzano, R. J., Pickering, D. J., & Pollock, J. E. (2005). *Classroom instruction that works: Research-based strategies for increasing student achievement.* Upper Saddle River, N.J: Pearson.

Marzano, R. J., Warrick, P. B., Rains, C. L., & DuFour, R. (2018). *Leading a high reliability school.* Bloomington, IN: Solution Tree Press.

Mason Crest Elementary School (n.d.). *Mission, vision, goals, and collective commitments.* Accessed at https://masoncrestes.fcps.edu/node/526 on February 17, 2020.

Mason Crest Elementary School. (2016). *Collective commitments from Mason Crest administrators* [Memo]. Annandale, VA: Author.

Mattos, M. (2017). *Timebomb: The cost of dropping out* [Video file]. Bloomington, IN: Solution Tree Press.

Mattos, M. (2019, May 2). *Eating the elephant.* Presentation at the RTI at Work Institute, Pasadena, CA.

McCloud, C., & Martin, K. (2018). *Fill a bucket: A guide to daily happiness for young children.* Chicago: Independent Publishers Group.

McDonald, P. (2018, March). Observing, planning, guiding: How an intentional teacher meets standards through play. *Young Children, 73*(1). Accessed at www.naeyc.org /resources/pubs/yc/mar2018/observing-planning-guiding on January 7, 2020.

McTighe, J., & Curtis, G. (2019). *Leading modern learning: A blueprint for visions-driven schools* [2nd ed.]. Bloomington, IN: Solution Tree Press.

Merrill, M. D. (2002). First principles of instruction. *Educational Technology Research and Development, 50*(3), 43–59. Accessed at https://mdavidmerrill.files.wordpress. com/2019/04/firstprinciplesbymerrill.pdf on January 7, 2020.

Michael Jr. (2017, January 8). *Know your why* [Video]. Accessed at https://youtube .com/watch?v=1ytFB8TrkTo on January 7, 2020.

Mitsumasa, A. (1986). *Anno's counting book.* New York: HarperCollins.

Muhammad, A. (2015). *Overcoming the achievement gap trap: Liberating mindsets to effect change.* Bloomington, IN: Solution Tree Press.

Muhammad, A., & Cruz, L. F. (2019). *Time for change: Four essential skills for transformational school and district leaders.* Bloomington, IN: Solution Tree Press.

Muhammad, A., & Hollie, S. (2012). *The will to lead, the skill to teach: Transforming schools at every level.* Bloomington, IN: Solution Tree Press.

National Association for the Education of Young Children. (n.d.). *What does a high-quality preschool program look like?* Accessed at https://naeyc.org/our-work/families /what-does-high-quality-program-for-preschool-look-like on September 30, 2019.

National Association for the Education of Young Children. (2009). *Developmentally appropriate practice in early childhood programs serving children from birth through age 8* [Position statement]. Accessed at https://academia.edu/6084771/Developmentally _Appropriate_Practice_in_Early_Childhood_Programs_Serving_Children_from _Birth_through_Age_8 on January 7, 2020.

National Association for the Education of Young Children. (2018, January). *Early learning program accreditation standards and assessment items.* Accessed at https://naeyc.org /accreditation/early-learning/standards on January 7, 2020.

National Association for the Education of Young Children. (2020). *Professional standards and competencies for early childhood educators* [Position Statement]. Accessed at https:// naeyc.org/sites/default/files/globally-shared/downloads/PDFs/resources/position -statements/professional_standards_and_competencies_for_early_childhood _educators.pdf on April 24, 2020.

National Association for the Education of Young Children & National Association of Early Childhood Specialists in State Departments of Education. (2003, November). *Early childhood curriculum, assessment and program evaluation: Building an effective, accountable system in programs for children birth through age 8* [Position statement]. Accessed at https://naeyc.org/sites/default/files/globally-shared/downloads/PDFs /resources/position-statements/pscape.pdf on March 17, 2020.

National Association for the Education of Young Children & National Council of Teachers of Mathematics. (2010). *Early childhood mathematics: Promoting good beginnings* [Position statement]. Accessed at https://naeyc.org/sites/default/files /globally-shared/downloads/PDFs/resources/position-statements/psmath.pdf on January 7, 2020.

National Council of Teachers of Mathematics. (2000). *Principles and standards for school mathematics: An overview.* Reston, VA: Author.

National Council of Teachers of Mathematics. (2014). *Principles to actions: Ensuring mathematical success for all.* Reston, VA: Author.

National Governors Association Center for Best Practices & Council of Chief State School Officers. (2010a). *Common Core State Standards for English language arts and literacy in history/social studies, science, and technical subjects.* Washington, DC: Authors. Accessed at www.corestandards.org/assets/CCSSI_ELA%20Standards.pdf on December 3, 2019.

National Governors Association Center for Best Practices & Council of Chief State School Officers. (2010b). *Standards for mathematics.* Accessed at www.corestandards .org/assets/CCSSI_Math%20Standards.pdf on March 17, 2020.

National Research Council (2001a). *Adding it up: Helping children learn mathematics.* Washington, DC: National Academies Press. Accessed at https://doi.org/10.17226 /9822 on March 17, 2020.

National Research Council. (2001b). *Eager to learn: Educating our preschoolers.* Washington, DC: National Academies Press. Accessed at https://doi.org/10.17226 /9745 on March 17, 2020.

National Research Council Committee on Science Learning. (2007). *Taking science to school: Learning and teaching science in grades K–8.* Washington, DC: National Academies Press. Accessed at https://doi.org/10.17226/11625 on March 17, 2020.

National Research Council & Institute of Medicine. (2000). *From neurons to neighborhoods: The science of early childhood development.* Washington, DC: National Academies Press.

National Science Teaching Association. (2018). *NSTA position statement: Elementary school science.* Accessed at www.nsta.org/about/positions/elementary.aspx on January 7, 2020.

National Turning Points Center. (2001). *Turning points: Transforming middle schools— Guide to collaborative culture and shared leadership.* Boston: Author.

Nielsen, M. (2019, Spring). Bringing the four critical questions to life. *AllThingsPLC Magazine,* 4–5.

O'Conner, R., De Feyter, J., Carr, A., Luo, J. L., & Romm, H. (2017). *A review of the literature on social and emotional learning for students ages 3–8: Teacher and classroom strategies that contribute to social and emotional learning (part 3 of 4).* ICF International and National Center for Education Evaluation and Regional Assistance. Accessed at https://files.eric.ed.gov/fulltext/ED572723.pdf on May 10, 2010.

O'Hora, D., & Maglieri, K. A. (2006). Goal statements and goal-directed behavior: A relational frame account of goal setting in organizations. *Journal of Organizational Behavior Management, 26*(1), 131–170.

Pre-Kindergarten Task Force. (2017, April 2). *The current state of scientific knowledge on pre-kindergarten effects.* Washington, DC: Brookings. Accessed at https://brookings .edu/wp-content/uploads/2017/04/duke_prekstudy_final_4-4-17_hires.pdf on January 7, 2020.

Reeves, D. (2005). *Accountability in action: A blueprint for learning organizations* (2nd ed.). Denver, CO: Advanced Learning Press.

Reeves, D. (2020). *Achieving equity and excellence: Immediate results from the lessons of high-poverty, high-success schools.* Bloomington, IN: Solution Tree Press.

Safer, N., & Fleischman, S. (2005). Research matters/How student progress monitoring improves instruction. *Educational Leadership, 62*(5), 81–83. Accessed at www.ascd .org/publications/educational-leadership/feb05/vol62/num05/How-Student-Progress -Monitoring-Improves-Instruction.aspx on January 7, 2020.

Sarama, J., Brenneman, K., Clements, D. H., Duke, N. K., & Hemmeter, M. L. (In press). *Connect4Learning: The preschool curriculum.* Lewisville, NC: Gryphon House.

Sarama, J., Clements, D. H., Wolfe, C. B., & Spitler, M. E. (2012). Longitudinal evaluation of a scale-up model for teaching mathematics with trajectories and technologies. *Journal of Research on Educational Effectiveness, 5*(2), 105–135.

Sarama, J., Lange, A. A., Clements, D. H., & Wolfe, C. B. (2012). The impacts of an early mathematics curriculum on emerging literacy and language. *Early Childhood Research Quarterly, 27*(3), 489–502. doi: 10.1016/j.ecresq.2011.12.002

Scherer, M. (2001). How and why standards can improve student achievement: A conversation with Robert J. Marzano. *Making Standards Work, 59*(1), 14–18.

Schmoker, M. (2004). Learning communities at the crossroads: Toward the best schools we've ever had. *Phi Delta Kappan, 86*(1), 84–88. Accessed at https://doi.org /10.1177/003172170408600114 on March 17, 2020.

Schuhl, S., Kanold, T. D., Deinhart, J., Lang-Raad, N. D., Larson, M. R., & Smith, N. N. (2021). *Mathematics unit planning in a PLC at Work®, grades preK–2.* Bloomington, IN: Solution Tree Press.

Sebe, M. (2011). *Let's count to 100!* Tonawanda, NY: Kids Can Press.

Sinek, S. (2009, September 28). *Start with why: How great leaders inspire action* [Video]. Accessed at www.youtube.com/watch?v=u4ZoJKF_VuA on May 14, 2020.

Smith, C. L., Wiser, M., Anderson, C. W., & Krajcik, J. (2006). Implications of research on children's learning for standards and assessment: A proposed learning progression for matter and atomic-molecular theory. *Measurement: Interdisciplinary Research and Perspectives, 14*(1&2), 1–98. Accessed at https://doi.org/10.1080/15366367.2006.9678 570 on March 24, 2020.

Snow, C. E., & Van Hemel, S. B. (2008). *Early childhood assessment: Why, what, and how?* Washington, DC: National Research Council of the National Academies. Accessed at www.acf.hhs.gov/sites/default/files/opre/early_child_assess.pdf on January 7, 2020.

Stiggins, R. J., Arter, J. A., Chappuis, J., & Chappuis, S. (2004). *Classroom assessment for student learning: Doing it right—using it well.* Portland, OR: Assessment Training Institute.

Suh, L. (2019, August 22). Building executive functioning skills can be fun. *Edutopia*. Accessed at https://edutopia.org/article/building-executive-function-skills-can-be-fun on January 7, 2020.

Texas Education Agency. (2015a). *Department of assessment and accountability: Division of performance reporting—Final 2015 accountability ratings*. Accessed at https://rptsvr1 .tea.texas.gov/perfreport/account/2015/statelist.pdf on February 17, 2020.

Texas Education Agency. (2015b). *Texas prekindergarten guidelines*. Accessed at https://tea .texas.gov/sites/default/ files/PKG_Final_2015_navigation.pdf on June 29, 2020.

Thomas, J. W. (2000, March). *A review of research on project-based learning*. San Rafael, CA: Autodesk Foundation. Accessed at http://live-buckinstitute.pantheonsite.io/sites /default/files/2019–01/A_Review_of_Research_on_Project_Based_Learning.pdf on January 7, 2020.

U.S. Department of Education. (n.d.). *Early learning: Frequently asked questions*. Accessed at https://ed.gov/budget14/faqs/early-learning on January 7, 2020.

Virginia Department of Education. (2013). *Virginia's foundation blocks for early learning: Comprehensive standards for four-year-olds*. Accessed at www.doe.virginia.gov/early -childhood/curriculum/foundation-blocks.pdf on May 9, 2020.

Webb, N. L. (1997). *Criteria for alignment of expectations and assessments in mathematics and science education* (Research monograph no. 8). Washington, DC: Council of Chief State School Officers.

Webb, N. (1999). *Alignment of science and mathematics standards and assessments in four states* (Research Monograph No. 18). University of Wisconsin-Madison, National Institute for Science Education.

Wiggins, G., & McTighe, J. (2005). *Understanding by design* (Expanded 2nd ed.). Alexandria, VA: Association for Supervision and Curriculum Development.

Wiliam, D. (2011). *Embedded formative assessment*. Bloomington, IN: Solution Tree Press.

Williams, K. C. (2010). *Do we have norms or "nice to knows"?* Accessed at www .allthingsplc.info/blog/view/90/do-we-have-team-norms-or-nice-to-knows on May 26, 2020.

Zins, J. E., Payton, J. W., Weissberg, R. P., & O'Brien, M. U. (2007). Social and emotional learning for successful school performance. In G. Matthews, M. Zeidner, & R. D. Roberts (Eds.), Series in affective science. *The science of emotional intelligence: Knowns and unknowns* (pp. 376–395). Oxford, England: Oxford University Press.

Williams, K. C., & Hierck, T. (2015). *Starting a movement: Building culture from the inside out in professional learning communities*. Bloomington, IN: Solution Tree Press.

Yoder, N. (2014, January). *Teaching the whole child: Instructional practices that support social-emotional learning in three teacher evaluation frameworks* (Rev. ed.). Washington, DC: American Institutes for Research. Accessed at https://gtlcenter.org /sites/default/files/TeachingtheWholeChild.pdf on January 7, 2020.

Index